THE
COMPLETE
BIBLE
ANSWER
BOOK
COLLECTOR'S
EDITION

A GIFT FOR

Bethany

FROM

Michelle

DATE

4/20/10

May this exploration bring you into deeper knowledge,
appreciation, and love of the Word.

THE
COMPLETE
BIBLE
ANSWER
BOOK
COLLECTOR'S
EDITION

FROM THE BIBLE ANSWER MAN
HANK HANEGRAAFF

THOMAS NELSON
Since 1798

NASHVILLE   DALLAS   MEXICO CITY   RIO DE JANEIRO   BEIJING

Published in Nashville, Tennessee, by Thomas Nelson. Thomas Nelson is a registered trademark of Thomas Nelson, Inc.

Designed by The DesignWorks Group, Sisters, Oregon.

Thomas Nelson, Inc., titles may be purchased in bulk for educational, business, fund-raising, or sales promotional use. For information, please e-mail SpecialMarkets@ThomasNelson.com.

www.thomasnelson.com

www.equip.org

ISBN: 978-1-4041-1381-7

CONTENTS

RELIGIONS AND CULTS

Eschatology / Revelation

Biblical Interpretation

Final Thoughts

INTRODUCTION

The Complete Bible Answer Book Collector's Edition is designed to answer questions that stumble seekers and solidify skeptics in their opposition to a biblical worldview—and was born out of two decades of hosting the nationally syndicated *Bible Answer Man* radio broadcast. I have taken my impromptu answers and chiseled them until only the gem emerges.

Questions you will encounter in this volume run the gamut from common to complex. In the category of common, I answer such questions as, *"Why do people end their prayers with 'Amen'?"* and *"What is Zen Buddhism?"* In the category of complex, I tackle questions such as, *"How can Christians legitimize a God who orders the genocide of entire nations?"* and *"Should Christians support a ban on embryonic stem cell research?"*

Perhaps the question I have been asked more than any other is *"Why does God allow bad things to happen to good people?"* At first blush it may seem as though there are as many responses to this question as there are religions. In reality, however, you will discover that there are only three basic answers—and only Christian theism can answer the question satisfactorily!

Along with questions I answered in previous Bible Answer Books, I have added answers to questions such as *"Does Mormonism really teach that Jesus is the spirit brother of Satan?"* and *"How should Christians think about global warming?"* In addition I have included acronyms such as *Y-O-G-A*, which are designed to take you from *reading* to *recall*. You'll also discover recommended resources for further study as well as Scripture passages specifically related to the subject matter at hand.

Finally, I would be remiss if I failed to thank the Thomas Nelson team—particularly Jack Countryman—for ensuring that the content of this volume was complemented by an elegance of presentation.

May *The Complete Bible Answer Book Collector's Edition* not only provide you with answers to your questions but equip you to answer questions raised by family and friends.

HANK HANEGRAAFF
Charlotte, North Carolina

BASIC CHRISTIAN THOUGHT

AND SPIRITUAL GROWTH

What must I do to be saved?

o one gets out of this world alive, so this is beyond a doubt the most important question you can ever ask yourself! In fact, the Bible was written, "so that you may know that you have eternal life" (1 John 5:13).

First, according to Scripture, you need to *realize* that you are a sinner. If you do not realize you are a sinner, you will not recognize your need for a savior. The Bible says we "all have sinned and fall short of the glory of God" (Romans 3:23).

Furthermore, you must *repent* of your sins. Repentance is an old English word that describes a willingness to turn from our sin toward Jesus Christ. It literally means a complete U-turn on the road of life—a change of heart and a change of mind. It means that you are willing to follow Jesus and to receive him as your Savior and Lord. Jesus said, "repent and believe the Good News" (Mark 1:15).

Finally, to demonstrate true belief means to be willing to *receive*. To truly receive is to trust in and depend on Jesus Christ alone to be the Lord of our lives here and now and our Savior for all eternity. It takes more than *knowledge* (the devil knows about Jesus and trembles). It takes more than *agreement* that the knowledge we have is accurate (the devil agrees that Jesus is Lord). What it takes is to *trust* in Jesus Christ alone for eternal life. The requirements for eternal life are based not on what *you can do* but on what *Jesus Christ has done*. He stands ready to exchange his perfection for your imperfection.

The requirements for eternal life are based not on what you can do but on what Jesus Christ has done.

According to Jesus Christ, those who *realize* they are sinners, *repent* of their sins, and *receive* him as Savior and Lord are "born again" (John 3:3)—not physically, but spiritually. The reality of our salvation is not dependant on our feelings but rather on the promise of the Savior who says: "I tell you the truth, whoever hears my word and believes him who sent me has eternal life and will not be condemned; he has crossed over from death to life" (John 5:24).

See also Hank Hanegraaff, "Does your relationship with God make you sure you will go to heaven when you die?" pamphlet, available through Christian Research Institute, www.equip.org. For further study, see John MacArthur, *Hard to Believe: The High Cost and Infinite Value of Following Jesus* (Nashville: Thomas Nelson Publishers, 2003).

JOHN 3:16

"For God so loved the world that he gave his one and only Son, that whoever believes in him shall not perish but have eternal life."

WHAT ARE THE SECRETS
TO SPIRITUAL GROWTH?

According to Jesus Christ, those who repent and receive him as Savior and Lord are "born again" (John 3:3)—not physically, but spiritually. And with this spiritual birth must come spiritual growth. It is crucial therefore to be intimately acquainted with the ABCs of spiritual growth.

First, no relationship can flourish without constant, heartfelt communication. This is true not only in human relationships but also in our relationship with God. If we are to nurture a strong relationship with our Savior, we must be in constant communication with him. The way to do that is through prayer.

Furthermore, it is crucial that we spend time reading God's written revelation of himself—the Bible. The Bible not only forms the foundation of an effective prayer life but also is foundational to every other aspect of Christian living. While prayer is our primary way of communicating with God, the Bible is God's primary way of communicating with us.

Nothing should take precedence over getting into the Word and getting the Word into us. If we fail to eat well-balanced meals on a regular basis, we will eventually suffer the physical consequences. What is true of the outer man is also true of the inner man. If we do not regularly feed on the Word of God, we will starve spiritually.

Finally, it is crucial for new believers to become active participants in a healthy, well-balanced church. In Scripture, the church is referred to as the body of Christ. Just as our body is one and yet has many parts, so too the body of Christ is one but is composed of many members. Those who receive Christ as the Savior and Lord of their lives are already a part of the church universal. It is crucial, however, that all Christians become vital, reproducing members of a local body of believers as well.

Adapted from *The FACE*

For further study, see Hank Hanegraaff, *The Covering: God's Plan to Protect You from Evil* (Nashville: W Publishing Group, 2002).

Hebrews 5:13–14

"Anyone who lives on milk, being still an infant, is not acquainted with the teaching about righteousness. But solid food is for the mature, who by constant use have trained themselves to distinguish good from evil."

WHAT IS ESSENTIAL CHRISTIAN DOCTRINE?

The importance of essential Christian doctrine can hardly be overstated. First, these are the very doctrines that form the line of demarcation between the kingdom of Christ and the kingdom of the cults. While we may debate nonessentials without dividing over them, when it comes to essential Christian doctrine there must be unity. Hence, the maxim: *In essentials unity, nonessentials liberty, and in all things charity.*

Furthermore, essential Christian doctrine is the North Star by which the course of Christianity is set. Just as the North Star is an unchanging reference point by which sailors safely guided their ships, so essential Christian doctrine has safely guided the church through the doctrinal storms that have sought to sink it. Shooting stars light the sky for a moment; following them, however, leads to shipwreck.

Finally, essential Christian doctrine is the foundation on which the gospel of Jesus Christ rests. From his deity to the eschatological certainty that he will appear a second time to judge the living and the dead, essential Christian doctrine is foundational to the gospel. All other religions compromise, confuse, or contradict these essentials. Muslims, for example, dogmatically denounce the doctrine of Christ's unique deity as the unforgivable sin of *shirk*. They readily affirm the sinlessness of Christ, but they adamantly deny his sacrifice upon the cross and his subsequent resurrection as the only hope of salvation.

I am so passionate about inscribing the essentials on the tablet of your heart that I've organized them around the acronym D–O–C–T–R–I–N–E. It is my prayer that you will become so familiar with essential Christian doctrine that when a counterfeit looms on the horizon you will know it instantaneously.

Deity of Christ—The biblical witness is clear and convincing that Jesus Christ is the eternal Creator God (John 1; Colossians 1; Hebrews 1; Revelation 1). Throughout his earthly ministry Jesus claimed to be God in word and deed (Mark 14:61–62; John 5:18, 20; 8:58; 10:30–33) and vindicated his claims to deity by living a sinless life (John 8:46; 2 Corinthians 5:21; Hebrews 4:15; 1 John 3:5; 1 Peter 2:22), by manifesting his power over nature (Mark 4:39), over fallen angels (Luke 4:35), over sickness

(Matthew 4:23), and even over death itself (John 4:50; 11:43–44; 1 Corinthians 15), and by accurately prophesying God's judgment on Jerusalem through the destruction of the Temple that occurred in AD 70 (Matthew 24:1–2, 32–35). (See *The Bible Answer Book Volume 1,* pp. 183–189)

ORIGINAL SIN—Sin is not just murder, rape, or robbery. "Sin" is a word that describes any thought, word, deed, or state of being that fails to meet God's standard of holiness and perfection. The Bible unambiguously proclaims that "all have sinned and fall short of the glory of God" (Romans 3:23). While the notion of generational curses and spirits is foreign to the text of Scripture, there is a sense in which all people are cursed as a result of an ancestor's sin. Adam's rebellion brought death to us all and tainted every aspect of our being (Genesis 3; 1 Corinthians 15:21–22; cf. Ephesians 2:3). God, however, has provided redemption through the atoning work of the "Second Adam," Jesus Christ (Romans 5:12–21). (See *The Bible Answer Book Volume 1,* pp. 18–21.)

CANON—The thirty–nine books of the Hebrew Scriptures along with the twenty–seven books of the Greek New Testament are divine rather than merely human in origin and constitute the entire Christian canon (meaning "standard of measurement"). In addition to the internal testimony of the Bible about itself (2 Timothy 3:16), the divine inspiration and preservation of the Bible can be demonstrated by the early dating and consistency of the many available manuscripts, the corroboration of archaeology, and the fulfillment of predictive prophecy. (See *The Bible Answer Book Volume 1,* pp. 157–159.)

TRINITY—Though the word 'Trinity' is found nowhere in the Bible, it aptly codifies the essential biblical truths that 1) there is only one God (Deuteronomy 6:4; Isaiah 43:10); 2) the Father is God, the Son is God, and the Holy Spirit is God (1 Corinthians 8:6; Hebrews 1:8; Acts 5:3–4); and 3) Father, Son, and Holy Spirit are eternally distinct (Matthew 28:19; John 15:26; 17:1–26). It is important to note that when Trinitarians speak of one God they are referring to the nature or essence of God. Moreover, when they speak of persons they are referring to personal self–distinctions within the Godhead. Put another way, Trinitarians believe in one *What* and three *Who's.* (See *The Bible Answer Book Volume 1,* pp. 180-182.)

RESURRECTION—All four canonical gospels record the bodily resurrection of Jesus Christ from the dead. The immutable fact of Jesus' resurrection is the cornerstone of Christian faith, because it not only vindicates Jesus' claims to deity but also ensures the future bodily resurrection unto eternal life of all who believe in Jesus Christ as their Savior and proclaim him as Lord (1 Corinthians 15; 1 Thessalonians 4:13–18). The historical reality of the resurrection can be demonstrated through the fatal torment of Jesus on the cross; the empty tomb—early Christianity could not have survived an identifiable tomb containing the corpse of Christ; the post–resurrection appearances of Jesus; and the transformation of believers throughout the ages whose lives have been radically altered upon experiencing the resurrected Lord. (See *The Bible Answer Book Volume 1,* pp. 192–196.)

INCARNATION—The doctrine of the Incarnation is aptly summed up in the words of the apostle John: "In the beginning was the Word, and the Word was with God, and the Word was God. . . . And the Word became flesh and dwelt among us, and we beheld His glory, the glory as of the only begotten of the Father, full of grace and truth" (John 1:1, 14). The clear testimony of Scripture is that, in the incarnation, Jesus Christ was fully God and fully man; that is, he existed as the perfect unity in one person of a divine and a human nature (John 1; Colossians 1). As *Theanthropos*

("God–Man"), the spotless "Lamb of God" (John 1:29) lived a perfectly sinless human life and died a sinner's death to sufficiently atone, once for all, for the sins of humanity (Romans 5:1–21; Hebrews 10:11–18). (See *The Bible Answer Book Volume 1*, pp. 183–187.)

NEW CREATION—The essential doctrine of New Creation is aptly codified in the words of the apostle Paul: "If anyone *is* in Christ, *he is* a new creation; old things have passed away; behold, all things have become new" (2 Corinthians 5:17, emphasis added). All who believe in the resurrection of Jesus Christ and confess him as Lord are reconciled to God and inherit eternal life in his glorious presence (John 3:16; Romans 10:9–10). Jesus' resurrection from the dead inaugurates the renewal of all things. The new creation of faithful believers and the new creation of the natural world will be consummated in the resurrection when Jesus returns bodily to earth as the conquering king (Romans 8:18–25).

ESCHATOLOGY—The word *eschatology* is an intimidating word with a simple meaning—the study of end times. While the meaning of eschatology is simple to grasp, its importance is difficult to overemphasize. Far from being a mere branch in the theological tree, eschatology is the root that provides life and luster to every fiber of its being. Put another way, eschatology is the thread that weaves the tapestry of Scripture into a harmonious pattern. It is the study of everything we long and hope for. Early in Genesis, Adam and Eve fell into a life of constant sin terminated by death. The rest of Scripture chronicles God's unfolding plan of redemption. Although Christians debate secondary aspects of eschatology, such as the timing of the tribulation or the meaning of the millennium, we are united in the truth that just as Christ came to earth once to bear the sins of the world, so too he will return again to gather the elect and to usher in the resurrection of all things (1 Thessalonians 4:13–18; Hebrews 9:27–28). On that day, the just will be resurrected to eternal life and the unjust to eternal conscious torment and separation from the love and grace of God (John 5:28–29). Paradise lost will become paradise restored, and the problem of sin and Satan will be fully and finally resolved (Revelation 20–22). (See *The Bible Answer Book Volume 1*, pp. 141–144; 211–220.)

For further study, see Bruce Milne, *Know the Truth: A Handbook of Christian Belief* (Downers Grove, Ill.: InterVarsity Press, 1999).

"Watch your life and doctrine closely.
Persevere in them, because if you do you will save
both yourself and your hearers."

The essential tenets of the Christian faith are:

> Deity of Christ
>
> Original sin
>
> Canon
>
> Trinity
>
> Resurrection
>
> Incarnation
>
> New creation
>
> Eschatology

— 4 —
WHAT IS THE BIBLICAL
DEFINITION OF FAITH?

The shield of faith described by the apostle Paul in his letter to the Ephesian Christians is of paramount importance because it is the grace "with which you can extinguish all the flaming arrows of the evil one" (Ephesians 6:16). This is not an uncertain promise. Rather, it is divine assurance that faith equips us to escape the very extremities of evil. But what is faith?

First, the Bible defines faith as "being sure of what we hope for and certain of what we do not see" (Hebrews 11:1). Thus, in biblical vernacular, faith is a *channel of living trust*—an assurance—that stretches from man to God. In other words, it is the *object* of faith that renders faith faithful.

Furthermore, faith is the assurance that God's promises will never fail, even if sometimes we do not experience their fulfillment in our mortal existence. Hebrews 11 underscores the fact that we trust God to fulfill his promises for the future (the unseen) based on what he has already fulfilled in the past.

Thus, our faith is not blind, but based squarely on God's proven faithfulness.

Finally, the faith that serves to protect us in spiritual warfare is not to be confused with mere knowledge. Millions worldwide believe in the trustworthiness of Billy Graham. They have heard him proclaim the good news on television and yet do not believe that his message corresponds to reality. Thus, they have the knowledge that it takes to be saved but do not have saving faith. Others hear the message, agree that it corresponds to reality, but due to the hardness of their hearts do not bow. Rather, like the demons, they continue to live in fearful anticipation of the judgment to come (James 2:19). Some, however, have what Scripture describes as genuine justifying faith—a faith that not only knows about the gospel and agrees that its content corresponds to reality, but a faith by which they are transformed.

IN PART ADAPTED FROM *The Covering.*

For further study, see Hank Hanegraaff, *The Covering: God's Plan to Protect You from Evil* (Nashville: W Publishing Group, 2002), chapter 7; and Hank Hanegraaff, *Christianity in Crisis* (Eugene, Ore.: Harvest House Publishers, 1993), Part 2.

JOB 13:15

"Though he slay me, yet will I hope in him."

Some, however, have what
Scripture describes as genuine
justifying faith—a faith that not only
knows about the gospel and
agrees that its content corresponds
to reality, but a faith by which
they are transformed.

WHAT IS SIN?

hile it has become politically incorrect to talk about sin, the Scriptures make it crystal clear that "all have sinned and fall short of the glory of God" (Romans 3:23). But what is sin from a biblical perspective?

First, sin is not just murder, rape, or robbery. Sin is failing to do the things we should and doing those things that we should not. In short, *sin* is a word that describes anything that fails to meet God's standard of perfection. Thus, sin is the barrier between you and a satisfying relationship with God. Just as light and dark cannot exist together, neither can God and sin.

Furthermore, sin is a barrier between us and other people. You need only read the newspaper or listen to a news report to see how true this really is. We live in a time when terrorism abounds and when the world as we know it can be instantly obliterated by nuclear aggression.

Finally, sin is the deprivation of good. As such, sin is characterized by a lack of something rather than being something in itself. As noted above, sin is a break in relationship to God and others rather than being an ontological substance.

ADAPTED FROM *THE FACE*

For further study, see Carl F. H. Henry, *Basic Christian Doctrines* (Grand Rapids: Baker Book House, 1962).

1 JOHN 3:4–6

"Everyone who sins breaks the law; in fact, sin is lawlessness. But you know that he appeared so that he might take away our sins. And in him is no sin. No one who lives in him keeps on sinning. No one who continues to sin has either seen him or known him."

SIN IS FAILING to do the things we should . . .

SINS OF OMISSION

Not forgiving (Matthew 6:15)

Failing to honor others (Romans 12:9)

Failing to keep your fervor (Romans, 12:9)

Failing to serve or give (Romans, 12:9)

Failing to live at peace (Romans 12:18)

Failing to love God (Deuteronomy 6:4; Mark 12:30)

Failing to love your neighbor as yourself (Mark 12:31)

Failing to trust God (Proverbs 3:5; Isaiah 26:4)

Failing to trust Christ (John 14:1)

Failing to worship God (Deuteronomy 6:13)

Failing to honor God (Proverbs 3:9; John 5:23)

Failing to honor the Son (John 5:23)

Failing to believe in Jesus (John 3:16–18; 6:29)

Failing to honor one's parents (Exodus 20:12)

Failing to give thanks to God (Psalm 105:1; Romans 1:21)

Failing to glorify God (Psalm 34:3; Romans 1:21)

Failing to fear the Lord (Deuteronomy 6:13; Proverbs 3:7)

Failing to test new teaching by Scripture (1 Thessalonians 5:21; Acts 17:11)

Failing to discern and guard against false teachers and prophets (Matthew 7:15–20; Acts 20:28–31)

Failing to learn and believe Scripture (Deuteronomy 6:6; 2 Timothy 2:15)

Failing to guard life and doctrine (1 Timothy 4:16)

Failing to repay debts (Romans 13:7)

Failing to care for orphans and widows in distress (James 1:20)

Failing to defend the faith (1 Peter 3:15)

Failing to share the gospel (Matthew 28:19)

and doing those things that we should not.

SINS OF COMMISSION

Wrong teaching
(Matthew 23:15)

Insincere love (Romans 12:9)

Causing someone else to sin
(Mark 9:42)

Sexual impurity (Romans 1:24)

Homosexuality
(Romans 1:26–27)

Idolatry (Romans 1:24)

Greed (Romans 1:29)

Blasphemy (Mark 3:29)

Misusing the Lord's name
(Exodus 20:7)

Selfish ambition
(Galatians 5:20)

Fits of rage (Galatians 5:20)

Slave trading (1 Timothy 1:10)

Lying (Exodus 23:1;
Revelation 21:8)

Hypocrisy (1 Peter 2:1)

Drunkeness
(1 Corinthians 6:10)

Stealing (Exodus 20:15;
1 Corinthians 6:10)

Sorcery (Deuteronomy 18:10)

Witchcraft
(Deuteronomy 18:10)

Divination
(Deuteronomy 18:10)

Interpreting Omens
((Deuteronomy 18:10)

Consulting the dead
(Deuteronomy 18:11)

Astrology (Deuteronomy
18:9–13; Isaiah 47:13–14)

Depravity (Romans 1:29)

Envy (Romans 1:29;
1 Peter 2:1)

Deceit (Romans 1:29;
1 Peter 2:1)

Murder (Romans 1:29)

Strife (Romans 1:29)

Malice (Romans 1:29;
1 Peter 2:1)

Gossip (Romans 1:29)

Slander (Romans 1:30;
1 Peter 2:1)

Hating God (Romans 1:30)

Insolence (Romans 1:30)

Arrogance (Romans 1:30)

Boastful (Romans 1:30)

Inventing evil (Romans 1:30)

Disobeying parents
(Romans 1:30)

– 6 –

HOW CAN I BE CERTAIN THAT I'VE
NOT COMMITTED THE UNFORGIVABLE SIN?

T his is one of the most frequently asked questions on the *Bible Answer Man* broadcast and stems from the following words spoken by Christ: "I tell you the truth, every sin and blasphemy will be forgiven men, but the blasphemy against the Spirit will not be forgiven. Anyone who speaks a word against the Son of Man will be forgiven, but anyone who speaks against the Holy Spirit will not be forgiven, either in this age or in the age to come" (Matthew 12:31–32). As a result of these words, Christians are often paralyzed by fear.

In response, let me first point out that from a historic perspective the Pharisees mentioned by Matthew militantly hated Christ and attributed his miracles to Beelzebub, the prince of demons. Unlike those who are afraid they have committed the unforgivable sin, the Pharisees were totally unconcerned about Christ's forgiveness. Instead, with premeditation and persistence, they willfully blasphemed the Holy Spirit's testimony that Christ was the Son of the living God. It is crucial to recognize that the unforgivable sin is not a single act but a continuous, ongoing rejection.

Furthermore, those who have committed the unpardonable sin have no godly regrets. As Paul emphasizes in the book of Romans, they not only continue in their evil ways but approve of others who do so as well (Romans 1:32). Conversely, "godly sorrow brings repentance that leads to salvation" (2 Corinthians 7:10). Sorrow for sin and the desire for Christ's forgiveness is proof positive that you have not rejected the Savior of your soul. Never forget that three times Peter denied his Lord with vile oaths. Yet, not only did Christ forgive him, but his confession, "You are the Christ, the Son of the living God" (Matthew 16:16) became the cornerstone of the Christian church.

Finally, the Bible consistently teaches that those who spend eternity separated from God do so because they willingly, knowingly, and continuously reject the gospel. John refers to this as the "sin that leads to death" (1 John 5:16) in the sense that those who refuse forgiveness through Christ will spend eternity separated from his grace and love. Be assured that those who sincerely desire God's forgiveness can be absolutely certain that they will never be turned away.

For further study see, Hank Hanegraaff, "The Unforgivable Sin," available from Christian Research Institute at http://www.equip.org.

To grow in your understanding of and relationship with God, see J. I. Packer, *Knowing God* (Downers Grove, Ill.: InterVarsity Press, 1993).

1 JOHN 5:13

"I write these things to you who believe in the name of the Son of God so that you may know that you have eternal life."

— 7 —

CAN CHRISTIANS
LOSE THEIR SALVATION?

Sincere believers are sharply divided on this question. Some say Christians *can* lose their salvation and subsequently must be born again and again if they fall away. Others contend that true believers *cannot* lose their salvation through sin, but they can apostatize or walk away from their salvation. Still others hold that salvation begins at the moment of conversion (not death) and continues for all eternity—I hold this view for several reasons.

First, outward appearances can be deceiving. Consider Judas. For three years, he was part of Christ's inner circle. From all outward appearances, he was a true follower of Christ. Yet, Jesus characterized Judas as "a devil" (John 6:70). The book of Hebrews warns us that there were Jews who, like Judas, tasted God's goodness and yet turned from his grace. They acknowledged Christ with their lips, but their apostasy proved that their faith was not real.

Furthermore, we would do well to remember that everlasting life means just that—life everlasting. This life does not begin when we die but when we embrace the Savior who died in our place. As our physical birth can never be undone, so too our spiritual birth can never be undone. Christ said "Ye must be born again" (John 3:7 KJV), not "ye must be born again and again and again." In Philippians, Paul praises God for the confidence that "he who began a good work in you will carry it on to completion" (1:6).

Finally, Scripture is replete with passages that testify to the security of the believer. John 5:24 assures us that "he who believes . . . *has* eternal life" (emphasis added); 1 Corinthians 1:8 promises that Christ will "keep you strong to the end;" And Jude 24 guarantees that God "is able to keep you from falling and to present you before his glorious presence without fault." Moreover, Ephesians provides the surety that "you were marked in him with a seal, the promised Holy Spirit, who is a deposit guaranteeing our inheritance until the redemption of those who are God's possession" (1:13–14). As has been well said, the Lord's trees are evergreen.

For further study, see Hank Hanegraaff, "Safe and Secure," available from CRI at www.equip.org.

*"My sheep listen to my voice;
I know them, and they follow me. I give them
eternal life, and they shall never perish; no one
can snatch them out of my hand.
My Father, who has given them to me,
is greater than all; no one can snatch them
out of my Father's hand."*

MUST CHRISTIANS ATTEND CHURCH?

irst, the Scriptures from first to last teach us that the Christian life is to be lived within the context of the family of faith (Ephesians 3:4–15; Acts 2). Indeed the Bible knows nothing of lone-ranger Christians! Far from being born again as rugged individuals, we are born into a body of believers of which Christ is the head. Thus, as Hebrews commands, "Let us not give up meeting together, as some are in the habit of doing" (10:25).

Furthermore, spiritual growth is impossible apart from membership in a healthy, well-balanced church. It is in the church that we receive the Word and sacraments as means of grace. Thus, it is crucial that we emulate the early Christians who "devoted themselves to the apostles' teaching and to the fellowship, to the breaking of bread and to prayer" (Acts 2:42).

Finally, while it is in the church that we enter into worship, experience fellowship, and are equipped to witness, church membership itself does not save us. As has been well said, walking into a church does not make you a Christian any more than walking into a garage makes you a car. We are rescued from God's wrath, forgiven of all our sins, and declared righteous before God solely by grace, through faith, on account of Jesus Christ (Romans 1:17; 3:21–4:8; Ephesians 2:8–9).

For further study, see Hank Hanegraaff, "How do I find a good church?" *The Bible Answer Book Volume One* (Nashville: J. Countryman, 2004): 39–46.

HEBREWS 10:25

"Let us not give up meeting together, as some are in the habit of doing, but let us encourage one another—and all the more as you see the Day approaching."

– 9 –

How do I find a good church?

One of the questions I am most frequently asked is "How do I find a good church?" This question has taken on added significance in recent years because of the massive impact televangelism has had on our culture. In all too may cases, worship has been replaced with entertainment, and fellowship has been transformed into individualism. In view of these cultural developments, it is critical that Christians have a handle on the ingredients of a healthy, well-balanced church.

The first sign of a healthy, well-balanced church is a pastor who is committed to leading the community of faith in the *worship* of God through prayer, praise, and proclamation. *Prayer* is so inextricably woven into the fabric of worship that it would be unthinkable to have a church service without it. From the very inception of the early Christian church, prayer has been a primary means of worshiping God. Through prayer, we have the privilege of expressing adoration and thanksgiving to the One who saved us, sanctifies us, and one day will glorify us. In fact, our Lord himself set the pattern by teaching his disciples the Prayer of Jesus (Matthew 6:9–13).

Praise is another key ingredient of worship. Scripture urges us to "speak to one another with psalms, hymns and spiritual songs" (Ephesians 5:19). Singing psalms is a magnificent means for intercession, instruction, and the internalization of Scripture. In addition, the great hymns of the faith have stood the test of time and are rich in theological tradition and truth. Spiritual songs, in turn, communicate the freshness of our faith. Thus, it is crucial that we preserve both a respect for our spiritual heritage and a regard for contemporary compositions.

Along with prayer and praise, *proclamation* is axiomatic to experiencing vibrant worship. Paul urged his protégé Timothy to "preach the Word; be prepared in season and out of season; correct, rebuke and encourage—with great patience and careful instruction. For the time will come when men will not put up with sound doctrine. Instead, to suit their own desires, they will gather around them a great number of teachers to say what their itching ears want to hear" (2 Timothy 4:2–3). Church leaders must once again produce in their people a holy hunger for the Word of God. For it is through the proclamation of God's Word that believers are edified, exhorted, encouraged, and equipped.

Furthermore, a healthy, well-balanced church is evidenced through its *oneness*. Christ breaks the barriers of gender, race, and background and unites us as one under the banner of his love. Such oneness is tangibly manifested through community, confession, and contribution.

Community is visible in baptism, which symbolizes our entrance into a body of believers who are one in Christ. It is a sign and a seal that we have been buried to our old life and raised to newness of life through his resurrection power. In like fashion, holy communion is an expression of oneness. As we all partake of the same elements, we partake of that which the elements symbolize— Christ, through whom we are one. Our fellowship on earth, celebrated through communion, is a foretaste of the heavenly fellowship we will share when symbol gives way to substance.

A further expression of our oneness in Christ is our common *confession* of faith—a core set of beliefs, which have been rightly referred to as "essential Christianity." These beliefs, which have been codified in the creeds of the Christian church, form the basis of our unity as the body of Christ. The well-known maxim bears repeating: "In essentials, unity; in nonessentials, liberty; and in all things, charity."

As with community and confession, we experience oneness through the *contribution* of our time, talent, and treasure. The question we should be asking is not "What can the church do for me?" but, "What can I do for the church?" The tragedy of modern Christianity is that when members of the body hurt, too often we relegate them to finding resources outside the walls of the church. That is precisely why the apostle Paul exhorts us to "share with God's people who are in need. Practice hospitality" (Romans 12:13).

Finally, a healthy, well-balanced church is one that is committed to equipping believers to be effective *witnesses* to what they believe, why they believe, and Who they believe. In the Great Commission, Christ called believers not to make mere converts but to make disciples (Matthew 28:19). A disciple is a learner or follower of the Lord Jesus Christ. Thus, we must be prepared to communicate *what* we believe. In other words, we must be equipped to communicate the evangel. If Christians do not know how to share their faith, they have never been through basic training. The gospel of Christ should become such a part of our vocabulary that presenting it becomes second nature.

We also must be equipped to share *why* we believe what we believe. As Peter put it, we must "always be prepared to give an answer to everyone who asks you to give the *reason* for the hope that you have. But do this with gentleness and respect" (1 Peter 3:15, emphasis added). Too many today believe that the task of apologetics is the exclusive domain of scholars and theologians. Not so! The defense of the faith is not optional; it is basic training for *every Christian*.

In addition to being prepared to communicate the what and why of our faith, we must be empowered to communicate the *Who* of our faith. Virtually every theological heresy begins with a misconception of the nature of God. Thus, in a healthy, well-balanced church believers are equipped to communicate glorious doctrines of the faith such as the Trinity and the deity of Jesus Christ. It is crucial that we, like the early Christian church, come to understand more fully the biblical concept of the priesthood of all believers. Clearly, it is not the pastor's calling to do the work of ministry single-handedly. Rather, the pastor is called "to prepare God's people for works of service, so that the body of Christ may be built up until we all reach unity in the faith and in the knowledge of the Son of God and become mature" (Ephesians 4:12–13).

In short, we know we have discovered a good church if God is *worshiped* in Spirit and in truth through prayer, praise, and the proclamation of the Word; if the *oneness* we share in Christ is tangibly manifested through community, confession, and contribution; and if the church is equipping its members as *witnesses* who can communicate what they believe, why they believe, and Who they believe—WOW!

ADAPTED FROM *Counterfeit Revival*
AND IN PART FROM *Christianity in Crsis*

For further study see Hank Hanegraaff, "How to Find a Healthy Church," available from CRI at www.equip.org.

ACTS 2:42
"They [followers of Christ] devoted themselves to the apostles' teaching and to the fellowship, to the breaking of bread and to prayer."

s the father of nine, I can tell you that I sometimes know what my children need before they ask. However, what I as an earthly father only sometimes know, our eternal Father always knows. Which inevitably leads to the question: If God knows what we need before we even ask, why bother asking at all?

First, it is crucial to recognize that supplication should not be seen as the sole sum and substance of prayers. Far from merely being a means of presenting our daily requests to God, prayer is a means of pursuing a dynamic relationship with him.

Furthermore, God ordains not only the ends but the means. Thus, to ask, "Why pray if God already knows what we need?" is akin to asking, "Why get dressed in the morning and go to work?" For that matter if God is going to do what he is going to do anyway, why bother doing anything? God has ordained that the work we do and the prayers we utter both produce results. The fact that

God knows the future does not imply that our futures are fatalistically determined any more than our knowledge that the sun will rise causes the sun to rise.

Finally, while our heavenly Father knows what we need before we even ask, our supplications are in and of themselves an acknowledgement of our dependence on him. And that alone is reason enough to pray without ceasing.

ADAPTED FROM *The Prayer of Jesus*

For further study, see Hank Hanegraaff, *The Prayer of Jesus: Secrets to Real Intimacy with God* (Nashville: W Publishing Group, 2001).

MATTHEW 6:7–8

"And when you pray, do not keep on babbling like pagans, for they think they will be heard because of their many words. Do not be like them, for your Father knows what you need before you ask him."

— 11 —

WHAT ARE SOME
SECRETS TO EFFECTIVE PRAYER?

veryone wants to know the secret to
something. Golfers want to know the
secret to playing golf like Tiger Woods.
Investors want to know the secret to making a
fortune on Wall Street. Parents want to know the
secret to raising healthy, happy kids. And
Christians desperately want to know the secrets to
effective prayer. So, what are the secrets to real
intimacy with God?

The first secret to effective prayer is secret
prayer. And Jesus provided the ultimate example.
As Dr. Luke puts it, he "often withdrew to lonely
places and prayed" (Luke 5:16). Unlike the
religious leaders of his day, Jesus did not pray to be
seen by men. He prayed because he treasured
fellowship with his Father. Hypocrites gain their
reward through public prayer. They may be
perceived as spiritual giants, but by the time they
are finished, they have received everything they will
ever get—their prayer's worth and nothing more.

A further secret is to recognize the connection between prayer and meditation. Our prayers are only as inspired as our intake of Scripture. Scripture feeds meditation, and meditation gives food to our prayers. Meditating on Scripture allows us to more naturally transition into a marvelous time of meaningful prayer. Donald Whitney, who rightly refers to meditation as the missing link between the intake of Scripture and prayer, notes that if there was a secret to the prayer life of evangelist George Müller, it was his discovery of the connection between meditation and prayer.

A final secret is to discover your secret place, a place where you can drown out the static of the world and hear the voice of your heavenly Father. The issue, of course, is not location but motivation. We are all unique creations of God. Thus, your secret place will no doubt be different than mine. The point is that we all desperately need a place away from the invasive sounds of this world so that we can hear the sounds of another place and another Voice.

ADAPTED FROM *The Prayer of Jesus* AND *The Covering*

For further study see, Hank Hanegraaff, *The Prayer of Jesus: Secrets to Intimacy with God* (Nashville: W Publishing Group, 2001).

"But when you pray, go into your room,
close the door and pray to your Father, who is unseen.
Then your Father, who sees what is done
in secret, will reward you."

A few prayers in the Bible:

Abraham's servant—Genesis 24:12–14—Prayed for success in finding a wife for Isaac

Jacob—Genesis 32:9–12—Prayed for protection

Job—Job 13:23—Prayed for conviction of sin

Moses—Exodus 32:11–13, 31–32; Deuteronomy 9:26–29—Prayed for mercy

Moses—Exodus 33:12–18—Prayed to know God and to see his glory

Manoah—Judges 13:8—Prayed for guidance in raising his son, Samson

Hannah—1 Samuel 2:1–10—Prayed to exalt God with thanksgiving and praise

Elijah—1 Kings 18:36–37—Prayed for vindication and proof of God's power

Hezekiah—2 Kings 19:15–19—Prayed for deliverance from enemies

Solomon—2 Chronicles 6:21—Prayed for forgiveness of sins for Israel

David—throughout Psalms—Prayed with thanksgiving and praise for mercy and grace, conviction of sin, forgiveness, instruction, and deliverance from enemies

Jeremiah—Jeremiah 20:7–18—Prayed to complain

Ezra—Ezra 9:6–15—Prayed to confess his people's sin

Daniel—Daniel 6:10–11—Prayed for help with thanksgiving

Daniel—Daniel 9:9–19—Prayed to confess his people's sin

Jonah—Jonah 2:1–9—Prayed for restoration

Jesus—Matthew 26:36–46—Prayed for God's will

Jesus—John 17:1–26—Prayed for himself, for the disciples, and for all believers

Jesus—Luke 23:34—Prayed for forgiveness for his enemies

Apostles—Acts 1:24–25—Prayed for selecting Judas' replacement

Apostles—Acts 4:29–30—Prayed for the bold proclamation of the gospel with miracles

Stephen—Acts 7:59–60—Prayed for the Lord to receive his spirit and to forgive his killers

WHY IS IT SO CRUCIAL TO PRAY
"YOUR WILL BE DONE"?

esus not only taught his disciples to pray, "Your will be done" (Matthew 6:10), but he modeled those very words in his own life and ministry. Which, of course, begs the question, "Why is it so crucial to pray in this way?"

First, to pray "your will be done" is to recognize the sovereignty of God over every aspect of our daily lives. In effect, it is a way of saying, "Thank God this world is under his control, not mine!" We would be in deep trouble if God gave us everything for which we asked. Fact is, we don't know what's best for us! We only see a snapshot of our lives—while God sees the entire panoply. Thus, his perspective is far superior to ours.

Furthermore, to pray "your will be done" is daily recognition that our wills must be submitted to his will. One of the most comforting thoughts that can penetrate a human mind yielded to the will of God is that he who has created us also knows what is best for us. Thus, if we walk according to his will, rather than trying to command him according to our own wills, we will indeed have, as he promised, not a panacea, but peace in the midst of the storm. In the yielded life there is great peace in knowing that the One who taught us to pray "your will be done" has every detail of our lives under control. Not only is God the object of our faith, he is also the originator of our faith. Indeed, he is the originator of our salvation and, yes, even the originator of our prayers. Thus, whatever we pray for, whether it's healing or a house, when our will is in harmony with his will, we will receive what we request 100 percent of the time. However, when we pray as Christ prayed, "Nevertheless, not my will but thy will be done," we can rest assured that even in sickness and tragedy "all things work together for good to those who love God and are called according to his purpose" (Romans 8:28).

Finally, to pray "your will be done" is daily recognition that God will not spare us from trial and tribulation, but rather he will use the fiery furnace to purge impurities from our lives. Ultimately, this is the message of the book of Job. Job endured more tragedy in a single day than most people experience in a lifetime. Yet in his darkest hour Job uttered the ultimate words of faith, "Though he slay me, yet will

I trust in him" (Job 13:15 KJV). For the child of God the hope is not perfect health and happiness in this lifetime, but a resurrected body and a heavenly dwelling in the life to come.

ADAPTED FROM THE Prayer of Jesus

For further study, see Hank Hanegraaff, *The Prayer of Jesus: Secrets to Real Intimacy with God* (Nashville: W Publishing Group, 2001).

JAMES 4:13–16

"Now listen, you who say, 'Today or tomorrow we will go to this or that city, spend a year there, carry on business and make money.' Why, you do not even know what will happen tomorrow. What is your life? You are a mist that appears for a little while and then vanishes. Instead, you ought to say, 'If it is the Lord's will, we will live and do this or that.' As it is, you boast and brag. All such boasting is evil."

— 13 —

WHY DO PEOPLE END THEIR
PRAYERS WITH "AMEN"?

veryone is familiar with the word "amen." But have you ever taken the time to consider what it really means? Is ending our prayers with "amen" a mere ritual? Or is there a majestic richness to the word that is often missed?

First, "amen" is a universally recognized word that is far more significant than simply signing off or saying, "That's all." With the word "amen" we are in effect saying, "May it be so in accordance with the will of God." It is a marvelous reminder that any discussion on prayer must begin with the understanding that prayer is a means of bringing us into conformity with God's will, not a magic mantra that ensures God's conformity to ours.

Furthermore, the word "amen" is a direct reference to Jesus, who taught us to pray "your will be done" (Matthew 6:10). In Revelation, he is referred to as the "Amen, the faithful and true witness, the ruler of God's creation" (3:14). Jesus not only taught us to pray, "your will be done" but also modeled those words in his life. In his passionate prayer in the Garden of Gethsemane he prayed, "My Father, if it is possible, may this cup be taken from me. Yet *not as I will, but as you will*" (Matthew 26:39, emphasis added).

Finally, although Jesus is our greatest example, he is certainly not our only example. His brother James warns those who are prone to "boast and brag" that they ought to pray instead, "If it is the Lord's will, we will live and do this or that" (James 4:15). Christ's closest friend during his earthly ministry, the apostle John, echoes the words of the Master when he writes, "This is the confidence we have in approaching God: that if we ask anything *according to his will*, he hears us" (1 John 5:14, emphasis added).

Next time you end your prayer time with the word "amen" it is my prayer that you will focus on the fact that far from being a formality, it is fraught with meaning. Not only is "amen" a direct reference to the Savior, but it is a reminder that even the seemingly insignificant details of our lives are under the Savior's sovereign control.

ADAPTED FROM *The Prayer of Jesus*

For further study, see Hank Hanegraaff, *The Prayer of Jesus: Secrets to Real Intimacy with God* (Nashville: W Publishing Group, 2001).

"This is the confidence we have in approaching God: that if we ask anything according to his will, he hears us. And if we know that he hears us—whatever we ask—we know that we have what we asked of him."

MUST I FORGIVE THOSE
WHO REFUSE FORGIVENESS?

esus taught his disciples to pray, "Forgive us our debts, as we also have forgiven our debtors" (Matthew 6:12). Does that mean we have to forgive someone even when they refuse reconciliation?

First, the debts we owe one another are small change compared to the infinite debt we owe our heavenly Father. Because we have been forgiven an infinite debt, it is a horrendous evil to even consider withholding forgiveness from those who seek it. Thus, we must always manifest the kind of love that is *willing* to forgive those who wrong us.

Furthermore, forgiveness is by definition a two-way street leading to the restoration of fellowship. It requires someone who is *willing* to forgive, and someone who is *wanting* to be forgiven. If you are to forgive me, I must be repentant; otherwise, there can be no restoration of fellowship (i.e., forgiveness).

Finally, we must never suppose that our standard of forgiveness is higher than God's standard. He *objectively* offers us forgiveness and the restoration of fellowship. His forgiveness is not *subjectively* realized, however, until we repent (Luke 6:37–38).

In part adapted from *The Prayer of Jesus*

For further study, see Hank Hanegraaff, *The Prayer of Jesus: Secrets to Real Intimacy with God* (Nashville: W. Publishing Group, 2001).

Matthew 5:23–24

*"Therefore, if you are offering your gift
at the altar and there remember that your brother has
something against you, leave your gift there in front of
the altar. First go and be reconciled to your brother;
then come and offer your gift."*

SPIRITUAL GIFTS

WHAT DOES IT MEAN TO SAY
THAT THE HOLY SPIRIT IS *IN* YOU?

 ver the past several decades, I have been asked the "in" question in a variety of different ways such as: What does it mean to say God is "in" my life; Jesus is "in" my heart; or the Holy Spirit is "in" me? Does it mean that everyone simultaneously has a little piece of God in them? Or is the Bible communicating something far more precious?

First, to say that the Holy Spirit is *in* you is not to point out *where* the Holy Spirit is physically located, but rather to acknowledge that you have come into an intimate, personal relationship with him through faith and repentance. As such, the preposition "*in*" is not a *locational* but a *relational* term. Similarly, when Jesus says, "The Father is in me, and I in the Father" (John 10:38), he is not speaking of physical location but intimacy of relationship.

Furthermore, to deny that the Holy Spirit is *spatially* locatable within us is not to deny that he is *actively* locatable within us, working redemptively to conform us to the image of Christ. Far from detracting from our nearness to the Holy Spirit, the classical Christian view intensifies the intimacy of our relationship to the Creator as well as the benefits of our redemption.

Finally, according to the Scriptures, the Holy Spirit is not a physical being, thus to ask *where* the Holy Spirit is, is to confuse categories. Asking spatial questions about a Being who does not have extension in space makes about as much sense as asking what the color blue tastes like. King Solomon reveals the utter futility of believing that the infinite Holy Spirit can be physically contained in any finite space, let alone the human body, when he exclaimed, "Will God really dwell on earth? The heavens, even the highest heaven, cannot contain you. How much less this temple I have built!" (1 Kings 8:27).

For further study, see Hank Hanegraaff, "The Indwelling of the Holy Spirit," from CRI at www.equip.org.

1 CORINTHIANS 6:19
"Do you not know that your body is a temple of the Holy Spirit, who is in you, whom you have received from God?"

– 16 –

IS THERE A DIFFERENCE BETWEEN *INDWELLING* AND *INFILLING*?

 irst, all members of true Israel are *indwelt* by the Holy Spirit (Romans 8:1–17; 1 Corinthians 12:13; Ephesians 1:13; 1 John 4:13). As such, the Spirit dwelt in Moses (Isaiah 63:11) as well as in Matthew (John 14:17), Joshua (Numbers 27:18), and James (see Acts 15). In every epoch of time, believers are regenerated and restored (John 3:3–6) as well as sanctified and sealed (Romans 15:16; Ephesians 1:13; 4:30) through the indwelling presence of the Holy Spirit.

While the indwelling of the Spirit happens at conversion, the infilling of the Spirit happens continually.

Furthermore, those who are in Christ are not only indwelt but *infilled* with the Holy Spirit. When Jesus said to his disciples, "I will ask the Father, and he will give you another Counselor to be with you forever" (John 14:16), he was not suggesting that the

Holy Spirit was not already working redemptively within his followers but that the Spirit would manifest in the special empowerment of each believer to proclaim the gospel (Acts 1:8; 13:52).

Finally, while the indwelling of the Spirit happens at conversion, the infilling of the Spirit happens continually (Ephesians 5:18). As such, we daily seek the Holy Spirit to empower us whether in our prayers to God or in our proclamations of the gospel. Indeed, whenever the gospel penetrates the human heart it is "'not by might nor by power, but by my Spirit,' says the Lord Almighty" (Zechariah 4:6).

For further study, see "Is speaking in tongues *the* evidence of the baptism of the Holy Spirit?" p. 74.

PSALM 51:10–13

"Create in me a pure heart, O God, and renew a steadfast spirit within me. Do not cast me from your presence or take your Holy Spirit from me. Restore to me the joy of your salvation and grant me a willing spirit, to sustain me. Then I will teach transgressors your ways, and sinners will turn back to you."

IS SPEAKING IN TONGUES *THE* EVIDENCE
OF THE BAPTISM OF THE HOLY SPIRIT?

 t has become increasingly common for Christians to suppose that the full gospel includes the baptism of the Holy Spirit with the evidence of speaking in tongues. Thus the question: Is speaking in tongues *the* evidence of being baptized by the Holy Spirit?

First, as the apostle Paul makes plain, believers are "all baptized by one Spirit into one body" (1 Corinthians 12:13), yet not all who believe speak in tongues (vv. 10, 30). Thus tongues may be a manifestation of the baptism of the Holy Spirit, but tongues cannot be *the* manifestation.

Furthermore, even if one does speak in tongues it is not a guarantee that they have been baptized in the Holy Spirit. For as Paul puts it, "If I speak in the tongues of men and angels, but have not love, I am only a resounding gong or a clanging cymbal" (1 Corinthians 13:1). Indeed, says Paul, without love, "I am nothing!" (v. 2). Moreover, socio–psychological manipulation tactics such as peer pressure or the subtle power of suggestion can induce ecstatic utterances wholly apart from the Spirit.

The normative sign of the baptism of the Holy Spirit is not speaking in tongues but the confession of Jesus Christ as Lord, repentance from sin, and obedience to God.

Finally, as Scripture makes clear, the normative sign of the baptism of the Holy Spirit is not speaking in tongues but the confession of Jesus Christ as Lord, repentance from sin, and obedience to God (Romans 8:1–17; 1 John 4:12–16; cf. Ephesians 1:13–15). "Those who live in accordance with the Spirit have their minds set on what the Spirit desires. The mind of sinful man is death, but the mind controlled by the Spirit is life and peace" (Romans 8:6). As such, the fruit of the Spirit is not merely speaking in tongues, but "love, joy, peace, patience, kindness, goodness, faithfulness, gentleness and self–control" (Galatians 5:22–23). In sum, righteousness, not tongues, is the core of Christianity compressed in a single word.

For further study, see Hank Hanegraaff, "What does it mean to say that the Holy Spirit is in you?" *The Bible Answer Book* Volume 1 (Nashville: J Countryman, 2004), 31–32.

"Do not get drunk on wine, which leads to debauchery.
Instead, be filled with the Spirit. Speak to
one another with psalms, hymns and spiritual songs.
Sing and make music in your heart to the Lord,
always giving thanks to God the Father for everything,
in the name of our Lord Jesus Christ.
Submit to one another out of reverence for Christ."

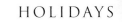

HOLIDAYS

SHOULD CHRISTIANS
CELEBRATE CHRISTMAS?

very year around Christmas time, serious
concerns are voiced regarding the
validity of celebrating Christmas. Some
note that the origins of Christmas are pagan, others
point out that the Bible overtly denounces
Christmas trees as idolatrous, and still others
suggest that Santa Claus is a dangerous fairy tale.

In response let me first acknowledge that when
Christmas was originally instituted, December 25
was indeed a pagan festival commemorating the
birthday of a false god. While this is historical fact,
what is frequently overlooked is that the church's
choice of December 25 was intentional. Instead of
Christianizing a pagan festival, the church
established a rival celebration. While the world has
all but forgotten the Greco-Roman gods of
antiquity, they are annually reminded that two
thousand years ago Christ invaded time and space.

Furthermore, the Bible nowhere condemns
Christmas trees as idolatrous. The oft-cited passage

in Jeremiah 10:2–4 might at first blush appear compelling, but context precludes the pretext. Jeremiah's description of a tree cut out of the forest adorned with silver and gold and fastened with a hammer and nails so that it would not totter is a reference to wooden idols, not Christmas trees. In fact, Christmas trees originated in Christian Germany two thousand years after Jeremiah's condemnation of manmade idols. They evolved over time from two Christian traditions. One was a "paradise tree" hung with apples as a reminder of the tree of life in the garden of Eden. The other was a triangular shelf holding Christmas figurines decorated by a star. In the sixteenth century, these two symbols merged into the present Christmas tree tradition. Next Christmas you might well consider using the Christmas tree in the home of an unbeliever as a springboard or opportunity to explain the reason for the season from the fall in Paradise to redemption in Christ.

Finally, believe it or not, even Santa can be saved! Far from merely being a dangerous fairy tale, "Santa Claus" in reality is an Anglicized form of the Dutch name *Sinter Klaas*, which in turn is a reference to Saint Nicholas. According to tradition, Saint Nick not only lavished gifts on needy children but also valiantly supported the doctrine of the Trinity at the Council of Nicea in AD 325. Thus, Christians may legitimately look to Saint Nick as a genuine hero of the faith.

This December 25 as you celebrate the coming of Christ with a Christmas tree surrounded by presents, may the selflessness of Saint Nick be a reminder of the Savior who gave the greatest gift of all: "Greater love has no one than this, that he lay down his life for his friends" (John 15:13).

For further study, see Paul Maier, *The First Christmas* (Grand Rapids: Kregel Publications, 2001).

LUKE 2:8–14

"And there were shepherds living out in the fields nearby, keeping watch over their flocks at night. An angel of the Lord appeared to them, and the glory of the Lord shone around them, and they were terrified. But the angel said to them, 'Do not be afraid. I bring you good news of great joy that will be for all the people. Today in the town of David a Savior has been born to you; he is Christ the Lord. This will be a sign to you: You will find a baby wrapped in cloths and lying in a manger.' Suddenly a great company of the heavenly host appeared with the angel, praising God and saying, 'Glory to God in the highest, and on earth peace to men on whom his favor rests.'"

HOW SHOULD CHRISTIANS
RESPOND TO HALLOWEEN?

yriad questions surround Halloween. Should we participate? Accommodate? Or should we vigorously denounce Halloween? To answer such questions, it's helpful to view Halloween from the perspective of history.

First, we should recognize that Halloween is indeed rooted in the ancient Celtic feast of *Samhain* (sah-ween). The Druids believed that on the eve of Samhain the veil between the present world and the world beyond was pierced, releasing demons, witches, and hobgoblins en masse to harass the living. In order to make themselves immune from attack, people disguised themselves as witches, devils, and ghouls; attempted to ward off evil spirits by carving grotesque faces on gourds illuminated with candles; and placated the spirits with a variety of treats.

Furthermore, we can learn a lot from how the early Christians responded to Halloween. October 31, the eve prior to All Saints Day was designated as a spiritually edifying holiday (holy day) on which to proclaim the supremacy of the gospel over the superstition of ghosts. Thus, "all Hallows Eve," from which the word *Halloween* is derived, was an attempt on the part of Christianity to overwhelm the tradition of ghouls with the truth of the gospel.

Finally, although Halloween is once again predominately pagan there is a silver lining. Like our forefathers, we can choose to celebrate "all Hallows Eve" by focusing on heroes of the faith—those who, like Martin Luther, were willing to stand for truth no matter what the cost. We might also use the occasion to introduce our children to such great classics as *Pilgrim's Progress*. In the end, the trick is to treat Halloween as a strategic opportunity rather than a time of satanic oppression.

See also Hank Hanegraaff, "Halloween: Oppression or Opportunity?" Available from CRI, www.equip.org.

HEBREWS 12:1
"Therefore, since we are surrounded by such a great cloud of witnesses, let us throw off everything that hinders and the sin that so easily entangles, and let us run with perseverance the race marked out for us."

WHY DO CHRISTIANS WORSHIP ON SUNDAY RATHER THAN ON THE SABBATH DAY?

lthough some Christian traditions denounce Sunday worship as the end time "mark of the beast," there are good reasons why millions of Christians gather on the first day of the week for worship.

First, in remembrance of the resurrection the early Christian church changed the day of worship from Saturday to Sunday. Within weeks, thousands of Jews willingly gave up a theological tradition that had given them their national identity. God himself had provided the early church with a new pattern of worship through Christ's resurrection on the first day of the week as well as the Holy Spirit's descent on Pentecost Sunday.

Furthermore, Scripture provides us with the reasons behind the symbol of the Sabbath. In Genesis, the Sabbath was a celebration of God's work in creation (Genesis 2:2–3; Exodus 20:11). After the Exodus, the Sabbath expanded to a celebration of God's deliverance from oppression in

Egypt (Deuteronomy 5:15). As a result of the resurrection, the Sabbath's emphasis shifted once again. It became a celebration of the "rest" we have through Christ who delivers us from sin and the grave (Hebrews 4:1–11). For the emerging Christian church, the most dangerous snare was a failure to recognize that Jesus was the substance that fulfilled the symbol of the Sabbath.

In the end, religious rites must
inevitably bow to redemptive realities.

Finally, if you insist on being slavishly bound to Old Testament laws you should also be forewarned that failing to keep the letter of the law might be hazardous to your health. According to the Mosaic Law, anyone who does any work on the Sabbath "must be put to death" (Exodus 35:2). As the apostle Paul explains, however, "Christ redeemed us from the curse of the law by becoming a curse for us, for it is written: 'Cursed is everyone who is hung on a tree'"(Galatians 3:13). The Sabbath was "a shadow of the things that were to come; the reality, however, is found in Christ" (Colossians 2:17).

In the end, religious rites must inevitably bow to redemptive realities.

For further study, see D. A. Carson, ed., *From Sabbath to Lord's Day: A Biblical, Historical, and Theological Investigation* (Eugene, Oregon: Wipf and Stock Publishers, 1999, originally published by Zondervan, 1982)

COLOSSIANS 2:16–17

"Do not let anyone judge you by what you eat or drink, or with regard to a religious festival, a New Moon celebration or a Sabbath day. These are a shadow of the things that were to come; the reality, however, is found in Christ."

THE NATURE AND

CHARACTER OF GOD

IS THE TRINITY BIBLICAL?

hile it has become increasingly popular to suggest that the doctrine of the Trinity is derived from pagan sources, in reality, this Christian essential is thoroughly biblical. The word "Trinity"—like "incarnation"—is not found in Scripture; however, it aptly codifies what God has condescended to reveal to us about his nature and being. In short, the Trinitarian platform contains three planks: (1) there is but one God; (2) the Father is God, the Son is God, and the Holy Spirit is God; (3) Father, Son, and Holy Spirit are eternally distinct.

The first plank underscores that there is only one God. Christianity is not polytheistic but fiercely monotheistic. "You are my witnesses, declares the LORD, and my servant whom I have chosen, so that you may know and believe me and understand that I am he. *Before me no god was formed, nor will there be one after me*" (Isaiah 43:10, emphasis added).

The second plank emphasizes that in hundreds of Scripture passages the Father, Son, and Holy Spirit are declared to be fully and completely God. As a case in point, the apostle Paul says that, "there is but one God the Father" (1 Corinthians 8:6). The Father, speaking of the Son, says, "Your throne, O God, will last forever and forever" (Hebrews 1:8). And when Ananias "lied to the Holy Spirit," Peter points out that he had "not lied to men but to God" (Acts 5:3–4).

The third plank of the Trinitarian platform asserts that the Father, Son, and Holy Spirit are eternally distinct. Scripture clearly portrays subject/object relationships between Father, Son, and Holy Spirit. For example, the Father and Son love one another, speak to each other (John 17:1–26), and together send the Holy Spirit (John 15:26). Additionally, Jesus proclaims that he and the Father are two distinct witnesses and two distinct judges (John 8:14–18). If Jesus were himself the Father, his argument would have been not only irrelevant but also fatally flawed; and if such were the case, he could not have been fully God.

It is important to note that when Trinitarians speak of one God they are referring to the nature or essence of God. Moreover, when they speak of persons they are referring to personal self-distinctions within the Godhead. Put another way, we believe in one *What* and three *Who's*.

For further study, see James R. White, *The Forgotten Trinity* (Minneapolis: Bethany House, 2001).

DEUTERONOMY 6:4

"Hear, O Israel: The LORD our God,
the LORD is one."

MATTHEW 28:19

"Therefore go and make disciples of all nations,
baptizing them in the name of the Father and of the
Son and of the Holy Spirit."

IF GOD IS ONE, WHY DOES THE BIBLE REFER TO HIM IN THE PLURAL?

ow could the Israelites be fiercely monotheistic and yet refer to their God using the plural *Elohim*?

First, this cannot be explained away as a "royal plural" or "plural of majesty." Biblical Hebrew knows of no other instance in which a first-person plural is used to refer solely to the speaker.

Furthermore, while the Bible from Genesis to Revelation reveals that God is one in nature or essence (Deuteronomy 6:4; Isaiah 43:10; Ephesians 4:6), it also reveals that this one God eternally exists in three distinct persons: the Father, the Son, and the Holy Spirit (1 Corinthians 8:6; Hebrews 1:8; Acts 5:3–4). Thus, the plural ending of *Elohim* points to a plurality of persons, not to a plurality of gods.

Finally, although *Elohim* is *suggestive* of the Trinity, this word alone is not *sufficient* to prove the Trinity. Thus, instead of relying on a singular grammatical construction, Christians must be equipped to demonstrate that the one God revealed in Scripture exists in three persons who are eternally distinct.

For further study, see Robert Letham, *The Holy Trinity: In Scripture, History, Theology, and Worship* (Phillipsburg, New Jersey: P&R Publishing, 2004).

DEUTERONOMY 6:4
"Hear, O Israel:
The LORD our God, the LORD is one."

- 2 3 -

WHAT DOES IT MEAN TO SAY
THAT GOD IS OMNIPRESENT?

◯

The Bible clearly portrays God's omnipresence. But what exactly does that mean? Is God dispersed throughout the universe? Or does omnipresence refer to God's nearness to all of creation all of the time?

First, when Scripture speaks of God as omnipresent or present everywhere (Psalm 139), it is not communicating that he is physically distributed throughout the universe, but that he is simultaneously present (with all his fullness) to every part of creation. Thus Scripture communicates God's creative and sustaining relationship to the cosmos rather than his physical location in the cosmos.

Furthermore, to speak of God's omnipresence in terms of his physical location in the world rather than his relationship to the world has more in common with the panentheism of heretical process theology (currently popular in liberal circles) than with classical Christian theism. Panentheism holds that God is intrinsically "in" the world (like a hand in a glove), while classical theism holds that God properly exists outside of time and space (Isaiah 57:15).

Finally, the danger of speaking about God in locational terms is that it logically implies that he is by nature a material being. The apostle John clearly communicates that "God is Spirit, and his worshipers must worship in spirit and in truth" (John 4:24).

For further study, see Gordon R. Lewis, "Attributes of God," in Walter A. Elwell, ed., *Evangelical Dictionary of Theology*, 2nd edition (Grand Rapids: Baker Academic, 2001), 492–499.

PSALM 139:7–10

"Where can I go from your Spirit?
Where can I flee from your presence?
If I go up to the heavens, you are there;
if I make my bed in the depths, you are there.
If I rise on the wings of the dawn,
if I settle on the far side of the sea,
even there your hand will guide me,
your right hand will hold me fast."

DOES GOD KNOW THE FUTURE?

 significant contingency in Christianity— open theists—are currently communicating that God does not have perfect knowledge of the future. How do we respond to this crisis within Christianity?

First, the Bible from beginning to end demonstrates the omniscience of God. In the words of Isaiah, God knows "the end from the beginning" (Isaiah 46:10). As such, God's knowledge is exhaustive, including even those things yet future (cf. Job 37:16; Psalm 139:1–6; 147:5; Hebrews 4:12–13).

Furthermore, if God's knowledge of the future is fallible, biblical predictions that depend on human agency might well have turned out wrong. Even Jesus' predictions in the Olivet Discourse could have failed, thus undermining his claim to deity. God himself could have failed the biblical test for a prophet (Deuteronomy 18:22). Indeed, if God's knowledge of the future is incomplete, we would be foolish to trust him to answer our prayers, thus negating the "confidence we have in approaching

God: that if we ask anything according to his will, he hears us. And if we know that he hears us—whatever we ask—we know that we have what we asked of him" (1 John 5:14–15).

Finally, while open theists suggest that God cannot know the future exhaustively because he changes his plans as a result of what people do, in reality it is not God who changes, but people who change in relationship to God. By way of analogy, if you walk into a headwind you struggle against the wind; if you make a u–turn on the road the wind is at your back. It is not the wind that has changed, but you have changed in relationship to the wind. As such, God's promise to destroy Nineveh was not aborted because he did not know the future but because the Ninevites, who had walked in opposition to God, turned from walking in their wicked ways. Indeed, all of God's promises to bless or to judge must be understood in light of the condition that God withholds blessing on account of disobedience and withholds judgment on account of repentance (Ezekiel 18; Jeremiah 18:7–10).

For further study, see "Does God repent?" on p. 98.

"Remember the former things, those of long ago; I am God, and there is no other; I am God, and there is none like me. I make known the end from the beginning, from ancient times, what is still to come. I say: My purpose will stand, and I will do all that I please."

DOES GOD REPENT?

The classic King James Version of the Bible says, "It repented the LORD that he had made man on the earth, and it grieved him at his heart" (Genesis 6:6). Elsewhere, God says, "It repenteth me that I have set up Saul to be king for he is turned back from following me, and hath not performed my commandments" (1 Samuel 15:11). If God is perfect, how could he repent?

First, the Bible unequivocally teaches that God is perfectly good and thus incapable of doing evil (Psalm 5:4–5; James 1:13; 3 John 1:11). As such, God's repentance must not be understood as entailing moral guilt. Indeed, the moral perfection of the Creator sets him apart from his sin–tainted creation (Leviticus 11:44–45; 19:2; 20:7; 1 Peter 1:15–16).

Furthermore, although God does not change, the meaning of the word "repent" has changed over time. Thus in place of the word "repent" most modern English translations substitute the word "regret" or "grieve." Indeed, as a human father grieves over rebellion on the part of his children, so our heavenly Father grieves over rebellion on the part of his creation.

Finally, God's repentance must be understood as an anthropomorphism communicating the full measure of God's grief over the horror of sin rather than a change of heart or a change of mind. With respect to the faithlessness of Saul, God says, "It repenteth me that I have set up Saul to be king" (1 Samuel 15:11). Yet, the very same context says that "the Strength of Israel will *not* lie *nor repent*: for he is not a man, that he should *repent*" (v. 29, emphasis added). Apart from an anthropomorphic understanding, such passages would be self-refuting.

For further study, see Millard J. Erickson, *What Does God Know and When Does He Know It?* (Grand Rapids: Zondervan, 2003).

1 SAMUEL 15:29
"He who is the Glory of Israel does not lie or change his mind; for he is not a man, that he should change his mind."

IF JEALOUSY IS SIN, HOW CAN GOD BE JEALOUS?

od is referred to in Scripture as jealous, and jealousy is referred to in Scripture as sin. The second commandment explicitly says that God is a jealous God (Exodus 20:4–5; cf. 34:14); yet, in Galatians Paul condemns jealousy in the same breath as idolatry (Galatians 5:19–20). How can this be?

First, there is such a thing as sanctified jealousy. As such, jealousy is the proper response of a husband or wife whose trust has been violated through infidelity. Indeed, when an exclusive covenant relationship is dishonored, sanctified jealousy is the passionate zeal that fights to restore that holy union. The jealousy of God for his holy name and for the exclusive worship of his people as such is sanctified.

Furthermore, as there is sanctified jealousy, so too there is sinful jealousy. In this sense jealousy is painfully coveting another's advantages. Accordingly, the apostle Paul lists jealousy as an act of the sinful nature. Says Paul, "The acts of the sinful nature are obvious: sexual immorality, impurity and debauchery; idolatry and witchcraft; hatred, discord, *jealousy*, fits of rage, selfish ambition, dissentions, factions and envy; drunkenness, orgies, and the like" (Galatians 5:19–21, emphasis added).

Finally, as God personifies sanctified jealousy, so those who reflect his character must be zealous for the things of God. The Bible is replete with heroes such as Elijah (1 Kings 19:10, 14), David (Psalm 69:9), and Paul (2 Corinthians 11:2) whose jealousy for God's glory motivated self–sacrifice and radical reform. The quintessential example, however, is found in the incarnate Christ who exercised the epitome of sanctified jealousy by overturning the tables of the moneychangers in the temple—a symbolic gesture condemning the Jewish leaders of his day for dishonoring God through their contemptible religiosity (Matthew 21:12–13; John 2:17; cf. Jeremiah 7:9–15).

For further study, see J. I. Packer, *Knowing God* (Downers Grove, Ill.: InterVarsity Press, 1982): 151–58.

2 CORINTHIANS 11:2
"I am jealous for you with a godly jealousy.
I promised you to one husband, to Christ, so that I
might present you as a pure virgin to him."

Does God have a gender?

t has become increasingly popular in Christian circles to apply politically correct sentiments to language for God. Some have even supplemented the Trinitarian language of Father, Son, and Holy Spirit with feminine formulations, such as Mother, Child, and Womb. This raises an important question: to wit, does God have a gender?

First, the Bible tells us "God created man in his own image, in the image of God he created him; male and female he created them" (Genesis 1:27). As God created both male and female in his image, he does not participate in one or the other gender, but rather transcends gender.

Furthermore, while the Bible uses masculine titles for God, such as Father and Son, it also employs feminine images for God, such as mother (Isaiah 49:14–15; 66:13) and midwife (Isaiah 66:9). Likewise, his judgment of Israel is likened to that of a mother bear robbed of her cubs (Hosea 13:8). Whether masculine or feminine, all such images are anthropomorphisms or personifications that reveal God to us in ways we can understand.

As God created both male and female in his image, he does not participate in one or the other gender, but rather transcends gender.

Finally, the language we use for God must *clarify* rather than *confuse*. In the absence of biblical warrant we ought to refrain from tampering with the traditional titles for God. Indeed, it would be a grave mistake to sacrifice theological clarity concerning the nature of God and the nature of the relationships between the divine persons of the Godhead on the altar of political correctness.

For further study, see Leslie Zeigler, "Christianity or Feminism?" in William A. Dembeski and Jay Wesley Richards, (eds.), *Unapologetic Apologetics* (Downers Grove, Ill.: InterVarsity Press, 2001): 179–86.

GALATIANS 3:28–29

"There is neither Jew nor Greek, slave nor free, male nor female, for you are all one in Christ Jesus. If you belong to Christ, then you are Abraham's seed, and heirs according to the promise."

CAN GOD CREATE A ROCK SO HEAVY
THAT HE CANNOT MOVE IT?

his question is a classic straw man that has most Christians looking like the proverbial deer in the headlights. At best, it challenges God's omnipotence. At worst, it undermines his existence.

First, there is a problem with the premise of the question. While it is true that God can do anything that is consistent with his nature, it is absurd to suggest that he can do everything. God cannot lie (Hebrews 6:18); he cannot be tempted (James 1:13); and he cannot cease to exist (Psalm 102:25–27).

It is crucial that we learn to question the question rather than assuming the question is valid.

Furthermore, just as it is impossible to make a one-sided triangle, so it is impossible to make a rock too heavy to be moved. What an all-powerful God can create he can obviously move. Put another way, God can do everything that is logically possible.

Finally, we should note that a wide variety of similar questions are raised to undermine the Christian view of God. Thus, it is crucial that we learn to question the question rather than assuming the question is valid.

For further study, see Norman L. Geisler, *Baker Encyclopedia of Christian Apologetics* (Grand Rapids: Baker Books, 1999), 553–554; see also 283–288. See also Hank Hanegraaff, "Indwelling of the Holy Spirit," available at www.equip.org.

PROVERBS 26:4–5

"Do not answer a fool according to his folly,
or you will be like him yourself.
Answer a fool according to his folly,
or he will be wise in his own eyes."

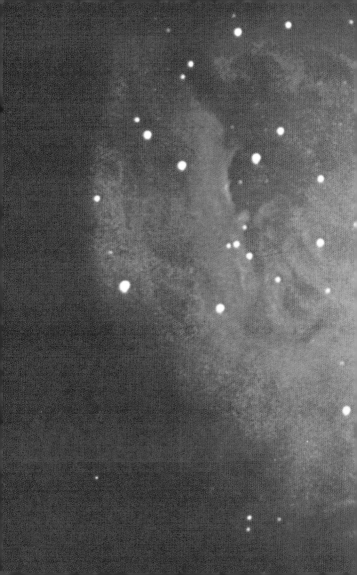

BASIC APOLOGETICS

WHAT IS APOLOGETICS?

As we move into what has been described as post–Christian America, it is increasingly important for Christians to know *what* they believe as well as *why* they believe it. The apostle Peter put it this way: "*Always* be prepared to give an answer *[apologia]* to everyone who asks you to give the reason for the hope that you have. But do this with gentleness and with respect" (1 Peter 3:15, emphasis added).

First, apologetics is the defense of the faith "once for all entrusted to the saints" (Jude 3). The word "apologetics" is derived from the Greek, *apologia*, which means "a reasoned defense." As such, it involves providing an *answer*, not an *apology* in the contemporary sense of the word. Just as good attorneys defend their clients in courts of law by presenting solid evidence and sound reasoning, so too apologists defend the truth of Christianity through well-reasoned answers to the questions of skeptics and seekers alike.

Furthermore, apologetics is *pre–evangelism*. As such, apologetics is the handmaiden to evangelism. It is using our logical answers as springboards or opportunities to share the good news of the gospel. The Christian faith is not a blind faith but rather a faith firmly rooted in history and evidence.

Finally, apologetics is *post–evangelism*. In the swirling waves of doubt and despair that often threaten to submerge our faith, it is crucial to be familiar with the pillars or posts on which our faith is founded—namely, that God created the universe; that Jesus Christ demonstrated he is God through the immutable fact of his resurrection; and that the Bible is demonstrably divine rather than human in origin.

This, in a nutshell, is what apologetics is all about. And remember—if you are looking for a truly rewarding experience, try becoming an apologist. Not only will you experience the power and presence of the Holy Spirit working through you, but you may just find yourself in the middle of an angelic praise gathering when you've helped a lost son or daughter of Adam find his or her way into the kingdom of God.

For further study, see William Lane Craig, *Reasonable Faith* (Wheaton, IL: Crossway, 1994).

"Be wise in the way you act toward outsiders; make the most of every opportunity. Let your conversation be always full of grace, seasoned with salt, so that you may know how to answer everyone."

IS APOLOGETICS REALLY NECESSARY?

Too often people suppose the task of apologetics to be the exclusive domain of scholars and theologians. Not so! The defense of the faith is not optional. It is basic training for *every Christian*. And that means *you!*

First, the Bible informs us that apologetics is not just a nicety; it is a necessity for every believer. Writing in a world steeped in mystery cults, the apostle Peter admonished believers to "always be prepared to give an answer [*apologia*] to everyone who asks you to give the reason for the hope that you have" (1 Peter 3:15). As such, Paul vigorously defended the gospel (Acts 17:15–34; 18:4) and charged Timothy and Titus to do the same (2 Timothy 2:23–26; 4:2–5; Titus 1:9–14).

Furthermore, apologetics is necessary for the preservation of the faith. Not only must the church defend against objections from without, she must also guard against false teachings from within. Thus, Paul admonishes Timothy to "preach the Word, be prepared in season and out of season; correct, rebuke and encourage—with great patience and careful instruction. For the time will come when men will not put up with sound doctrine. They will turn their ears away from the truth and turn aside to myths" (2 Timothy 4:2–4). Defending essential Christian doctrine against perversions by pseudo–Christian cults is a crucial task of the Christian apologist.

Finally, apologetics is necessary for the cultural relevance of the church. In a post–Christian society in which theism is no longer *en vogue* and belief in the possibility of miracles is viewed as simpleminded superstition, apologetics creates intellectual room for the acceptance of the gospel. In place of merely pontificating dogmatic assertions, Christian apologists are commanded to provide defensible arguments "with gentleness and respect" (1 Peter 3:15).

For further study, see J. P. Moreland, *Love Your God with All Your Mind: The Role of Reason in the Life of the Soul* (Colorado Springs: NavPress, 2007); see also Hank Hanegraaff and Tom Fortson, *7 Questions of a Promise Keeper* (Nashville: J. Countryman, 2006).

JUDE 3

"Dear friends, although I was very eager to write to you about the salvation we share, I felt I had to write and urge you to contend for the faith that was once for all entrusted to the saints."

— 3 1 —

CAN A PERSON BE ARGUED
INTO THE KINGDOM OF GOD?

A common mistake Christians make derives from the notion that someone can be talked into the kingdom of God. While the motivation may be sincere, the consequences are often devastating.

First, no matter how eloquent you may or may not be, you cannot change anyone else's heart—only the Holy Spirit can do that. Thus while it is your responsibility to "always be prepared to give an answer to everyone who asks you to give the reason for the hope that you have" (1 Peter 3:15–16), it is God who changes the heart.

Furthermore, the problem is not that people *cannot* believe, it is that they *will not* believe. In other words, it is often not a matter of the mind but a matter of the will. To wit, the maxim: "A man convinced against his will is of the same opinion still." As Jesus Christ declared, "This is the verdict: Light has come into the world, but men loved darkness instead of light because their deeds were evil.

Everyone who does evil hates the light, and will not come into the light for fear that his deeds will be exposed" (John 3:19–20). The Christian faith is reasonable, but reason alone will not compel a person to embrace Christ.

Finally, I am utterly convinced that if we are "prepared to give an answer," God will bring into our paths those whose hearts he has prepared. Thus, it is our responsibility to prepare ourselves to be the most effective tools in the hands of Almighty God.

For further study, see William Lane Craig, *Reasonable Faith* (Crossway Books, 1994), chapter one.

1 PETER 3:15–16

"But in your hearts set apart Christ as Lord.
Always be prepared to give an answer to everyone who
asks you to give the reason for the hope
that you have. But do this with gentleness and respect,
keeping a clear conscience, so that those
who speak maliciously against your good behavior in
Christ may be ashamed of their slander."

WHAT ARE THE MOST
SIGNIFICANT APOLOGETIC ISSUES?

hankfully, learning to defend our faith is not nearly as difficult as one might think. In fact, it all boils down to being able to deal with three major apologetic issues.

First and foremost is the issue of *origins*. How people view their origins will determine how they live their lives. If you suppose you are merely a function of random processes you will live your life by a different standard than if you know you are created in the image of God and accountable to him. In the final analysis more consequences for society hinge on this issue than on any other.

Furthermore, because of its centrality to Christianity, those who take the sacred name of Christ upon their lips must be prepared to defend the historical reality of his *resurrection*. The resurrection is not merely important to the historic Christian faith; without it, there would be no Christianity. It is the singular doctrine that elevates Christianity above all other world religions. Through the resurrection,

Christ demonstrated that he does not stand in a line of peers with Abraham, Buddha, or Confucius. He is utterly unique. He has the power not only to lay down his life but to take it up again. The apostle Paul put it plainly, "If Christ has not been raised, our preaching is useless and so is your faith" (1 Corinthians 15:14).

Without the enduring reference point of scriptural authority, societal norms are reduced to mere matters of preference.

Finally, we must be equipped to demonstrate that the *Bible* is divine rather than merely human in origin. If we can successfully accomplish this, we can answer a host of other objections by simply appealing to the authority of Scripture. If the Bible is merely human in origin, then it stands in a long line of peers with other holy books. If, however, we can demonstrate the Old and New Testaments to be divine in origin, they are *the* authority by which to govern our lives. Without the enduring reference point of scriptural authority, societal norms are reduced to mere matters of preference.

Because of the transcendent importance of these apologetic issues, I have organized a memorable acronym for each of them. First is the F–A–C–E that demonstrates the farce of evolution (Fossil record,

Ape–men fictions, Chance, Empirical science). Furthermore, resurrection is the greatest F–E–A–T in the annals of recorded history (Fatal torment, Empty tomb, Appearances of Christ, Transformation). Finally, Bibles contain M–A–P–S demonstrating that its details and descriptions are rooted in history and evidence (Manuscripts, Archaeology, Prophecy, Statistics).

For further study, see Hank Hanegraaff, *The FACE That Demonstrates the Farce of Evolution* (Nashville: Word Publishing, 1998); and, Hank Hanegraaff, *Resurrection* (Nashville: Word Publishing, 2000). For a treatment of M–A–P–S, see *The FACE That Demonstrates the Farce of Evolution*, appendix B.

1 PETER 3:15

"But in your hearts set apart Christ as Lord.
Always be prepared to give an answer to everyone who
asks you to give a reason for the hope that you have.
But do this with gentleness and respect."

How do we know that the Bible is divine rather than human in origin?

 o defend the faith we must be equipped to demonstrate that the Bible is divine rather than human in origin. When we can successfully accomplish this, we can answer a host of other objections by appealing to Scripture.

To begin with, the Bible has stronger manuscript support than any other work of classical history—including Homer, Plato, Aristotle, Caesar, and Tacitus. Equally amazing is the fact that the Bible has been virtually unaltered since the original writing, as is attested by scholars who have compared the earliest extant manuscripts with manuscripts written centuries later. Additionally, the reliability of the Bible is affirmed by the testimony of its authors, who were eyewitnesses—or close associates of eyewitnesses—to the recorded events, and by secular historians who confirm the many events, people, places, and customs chronicled in Scripture.

Furthermore, archaeology is a powerful witness to the accuracy of the New Testament documents.

Repeatedly, comprehensive archaeological fieldwork and careful biblical interpretation affirm the reliability of the Bible. For example, recent archaeological finds have corroborated biblical details surrounding the trial that led to the fatal torment of Jesus Christ—including Pontius Pilate, who ordered Christ's crucifixion, as well as Caiaphas, the high priest who presided over the religious trials of Christ. It is telling when secular scholars must revise their biblical criticisms in light of solid archaeological evidence.

Finally, the Bible records predictions of events that could not be known nor predicted by chance or common sense. For example, the book of Daniel (written before 530 BC) accurately predicts the progression of kingdoms from Babylon through the Median and Persian empires to the further persecution and suffering of the Jews under Antiochus IV Epiphanes with his desecration of the temple, his untimely death, and freedom for the Jews under Judas Maccabeus (165 BC). It is statistically preposterous that any or all of the Bible's specific, detailed prophecies could have been fulfilled through chance, good guessing, or deliberate deceit.

ADAPTED FROM *Resurrection* AND IN PART FROM *The FACE*

For further study, see Lee Strobel, *The Case for Christ: A Journalist's Personal Investigation of the Evidence for Jesus* (Grand Rapids: Zondervan, 1998).

2 TIMOTHY 3:16

"All Scripture is God-breathed and is useful for teaching, rebuking, correcting and training in righteousness."

34

IS THERE EVIDENCE FOR LIFE AFTER DEATH?

A theists believe that death is the cessation of being. In their view, humans are merely bodies and brains. Though they reject metaphysical realities such as the soul *a priori* (prior to examination), there are convincing reasons to believe that humans have an immaterial aspect to their being that transcends the material and thus can continue to exist after death. Christian philosopher J. P. Moreland advances several sound arguments for the existence of the immaterial soul.

First, from the perspective of logic, we can demonstrate that *the mind is not identical to the brain* by proving that the mind and brain have different properties. As Moreland explains: "The subjective texture of our conscious mental experiences—the feeling of pain, the experience of sound, the awareness of color—is different from anything that is simply physical. If the world were only made of matter, these subjective aspects of consciousness would not exist. But they *do* exist! So there must be more to the world than matter." An obvious example is color. A moment's reflection is enough to convince thinking people everywhere that the experience of color involves more than a mere wavelength of light.

Furthermore, from a legal perspective, if human beings were merely material, they could not be held accountable this year for a crime committed last year, because physical identity changes over time. Every day we lose multiplied millions of microscopic particles—in fact, every seven years, virtually every part of our material anatomy changes, apart from aspects of our neurological system. Therefore, from a purely material perspective, the person who previously committed a crime is presently not the same person. A criminal who attempts to use this line of reasoning as a defense would not get very far. Legally and intuitively, we recognize a *sameness of soul* that establishes personal identity over time.

Finally, libertarian freedom (freedom of the will) presupposes that we are more than mere material robots. If I am merely material, my choices are merely a function of such factors as genetic makeup and brain chemistry. Therefore, my decisions are not free; they are fatalistically determined. The implications of such a notion are profound. In a worldview that embraces fatalistic determinism, I cannot be held morally accountable for my actions, because reward and punishment make sense only if we have freedom of the will.

While the logical, legal, and libertarian freedom arguments are convincing in and of themselves, there is an even more powerful and persuasive argument demonstrating the reality of life beyond the grave. That argument flows from the resurrection of Jesus Christ. The best minds of ancient and modern times have demonstrated beyond a shadow of doubt that Christ's physical trauma was fatal; that the empty tomb is one of the best-attested facts of ancient history; that Christ's followers experienced on several occasions tangible post-resurrection appearances of Christ; and that within weeks of the resurrection, not just one, but an entire community of at least ten thousand Jews experienced such an incredible transformation that they willingly gave up sociological and theological traditions that had given them their national identity.

Through the resurrection, Christ not only demonstrated that he does not stand in a line of peers with Abraham, Buddha, or Confucius but also provided compelling evidence for life after death.

ADAPTED FROM *Resurrection*

For further study, see Gary R. Habermas and J. P. Moreland, *Beyond Death: Exploring the Evidence for Immortality* (Wheaton, Ill.: Crossway Books, 1998).

MATTHEW 10:28

"Do not be afraid of those who kill the body but cannot kill the soul. Rather, be afraid of the One who can destroy both soul and body in hell."

35

CAN CHANCE ACCOUNT FOR THE UNIVERSE?

stronaut Guy Gardner, who has seen the earth from the perspective of the moon, points out that "the more we learn and see about the universe the more we come to realize that the most ideally suited place for life within the entire solar system is the planet we call home." In other words, life on earth was designed by a benevolent Creator rather than directed by blind chance.

First, consider the ideal temperatures on planet Earth—not duplicated on any other known planet in the universe. If we were closer to the sun, we would fry. If we were farther away, we would freeze.

Furthermore, ocean tides, which are caused by the gravitational pull of the moon, play a crucial role in our survival. If the moon were significantly larger, thereby having a stronger gravitational pull, devastating tidal waves would submerge large areas of land. If the moon were smaller, tidal motion would cease, and the oceans would stagnate and die.

Finally, consider plain old tap water. The solid state of most substances is denser than their liquid state, but the opposite is true for water, which explains why ice floats rather than sinks. If water were like virtually any other liquid, it would freeze from the bottom up rather than from the top down, killing aquatic life, destroying the oxygen supply, and making earth uninhabitable.

From the temperatures to the tides and the tap water, and myriad other characteristics that we so easily take for granted, the earth is an unparalleled planetary masterpiece. Like Handel's *Messiah* or da Vinci's *Last Supper*, it should never be carelessly pawned off as the result of blind evolutionary processes.

ADAPTED FROM *Fatal Flaws*

For further study, see R.C. Sproul, *Not a Chance: The Myth of Chance in Modern Science and Cosmology* (Grand Rapids: Baker Book House, 1994).

GENESIS 1:1
*"In the beginning
God created the heavens and the earth."*

HOW MANY EXPLANATIONS ARE THERE FOR THE EXISTENCE OF OUR UNIVERSE?

hilosophical naturalism—the worldview undergirding evolutionism—can provide only three explanations.

First, the universe is merely an illusion. This notion carries little weight in an age of scientific enlightenment.

Second, the universe sprang from nothing. This proposition flies in the face of both the laws of cause and effect and energy conservation. As has been well said, "Nothing comes from nothing, nothing ever could." Or, to put it another way, there simply are no free lunches. The conditions that hold true in this universe prevent any possibility of matter springing out of nothing.

Third, the universe eternally existed. The law of entropy, which predicts that a universe that has eternally existed would have died an "eternity ago" of heat loss, devastates this hypothesis.

There is, however, one other possibility. It is found in the first chapter of the first book of the

Bible: "In the beginning God created the heavens and the earth." In an age of empirical science, nothing could be more certain, clear, or correct.

For further study, see James W. Sire, *The Universe Next Door: A Basic Worldview Catalog*, third ed. (Downers Grove, Ill.: InterVarsity Press, 1997); C. S. Lewis, *Mere Christianity* (New York: Macmillan, 1952).

ADAPTED FROM *Fatal Flaws*

ROMANS 1:20

"For since the creation of the world God's invisible qualities—his eternal power and divine nature— have been clearly seen, being understood from what has been made, so that men are without excuse."

WHO MADE GOD?

None of the arguments forwarded by philosophical naturalism—(1) the universe is merely an illusion; (2) the universe sprang from nothing; (3) the universe eternally existed—satisfactorily account for the existence of the universe. Logically, we can turn only to the possibility that "God created the heavens and the earth" (Genesis 1:1). If that's the case, however, it immediately brings up the question—who made God?

First, unlike the universe, which according to modern science had a beginning, God is infinite and eternal. Thus, as an infinite eternal being, God logically can be demonstrated to be the uncaused First Cause.

Furthermore, to suppose that because the universe had a cause, the cause of the universe must have had a cause simply leads to a logical dead end. An infinite regression of finite causes does not answer the question of *source*; it merely makes the *effects* more numerous.

Finally, simple logic dictates that the universe is not merely an illusion; it did not spring out of nothing (nothing comes from nothing; nothing ever could); and it has not eternally existed (the law of entropy predicts that a universe that has eternally existed would have died an "eternity ago" of heat loss). Thus, the only philosophically plausible possibility that remains is that the universe was made by an unmade Cause greater than itself.

ADAPTED FROM *Fatal Flaws*

For further study, see Paul Copan, *That's Just Your Interpretation: Responding to Skeptics Who Challenge Your Faith* (Grand Rapids: Baker Books, 2001), 69–73.

PSALM 90:2

*"Before the mountains were born
or you brought forth the earth and the world,
from everlasting to everlasting you are God."*

IF WE CAN'T SEE GOD,
HOW CAN WE KNOW HE EXISTS?

t is not uncommon for skeptics to suppose that Christians are irrational for believing in a God they cannot see. In reality, it is irrational for such skeptics to suppose that what cannot be seen does not exist.

First, the fact that something cannot be seen does not presuppose that it doesn't exist. We know that black holes, electrons, the laws of logic, and the law of gravity exist despite the fact that we cannot see them. Indeed, even a full–blown empiricist holds fast to the law of gravity while standing atop the Eiffel tower.

Furthermore, as King David exudes, "The heavens declare the glory of God; the skies proclaim the work of his hands" (Psalm 19:1). Or in the words of the apostle Paul, "God's invisible qualities—his eternal power and divine nature—have been clearly seen, being understood from what has been made, so that men are without excuse" (Romans 1:20). Put another way, the order and complexity of the visible, physical universe eloquently testify to the existence of an uncaused first cause.

Finally, God can be seen through the person and work of Jesus Christ. As Paul explains, "In Christ all the fullness of the Deity lives in bodily form" (Colossians 2:9). Indeed, the incarnation of Jesus Christ is the supreme act of God's self–revelation. Through the ministry of the Holy Spirit we experience the power and presence of God in a way that is more fundamentally real than even our perceptions of the physical world in which we live.

For further study, see J. P. Moreland and William Lane Craig, *Philosophical Foundations for a Christian Worldview* (Downers Grove, Ill: InterVarsity Press, 2003); see also Lee Strobel, *The Case for a Creator* (Grand Rapids: Zondervan, 2004).

1 CORINTHIANS 13:12

"Now we see but a poor reflection as in a mirror; then we shall see face to face. Now I know in part; then I shall know fully, even as I am fully known."

WHAT IS TRUTH?

T his is the very question Pontius Pilate asked Jesus. In the irony of the ages, he stood toe to toe with the personification of truth and yet missed its reality. Postmodern people are in much the same position. They stare at truth but fail to recognize its identity.

First, truth is an aspect of the nature of God himself. Thus, to put on truth is to put on Christ. For Christ is "truth" (John 14:6), and Christians are to be the bearers of truth. As Os Guinness explains, Christianity is not true because it works (pragmatism); it is not true because it feels right (subjectivism); it is not true because it is "my truth" (relativism). It is true because it is anchored in the person of Christ.

Furthermore, truth is anything that corresponds to reality. As such, truth does not yield to the size and strength of the latest lobby group. Nor is truth merely a matter of preference or opinion. Rather truth is true even if everyone denies it, and a lie is a lie even if everyone affirms it.

Finally, truth is essential to a realistic worldview. When sophistry, sensationalism, and superstition sabotage truth, our view of reality is seriously skewed. The death of truth spells the death of civilization. However, as Aleksandr Solzhenitsyn discovered, "One word of truth outweighs the entire world."

ADAPTED FROM *The Covering*

For further study, See Os Guinness, *Time for Truth* (Grand Rapids: Baker Books, 2000).

JOHN 18:37–38

"'You are a king, then!' said Pilate. Jesus answered, 'You are right in saying I am a king. In fact, for this reason I was born, and for this I came into the world, to testify to the truth. Everyone on the side of truth listens to me.'" 'What is truth?' Pilate asked."

WHY DOES GOD ALLOW BAD THINGS
TO HAPPEN TO GOOD PEOPLE?

his is perhaps the most common question Christian celebrities are asked to answer on shows such as *Larry King Live*. At first blush, it may seem as though there are as many responses as there are religions. In reality, however, there are only three basic answers, namely pantheism, philosophical naturalism, and theism. *Pantheism* denies the existence of good and evil because in this view god is all and all is god. *Philosophical naturalism* (the worldview undergirding evolutionism) supposes that everything is a function of random processes, thus there is no such thing as good and evil. *Theism* alone has a relevant response—and only *Christian* theism can answer the question satisfactorily.

First, Christian theism acknowledges that God created the *potential* for evil because God created humans with freedom of choice. We choose to love or hate, to do good or evil. The record of history bears eloquent testimony to the fact that humans of their own free will have actualized the reality of evil through such choices.

Furthermore, without choice, love is meaningless. God is neither a cosmic rapist who forces his love on people, nor a cosmic puppeteer who forces people to love him. Instead, God, the personification of love, grants us the freedom of choice. Without such freedom, we would be little more than preprogrammed robots.

Finally, the fact that God created the potential for evil by granting us freedom of choice ultimately will lead to the best of all possible worlds—a world in which "there will be no more death or mourning or crying or pain" (Revelation 21:4). Those who choose Christ will be redeemed from evil by his goodness and will forever be able *not* to sin.

ADAPTED FROM *Resurrection*

For further study, see Joni Eareckson Tada and Steven Estes, *When God Weeps* (Grand Rapids: Zondervan, 1997); Lee Strobel, *The Case for Faith* (Grand Rapids: Zondervan, 2000), chapter one.

ROMANS 8:28

"We know that in all things God works for the good of those who love him, who have been called according to his purpose."

IS RELIGION THE ROOT OF EVIL?

Acommon refrain sung in the twenty–first century is that religion is the root cause of the great atrocities of human history. In reality, more people died as a result of secularist ideologies in the last century alone than have died in all the religiously motivated conflicts of Western history.

First, the Nazi philosophy that Jews were subhuman and that Aryans were Supermen led to the extermination of six million Jews. In the words of Sir Arthur Keith, a militant anti–Christian physical anthropologist: "The German Fuhrer, as I have consistently maintained, is an evolutionist; he has consistently sought to make the practices of Germany conform to the theory of evolution." Far from religiously motivated, Hitler's "Final Solution to the Jewish problem" was grounded in the naturalistic philosophy of survival of the fittest. In fact, Hitler overtly distanced himself from Christianity, proclaiming, "I shall never come to terms with the Christian lie" and "Our epoch will certainly see the end of the disease of Christianity."

Furthermore, the inherently atheistic utopian philosophy of communism eclipsed even the carnage of Hitler's Germany. Karl Marx saw in philosophical naturalism the scientific and sociological support for an economic experiment that led to the mass murder of multiplied millions worldwide. Mao Tse–tung's communist dictatorship of China accounted for the deaths of an estimated sixty–five million people, while the U.S.S.R. under Stalin saw between twenty and thirty million murdered as a result of agrarian collectivization and the Great Purge. Add to that two million Cambodians—nearly a quarter of that nation's population—massacred by Pol Pot's Khmer Rouge regime, and the death toll resulting from the secular ideology of communism becomes a horror beyond comprehension.

More people died as a result of secularist ideologies in the last century alone than have died in all the religiously motivated conflicts of Western history.

Finally, a third ideology of modern secularism has led to even more ghastly consequences. Though not formally organized under a deranged dictator, this invisible holocaust continues to claim the lives of untold millions around the globe. Four thousand helpless victims—more than the total casualties of 9/11—die each day in the United States alone. The secularist ideology to which I refer, of course, is abortionism. Indeed, the modern bioethical holocaust has eclipsed the carnage of Nazism and communism combined.

Even apart from the ongoing genocide of the unborn, over one hundred million people died at the hands of secularist regimes during the twentieth century. Coupled with recognition of the innumerable humanitarian aid efforts motivated by religious commitments, these statistics should motivate secularists toward humble introspection, rather than haughty inculpation of religion.

For further study, see Os Guinness, *Unspeakable: Facing up to Evil in an Age of Genocide and Terror* (San Francisco: Harper San Francisco, 2005); see also, Hank Hanegraaff, "If Christianity is true, why are so many atrocities committed in the name of Christ?" *The Bible Answer Book Volume 1* (Nashville: J Countryman, 2004).

PROVERBS 21:15
"When justice is done, it brings joy to the righteous but terror to evildoers."

IF CHRISTIANITY IS TRUE,
WHY ARE SO MANY ATROCITIES
COMMITTED IN THE NAME OF CHRIST?

his is a classic smokescreen question often asked to avoid having to grapple with the evidence for authentic Christianity. At best, it involves a hasty generalization. At worst, it's a way of "poisoning the well."

To begin with, this question was anticipated by Christ, who long ago proclaimed that his followers would be recognized by the way they lived their lives (John 15:8). Thus to classify as Christian those who are responsible for instigating atrocities, is to beg the question of who Christ's disciples are to begin with. As Jesus pointed out, not everyone who calls him "Lord" is the real deal (Matthew 7:21–23).

Furthermore, this question implies that Christianity must be false on the basis that atrocities have been committed in Christ's name. There is no reason, however, why we can't turn the argument around and claim that Christianity must be true because so much good has been done in the name of Christ. Think of the countless hospitals, schools, universities, and relief programs that have been instituted as a direct result of people who have the sacred name of Christ upon their lips.

Finally, those who use this argument fail to realize that the validity of Christianity does not rest on sinful men but rather on the perfection of Jesus Christ alone (Hebrews 7:26; 1 Peter 2:22). Moreover, the fact that professing Christians commit sins only serves to prove the premise of Christianity—namely, "all have sinned and fall short of the glory of God" (Romans 3:23); thus all are in need of a Savior (1 John 3:4–5).

For further study, see R. C. Sproul, *Reason to Believe* (Grand Rapids: Zondervan, 1982); Lee Strobel, *The Case for Faith* (Grand Rapids: Zondervan, 2000), chapters 4 and 7.

MATTHEW 7:21–23

"Not everyone who says to me, 'Lord, Lord,' will enter the kingdom of heaven, but only he who does the will of my Father who is in heaven. Many will say to me on that day, 'Lord, Lord, did we not prophesy in your name, and in your name drive out demons and perform many miracles?' Then I will tell them plainly, 'I never knew you. Away from me you evildoers!'"

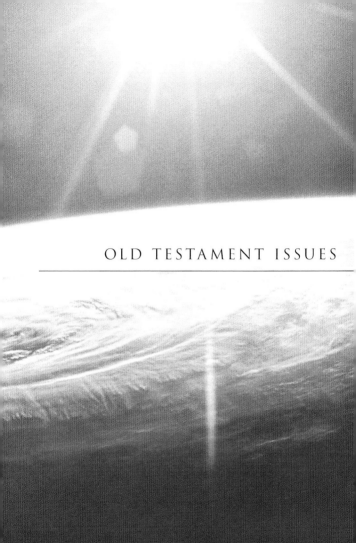

OLD TESTAMENT ISSUES

WHO WAS CAIN'S WIFE?

ne of the most common objections to the Genesis account of Creation concerns the reference to Cain's wife in Genesis 4:17. Unless God supernaturally created a wife for Cain as he had for Adam, he would have had to engage in incest with one of his sisters.

First, we should note that Adam lived almost a thousand years (Genesis 5:5) and fulfilled God's charge to "be fruitful and increase in number" (Genesis 1:28). Thus while Scripture does not tell us where Cain got his wife, the logical implication is that he married either a sister or a niece.

Furthermore, because genetic imperfections accumulated gradually over time, there was no prohibition against incest in the earliest stages of human civilization. The Levitical law against incestuous relationships was given by God hundreds of years after Cain at the time of Moses. Thus familial relationships were preserved and birth defects were prevented (Leviticus 18:6, 9).

Finally, the speculation that God may have created a wife for Cain as he had for Adam is completely *ad hoc*. The consistent teaching of Scripture is that "from one man God made every nation of men, that they should inhabit the whole earth; and he determined the times set for them and the exact places where they should live. God did this so that men would seek him and perhaps reach out for him and find him; though he is not far from each one of us" (Acts 17:26–27).

For further study, see Gleason Archer, *Encyclopedia of Bible Difficulties* (Grand Rapids: Zondervan, 1982).

GENESIS 4:17
"Cain lay with his wife, and she became pregnant and gave birth to Enoch."

– 44 –

Does the Bible promote polygamy?

Polygamy, the practice of one man having multiple wives, was common in antiquity. Though practiced in the Old Testament, polygamy was never God's perfect plan.

First, the ideal pattern of monogamous marriage of one woman and one man was established early in Genesis: "For this reason a man will leave his father and mother and be united to his wife, and they will become one flesh" (2:24). Moreover this very passage was quoted by both Jesus and Paul in defense of the sacredness and exclusivity of monogamous marriage (Matthew 19:3–9; 1 Corinthians 6:15–17; cf. 1 Corinthians 7:2).

Furthermore, the Bible explicitly condemns the polygamy of Old Testament kings (Deuteronomy 17:17). Likewise, New Testament elders and deacons are called to be "the husband of but one wife" (1 Timothy 3:2, 12; Titus 1:6). Just as the requirements for church leaders set the standards of morality and spiritual maturity for all believers, so too the admonition against polygamy for the kings of Israel demonstrates the danger of this practice for all.

Solomon is the quintessential example of one whose legacy of faithfulness was compromised because of his polygamous behavior.

Finally, God's disdain for polygamy is seen in its consequences. The Old Testament clearly reveals the familial strife and temptations that accompany the practice. Solomon is the quintessential example of one whose legacy of faithfulness was compromised because of his polygamous behavior. Despite his world–renowned wisdom, Solomon's peaceful and prosperous rule ended in idolatrous scandal and civil strife, for "his wives turned his heart after other gods" (1 Kings 11:4).

For further study, see Gleason Archer, *Encyclopedia of Bible Difficulties* (Grand Rapids: Zondervan, 1982).

MATTHEW 19:4–6
"Haven't you read," he replied, "that at the beginning the Creator 'made them male and female,' and said, 'For this reason a man will leave his father and mother and be united to his wife, and the two will become one flesh?' So they are no longer two, but one."

DOES THE BIBLE PROMOTE SLAVERY?

 myth propped up by secular skeptics is that Scripture sanctions slavery. Nothing could be farther from the truth.

First, it should be noted that far from extolling the virtues of slavery, the Bible denounces slavery as sin. The New Testament goes so far as to put slave traders in the same category as murderers, adulterers, perverts, and liars (1 Timothy 1:10).

Furthermore, slavery within the Old Testament context was sanctioned due to economic realities rather than racial or sexual prejudices. Because bankruptcy laws did not exist, people would *voluntarily* sell themselves into slavery. A craftsman could thus use his skills in servitude to discharge a debt. Even a convicted thief could make restitution by serving as a slave (Exodus 22:3).

Finally, while the Bible as a whole recognizes the reality of slavery, it never promotes the practice of slavery. In fact, it was the application of biblical principles that ultimately led to the overthrow of slavery, both in ancient Israel and in the United

States of America. Israel's liberation from slavery in Egypt became the model for the liberation of slaves in general. In America, many are beginning to wake up to the liberating biblical truth that *all* people are created by God with innate equality (Genesis 1:27; Acts 17:26–28; Galatians 3:28).

For further study, see Paul Copan, *That's Just Your Interpretation: Responding to Skeptics Who Challenge Your Faith* (Grand Rapids: Baker Books, 2001), 171–178. See also Hank Hanegraaff, "President Bartlett's Fallacious Diatribe." Available from CRI at www.equip.org.

1 Timothy 1:8–11

"We know that the law is good if one uses it properly. We also know that law is made not for the righteous but for lawbreakers and rebels, the ungodly and sinful, the unholy and irreligious; for those who kill their fathers or mothers, for murderers, for adulterers and perverts, for slave traders and liars and perjurers— and for whatever else is contrary to the sound doctrine that conforms to the glorious gospel of the blessed God, which he entrusted to me."

– 4 6 –

WAS JONAH SWALLOWED BY A WHALE?

he book of Jonah contains the familiar story of a prophet named Jonah who was preserved three days and three nights in the belly of a large fish (1:17). Though skepticism has led many to allegorize this fish tale, there are good reasons to interpret it as an actual historical account.

First, details and descriptions in the narrative defy allegorization. The book of Jonah is written in the genre of historical narrative. The brief mention of the fish does not deter literarily from the descriptions of Jonah's journey to Joppa, his payment of the fare, his conversations with the sailors during the storm, and his eventual trip to Nineveh.

Furthermore, the Christian worldview presupposes the miraculous. The universe itself is an effect that presupposes a cause equal to or greater than itself. Just as the uncaused First Cause created the universe, so the uncaused First Cause is capable of supernaturally intervening in the universe he created. Because God created the universe *ex nihilo* ("out of nothing"), preserving Jonah in the belly of a great fish poses no problem whatsoever.

The Christian worldview presupposes the miraculous.

Finally, when we hear a miraculous account of this magnitude we would do well to seek a second opinion. In the case of Jonah, corroboration is provided by no less an authority than Jesus Christ. Our Lord not only referred to Jonah's preservation for "three days and three nights in the belly of a fish" as a miracle, he used it as the basis for prophesying that he too would be preserved for "three days and three nights in the heart of the earth" (Matthew 12:40). As such, Jonah's marine rescue is a type of Jesus' miraculous resurrection.

For further study, see Walter C. Kaiser Jr., Peter H. Davids, F. F. Bruce, and Manfred T. Brauch, (eds.), *Hard Sayings of the Bible* (Downers Grove, Ill.: InterVarsity Press, 1996).

MATTHEW 12:40

"For as Jonah was three days and three nights in the belly of a huge fish, so the Son of Man will be three days and three nights in the heart of the earth."

How could the Bible command a rape victim to marry her rapist?

ccording to Mosaic Law, "If a man happens to meet a virgin who is not pledged to be married and rapes her and they are discovered, he shall pay the girl's father fifty shekels of silver. He must marry the girl, for he has violated her. He can never divorce her as long as he lives" (Deuteronomy 22:28–29). Isn't that barbaric?

First, the Mosaic Law is hardly about letting a rapist off easy. The consequence for raping a woman engaged to be married was stoning (Deuteronomy 22:25). If the woman was not engaged, the rapist was spared for the sake of the woman's security. Having lost her virginity, she would have been deemed undesirable for marriage—and in the culture of the day, a woman without a father or husband to provide for her would be subject to a life of abject poverty, destitution, and social ostracism. As such, the rapist was compelled to provide for the rape victim for as long as he lived. Thus, far from barbaric, the law was a cultural means of protection and provision.

Furthermore, there was precedent under the Mosaic Law for the victimized woman not to marry the victimizer if her father determined that she could be provided for in a more suitable manner (Exodus 22:16–17). Thus, the law was not designed to force the rape victim into an unbearable marriage, but to secure her future and that of her children.

Finally, neither then nor now, there is no perfect resolution for a woman who has been violated through the horror of rape. The modern–day solution of aborting a child conceived through rape only compounds the horror. Indeed, if we are completely satisfied by any earthly solution—even the death penalty—our moral sensibilities are seriously skewed. Ultimately, only eternity will make all wrongs right.

For further study on Mosaic laws, see Hank Hanegraaff, "T.V.'s *The West Wing* vs. The Bible," available through the Christian Research Institute (CRI) at www.equip.org.

ISAIAH 25:8
"The Sovereign LORD will wipe away the tears
from all faces;
he will remove the disgrace of his people
from all the earth."

– 4 8 –

HOW COULD A GOOD GOD SANCTION THE
STONING OF A DISOBEDIENT CHILD?

he Mosaic Law included the following provision for dealing with a disobedient son: "His father and mother shall take hold of him and bring him to the elders at the gate of his town. They shall say to the elders, 'This son of ours is stubborn and rebellious. He will not obey us. He is a profligate and a drunkard.' Then all the men of the town shall stone him to death. You must purge the evil from among you" (Deuteronomy 21:19–21). At first blush such language jars modern moral sensibilities. A closer examination, however, turns such moral pretension on its head.

First and foremost, the son in question should not be thought of as an adolescent guilty of nothing more than slamming doors or stubbornly asserting his independence. Rather, the son described above is old enough to be morally culpable of extravagantly wicked behavior that threatens the health and safety of the entire community. As such, the prescribed punishment is not for adolescent decadence, but for adult degeneracy.

Furthermore, the parents' desire to spare their own son serves as a built–in buffer against an unwarranted or frivolous enforcement of the law. Likewise, ratification by the elders precludes a precipitous judgment on the part of the parents. Thus, the standard of evidence prescribed by the Mosaic Law exceeds that of modern jurisprudence.

Finally, for modern skeptics to claim the moral high ground over the ancient Scriptures is the height of hypocrisy. Rather than the civility of the Mosaic Law, our culture reflects the carnality of Israel's neighbors who sacrificed their sons and daughters. Indeed, for over three decades Western society has sanctioned the systematic slaughter of children, guilty of nothing more than being unloved.

For further study, see Walter C. Kaiser Jr., Peter H. Davids, F. F. Bruce, and Manfred T. Brauch, (eds.), *Hard Sayings of the Bible* (Downers Grove, Ill.: InterVarsity Press, 1996); on related issues, see Hank Hanegraaff, "TV's *The West Wing* vs. The Bible" available through the Christian Research Institute (CRI) at www.equip.org.

EZEKIEL 18:23

"Do I take any pleasure in the death of the wicked? declares the Sovereign Lord. Rather, am I not pleased when they turn from their wicked ways and live?"

How can Christians legitimize a God who orders the genocide of entire nations?

he very notion that God would command the obliteration of entire nations is abhorrent to skeptics and seekers alike. In context, however, God's commands are perfectly consistent with his justice and mercy.

First, a text without a context is a pretext. God's commands to destroy the nations inhabiting the promised land of Canaan must never be interpreted in isolation from their immediate contexts. The command to "destroy them totally" (Deuteronomy 7:2) is contextualized by the words: "Do not intermarry with them . . . for they will turn your sons and daughters away from following me to serve other gods. . . . This is what you are to do to them: Break down their altars, smash their sacred stones, cut down their Asherah poles and burn their idols in the fire" (vv. 3–5). As such, the aim of God's command was not the obliteration of the wicked but the obliteration of wickedness.

Furthermore, God's martial instructions are qualified by his moral intentions to spare the repentant. As the author of Hebrews explains, "By faith the prostitute Rahab, because she welcomed the spies, was not killed with those who were disobedient" (11:31). Not only were Rahab and her family spared on account of her faith, she was allowed to live among the Israelites (Joshua 6:25) and came to hold a privileged position in the lineage of Jesus Christ (Matthew 1:5). God's desire to spare the pagan city of Nineveh further illustrates the extent of his mercy for the repentant (see Jonah).

"Cursed is the man who withholds justice
from the alien, the fatherless, or the widow."

Finally, God unequivocally commanded Israel to treat the aliens living among them with respect and equality. Foreigners living among the Israelites were allowed to celebrate Passover (Numbers 9:14; cf. 15:15), benefited from an agrarian system of welfare (Leviticus 19:9), and enjoyed full legal protection (Deuteronomy 1:16–17). Even descendants of Israel's enemies, the Edomites and the Egyptians, were allowed to enter the assembly of the Lord (Deuteronomy 23:7–8). In fact, God condemned oppression of aliens in the harshest possible language: "Cursed is the man who withholds justice from the alien, the fatherless, or the widow" (Deuteronomy 27:19). Such concern for foreigners clearly demonstrates that mercy was to be shown to those who by faith repented of their idolatry and were thereby grafted into true Israel (cf. Romans 11:11–24).

For further study, see Gary M. Burge, *Whose Land? Whose Promise?* (Cleveland, OH: The Pilgrim Press, 2003): 82–93.

JEREMIAH 7:5–7

"If you really change your ways and your actions and deal with each other justly, if you do not oppress the alien, the fatherless or the widow and do not shed innocent blood in this place, and if you do not follow other gods to your own harm, then I will let you live in this place, in the land I gave your forefathers for ever and ever."

How could Pharaoh be morally responsible if God hardened his heart?

he apostle Paul explicitly states that God hardened Pharaoh's heart (Romans 9:17–18). That, of course, begs the question: If God determined to harden Pharaoh's heart, then how is God just in holding Pharaoh morally responsible for his sins?

First, though God promised Moses that he would harden Pharaoh's heart (Exodus 4:21; 7:3), the Exodus account underscores the fact that Pharaoh was responsible for hardening his own heart (Exodus 7:13, 22; 8:15, 19, 32; 9:7; cf. 9:34).

Furthermore, far from hardening Pharaoh's heart in a direct or deterministic fashion, God presented Pharaoh with ample opportunity to either repent or continue in rebellion. Every time God showed Pharaoh mercy and removed a plague from Egypt, Pharaoh responded in stubborn disobedience. As such, God's mercy was the occasion for the hardening of Pharaoh's heart.

Finally, in dealing with this issue, the apostle Paul begins with the presupposition that God judges all men justly (Romans 3:5–8). He emphasizes the fact that people like Pharaoh are "prepared for destruction" because that is ultimately what they will. Every time God provides an opportunity to repent, like Pharaoh they harden their hearts in disobedience and unbelief.

For further study, see Paul Marston and Roger Forster, *God's Strategy in Human History*, 2nd ed. (Wipf and Stock Publishers, 2000).

EXODUS 9:34–35

"When Pharaoh saw that the rain and hail and thunder had stopped, he sinned again: He and his officials hardened their hearts. So Pharaoh's heart was hard and he would not let the Israelites go, just as the LORD had said through Moses."

Does Isaiah 53:5

guarantee our healing today?

he mantra "by his stripes we are healed" is repeated endlessly in Christian circles. However, these words extracted from Isaiah 53:5 focus on *spiritual* rather than *physical* healing.

First, a quick look at the context makes it clear that Isaiah had *spiritual* rather than *physical* healing in mind: Christ "was wounded for our *transgressions*, He was bruised for our *iniquities*; The chastisement for our peace was upon Him, And by His stripes we are healed" (Isaiah 53:5 NKJV, emphasis added). Peter builds on this understanding when he writes, "He himself bore our *sins* in his body on the tree, so that we might die to *sins* and live for righteousness; by his wounds you have been healed" (1 Peter 2:24, emphasis added).

Furthermore, while healing for the body is not referred to in Isaiah 53:5, it is referred to in the verse *immediately* preceding it. Here Isaiah writes, "Surely he has borne our griefs and carried our sorrows; Yet we esteemed Him stricken, Smitten by God, and afflicted" (Isaiah 53:4 NKJV). *Physical* healing here is not only clear in context but affirmed by the Gospels where it is given an important qualification: "When evening came, many who were demon-possessed were brought to him, and he drove out the spirits with a word and healed all the sick. This was to fulfill what was spoken through the prophet Isaiah: 'He took up our infirmities and carried our diseases'" (Matthew 8:16–17). Thus, the healing here was *fulfilled* during the ministry of Christ and does not *guarantee* healing today.

Finally, I should note that in a real sense Christ's atonement on the cross *does* extend to *physical* healing. One day, "there will be no more death or mourning or crying or pain, for the old order of things has passed away" (Revelation 21:4). However, as Paul points out, "We hope for *what we do not yet have*, we *wait* for it patiently" (Romans 8:25, emphasis added). In the meantime, we will all experience sickness and suffering. Indeed, those who live before Christ returns will all die of their last disease—the death rate is one per person and we're all going to make it!

For further study, see Hank Hanegraaff, *Christianity in Crisis* (Eugene, Ore.: Harvest House Publishers, 1993).

NEW TESTAMENT ISSUES

IS BAPTISM NECESSARY FOR SALVATION?

hose who suppose baptism is necessary for salvation frequently cite Peter's words in Acts 2:38, "Repent and be baptized," as evidence that belief *plus* baptism results in salvation. Scripture clearly does not support this view.

First, as the book of Acts itself demonstrates, baptism is a *sign* of conversion, not the *means* of conversion. Indeed, Acts 10:47 describes believers who were indwelt by the Holy Spirit (and therefore saved—see Romans 8:9) prior to being baptized. Moreover, when the thief on the cross placed his faith in Christ, Jesus said to him, "Today you will be with me in paradise" (Luke 23:43), even though the dying thief had no chance to be baptized.

Furthermore, the Bible as a whole clearly communicates that we are saved by faith and not by works (Ephesians 2:8–9). As Paul pointed out in Romans, our righteous standing before God is "by faith from first to last" (Romans 1:17). When the jailer asked the apostle Paul, "What must I do to be saved?" Paul responded, "Believe in the Lord Jesus, and you will be saved" (Acts 16:30–31).

Finally, although baptism is not the means by which we are saved, it is the means by which we are set apart. Through baptism we testify that we are no longer our own—we have been bought by Christ's blood and have been brought into the community of faith. Thus in Acts 2:38 Peter was not suggesting that his hearers could not be saved apart from baptism; rather, he was saying that their genuine repentance would be evidenced by their baptism. As St. Augustine taught, it is not the absence of baptism but the despising of baptism that damns.

Indeed, behind the symbol of baptism is the substance of baptism—the blood of Jesus Christ which cleanses from sin. As water cleanses the skin from soil and sweat, so the blood of Jesus Christ cleanses the soul from the stain of sin.

For further study, see Hank Hanegraaff, "Bringing Baptism into Biblical Balance," *Christian Research Journal*, vol. 19, no. 1 (1996) available through the Christian Research Institute at www.equip.org.

GALATIANS 3:26-27
"You are all sons of God through faith in Christ Jesus, for all of you who were baptized into Christ have clothed yourselves with Christ."

DOES JAMES TEACH SALVATION BY WORKS?

Critics of the Bible have long argued that the book of James contradicts the rest of Scripture in teaching "that a person is justified by what he does and not by faith alone" (James 2:24). Upon closer examination, however, the book of James, like the rest of Scripture, confirms that we are saved not by what we do but by what Jesus Christ has *done*.

First, in context James teaches that we are saved not by works but by the kind of faith that produces good works. As James puts it, "What good is it, my brothers, if a man claims to have faith but has no deeds? Can such faith save him?" (2:14). The answer is "no." "As the body without the spirit is dead, so faith without deeds is dead" (v. 26).

Furthermore, when James says a person is not justified by faith alone, he means that a person is not justified by mental *assent* alone. As such, he says, "Show me your faith without deeds, and I will show you my faith by what I do. You believe that there is one God. Good! Even the demons believe that—and shudder" (vv. 18–19). In other words, demons believe in the sense of giving mental *assent* to the fact that there is only one true God, all the while failing to place their hope and trust in him.

"Justification is by faith alone, but not by a faith that *is* alone."

Finally, while James says "a person is justified by what he does and not by faith alone" and Paul says "man is justified by faith apart from observing the law" (Romans 3:28), their words are in complete harmony. James is countering the false assertion that a *said faith* is a substitute for a *saving faith*, while Paul is countering the equally fallacious notion that salvation can be earned by observing the law. As the Reformers were wont to say, "Justification is by faith alone, but not by a faith that *is* alone."

For further study, see R. C. Sproul, *Justified by Faith Alone* (Wheaton, IL: Crossway Books, 1999).

JAMES 2:21–22

"Was not our ancestor Abraham considered righteous for what he did when he offered his son Isaac on the altar? You see that his faith and his actions were working together, and his faith was made complete by what he did."

CAN AN UNBELIEVER BE SAVED BY MARRYING A BELIEVER?

n his first letter to the Corinthian Christians, Paul says "the unbelieving husband has been sanctified through his wife, and the unbelieving wife has been sanctified through her husband" (7:14). Does this mean that unbelievers are saved by virtue of being married to believers?

First, if unbelievers can be saved through marriage, there would be at least two ways to be saved: one by God's grace through faith in Jesus Christ alone; the other by marriage to a believer. Not only so, but unbelievers would be forced into the kingdom of Christ against their wills.

Furthermore, being *sanctified* is not the same as being *saved*. In context, to be sanctified means to be *set apart*. As such, the unbeliever has been sanctified for the sake of the marriage, not for the sake of salvation. In other words, the believer is not defiled by the spiritual deadness of the unbeliever. Rather the unbeliever comes under the special influence of the Holy Spirit.

Being *sanctified* is not the same as being *saved*.

Finally, in the self–same context, Paul distinguishes between being sanctified and being saved by writing, "How do you know, wife, whether you will *save* your husband? Or, how do you know, husband, whether you will *save* your wife?" (v. 16, emphasis added). As such, sanctification is not synonymous with salvation.

For further study, see Gordon Fee and Douglas Stuart, *How to Read the Bible for All Its Worth*, 3rd ed. (Grand Rapids: Zondervan, 2003).

JOHN 14:6

"Jesus answered, 'I am the way and the truth and the life. No one comes to the Father except through me.'"

CAN A WOMAN BE SAVED
THROUGH CHILDBEARING?

n his first letter to Timothy, Paul says that "women will be saved through childbearing" (2:15). If this is the case, there must be more than one way to be saved.

First, in the Jewish culture of Paul's day, it was believed that if women died in childbirth it was a direct punishment for Eve's role in the Fall. Thus, Paul may well be assuring believers that women will be kept safe through the process of childbirth "if they continue in faith, love and holiness with propriety" (2:15). As such, Paul's words refute the denigration of women both in the culture and in the church.

Furthermore, men and women alike are ultimately saved as a result of the most significant birth in the history of humanity. Thus, Paul may also be alluding to the fact that just as "the woman [Eve] was deceived and became a sinner" (v. 14), so the woman (Mary) conceived and brought forth the Savior.

Finally, salvation here cannot mean salvation in the ultimate sense. If it did, women would not be saved by God's grace through faith *alone*. Unlike men, they would also have to bear children. This not only is absurd but stands in direct opposition to the unambiguous teaching of Scripture (John 14:6; Ephesians 2:8–9; Galatians 3:28). Remember, that which is cloudy must always be interpreted in the light of that which is clear.

For further study, see Philip H. Towner, *The Letters to Timothy and Titus* (Grand Rapids: Eerdmans Publishing Co., 2006), 233–37.

EPHESIANS 2:8–9

"For it is by grace you have been saved, through faith—and this is not from yourselves, it is the gift of God—not by works, so that no one can boast."

MUST WOMEN BE SILENT IN CHURCH?

he following words by the apostle Paul are frequently used to denigrate the Bible as sexist—"I do not permit a woman to teach or to have authority over a man; *she must be silent.* For Adam was formed first, then Eve. And Adam was not the one deceived; it was the woman who was deceived and became a sinner" (1 Timothy 2:12–13, emphasis added). The criticism that Paul's teaching is sexist is silenced by a careful consideration of context.

First, Paul obviously does not intend to say that women must always be silent in church. Rather, in a culture in which women were largely illiterate and unlearned, Paul is saying that until a woman learns she must not presume to teach. If Paul had intended to say a woman must always be silent, he would not have given women instructions on how to pray or prophesy publicly in church (1 Corinthians 11:5).

Furthermore, by alluding to Eve's deception in the garden, Paul underscores how crucial it is that women, like men, involve themselves in learning. Far from chastising Eve for her role in the Fall, Paul chastises the Jewish men of his day for excluding women from learning, thus leaving them vulnerable to deception. Just as Adam was responsible for failing to protect Eve from deception, so too the men of Paul's day would be held responsible if they hindered women from studying and growing in their faith.

Finally, Paul's words refute the matriarchal authoritarianism practiced by pagan cults in that day. Ephesus, where Timothy ministered, was the home of a cult dedicated to the pagan goddess Artemis. Worship of Artemis was conducted under the authority of an entirely female priesthood that exercised authoritarian dominion over male worshipers. Thus, Paul emphasizes that women should not presume undue authority over men. Paul neither elevates women over men nor men over women, but is rather concerned that men and women be granted equal opportunity to learn and grow in submission to one another and to God (1 Timothy 2:11; cf. Ephesians 5:21).

For further study, see N.T. Wright, "Women's Service in the Church: The Biblical Basis," available at www.ntwrightpage.com.

EPHESIANS 5:21
"Submit to one another out of reverence for Christ."

WERE MARK AND MESSIAH MISTAKEN
ABOUT MUSTARD SEEDS?

 tired old canard making the rounds these days is that the gospel of Mark and the God-man Messiah were both mistaken about the size of mustard seeds. The argument is typically framed as follows: Orchid seeds are smaller than mustard seeds. Thus when Mark records Messiah as saying that a mustard seed is the smallest of all seeds he was patently mistaken. It follows therefore that if Jesus was mistaken, Jesus is not God. And if Mark records Messiah's mistake, the Bible is not infallible. What's wrong with this picture?

First, in order to interpret the Bible literally we must pay special attention to what is known as form or genre. Put another way, to interpret the Bible literally we must first consider the *form* of literature we are interpreting. As a legal brief differs in form from fantasy literature, so, too, a parable concerning a mustard seed would likely differ in form and function from a technical discussion on horticulture.

Furthermore, when Jesus asks, "What shall we say the kingdom of God is *like*?" (Mark 4:30, emphasis added) we should immediately be alerted to the fact that Jesus is about to use an extended simile (parable) to teach his disciples a principle about the kingdom. Indeed, Jesus says as much when he continues, "or what *parable* should we use to describe it" (v. 30, emphasis added). As with metaphors, the danger is to interpret extended similes in a strictly wooden literal sense. The kingdom of God is obviously not like a mustard seed in every way. Nor does Jesus intend to make his parable "walk on all fours." A kingdom does not look like a mustard seed, nor is a mustard seed the smallest seed in the kingdom. Rather the kingdom of God is like a mustard seed in the sense that it begins small and becomes large (cf. Daniel 2:31–45).

Finally, while the One who caused the universe to leap into existence (another figure of speech) by simple speaking would obviously know that an orchid seed is smaller than a mustard seed, an orchid seed would have been profoundly inept for the purpose of the parable. Jesus used the smallest seed familiar to a Palestinian farmer—a small seed that unlike an orchid seed grows to have "big branches that the birds in the air can perch in"—to illustrate that the kingdom of God began in obscurity but would one day "fill the earth."

In sum, to avoid the dangers of the hyper-literalism of fundamentalist scholars on the left, it is crucial to read the Bible as literature, paying close attention to *form*. As we do, you and I must ever be mindful that the Bible is not *merely* literature. Instead, the Scriptures are uniquely inspired by the Spirit. Thus, we must fervently pray that the Spirit, who inspired the Scriptures, illumines our minds as we learn to read the Bible for all it's worth.

For further study, see "What does it mean to interpret the Bible literally?" on p. 522.

MARK 4:30-32

"Again [Jesus] said, "What shall we say the kingdom of God is like, or what parable shall we use to describe it? It is like a mustard seed, which is the smallest seed you plant in the ground. Yet when planted, it grows and becomes the largest of all garden plants, with such big branches that the birds of the air can perch in its shade."

– 5 8 –

Did Jesus make a crucial historical
blunder in the Gospel of Mark?

One of the reasons cited by famed New Testament scholar and best-selling author Bart Ehrman for his transition from fundamentalist Christian to fundamentalist agnostic is that the gospel of Mark is riddled with factual and historical errors. A prominent example is that David and his men ate the showbread "when Abiathar was the high priest." In reality, argues Ehrman, Ahimelech (Abiathar's father) was high priest at the time. Did Mark make a mistake, or is it Ehrman who is dead wrong?

First, it should be noted that it is Ehrman, not Mark, who makes a crucial blunder. A quick reading of the text in question reveals that far from saying that Abiathar was high priest, Mark states that David and his men ate the showbread *"in the days of* Abiathar the high priest" (Mark 2:26, emphasis added). Put another way, there is no direct indication that Abiathar was serving in the office of high priest at the time, only that he was alive. Had Jesus erred, the Jewish leaders who were intimately acquainted with their history would have jumped all over him.

Furthermore, the reason Jesus references Abiathar rather than his father Ahimelech should be self-evident—particularly to a New Testament scholar. Namely, while David has little interaction with Ahimelech in biblical history, he is inextricably linked to Abiathar. In fact, after Saul killed Ahimelech (1 Samuel 22:1–19), Abiathar found protection under David (1 Samuel 22:23), became priest to David (1 Samuel 23:6, 9; 2 Samuel 8:17), and eventually was exalted to the highest priestly office under David (1 Chronicles 15:11; 1 Kings 2:35). Put another way, Abiathar was the star— Ahimelech was but a footnote.

Finally, one thousand years from now people may well say that Desert Storm occurred in the days of President George W. Bush, though he was *not* president at the time—his dad was. Indeed, the entire Iraq crisis from 9/11 to the toppling and trial of Saddam, including all the attendant circumstances leading up to those events (e.g., the challenges of the U.N. weapon's inspections prior to 9/11), are associated with George W. Bush's Iraq war, not with George Herbert Walker Bush. In much the same way,

Jesus is justified in speaking of David eating the showbread "in the days of Abiathar the high priest."

Through a fair and balanced application of interpretive principles, this and a host of apparent contradictions are easily resolved.

For further study, see "Do the gospel accounts contradict one another?" on p. 180 and Hank Hanegraaff, *The Apocalypse Code: Find Out What the Bible Really Says about the End Times...and Why It Matters Today* (Nashville: Thomas Nelson, 2007).

PROVERBS 18:17

"The first to present his case seems right,
till another comes forward and questions him."

Do the gospel accounts
contradict one another?

uring a prime-time television special titled *The Search for Jesus*, Peter Jennings asserted that according to some scholars, "the New Testament has four different and sometimes contradictory versions of Jesus' life." The Jesus Seminar scholars Jennings referenced, however, are famous for an idiosyncratic brand of fundamentalism that supplants reason and evidential substance with rhetoric and emotional stereotypes. They have made a virtual art form out of exploiting "discrepancies" in the secondary details of the Gospels.

One of the most frequently cited alleged contradictions involves the female discoverers of the empty tomb. According to Matthew, the discoverers were Mary Magdalene and another Mary (28:1); Mark says they were Mary Magdalene, Mary the mother of James, and Salome (16:1); Luke claims Mary Magdalene, Joanna, Mary the mother of James, and others (24:10); and John focuses solely on Mary Magdalene (20:18).

In providing a defensible argument against such dogmatic assertions, it is first helpful to point out that the Gospels are *complementary* rather than *contradictory*. If John, in the example cited above, had stipulated that Mary Magdalene was the *only* female to discover the empty tomb while the other gospels claimed that more than one woman was involved, we would be faced with an obvious contradiction. Instead, the complementary details provided by the four gospel writers simply serve to flesh out the rest of the story.

Furthermore, credible scholars look for a reliable *core* set of facts in order to validate historical accounts. In this case, liberal and conservative scholars alike agree that the body of Jesus was buried in the tomb of Joseph of Arimathea. As a member of the Jewish court that convicted Jesus, Joseph is unlikely to be Christian fiction. Additionally, when we consider the role of women in first-century Jewish society, what is remarkable is that the empty tomb accounts would feature females as heroes of the story. This demonstrates that the gospel writers factually recorded what happened even if it was culturally embarrassing.

Finally, if each of the gospel writers presented secondary details in exactly the same manner, critics would dismiss their accounts on the basis of *collusion*. Instead, the Gospels provide unique yet mutually consistent perspectives on the events surrounding the empty tomb.

The principles above not only resolve the circumstances in the case at hand but all supposed contradictions highlighted by Peter Jennings in *The Search for Jesus*. We can safely conclude that far from being contradictory, the gospel accounts are clearly *complementary*; a consensus of credible scholarship considers the *core* set of facts presented by the gospel writers to be authentic and reliable; and the unique perspectives provided by Matthew, Mark, Luke, and John preclude the possibility of *collusion*.

For further study concerning alleged contradictions in the Bible, see Gleason L. Archer, *New International Encyclopedia of Bible Difficulties* (Grand Rapids: Zondervan, 1982); concerning evidences for Christ's resurrection, see Hank Hanegraaff, *The Third Day* (Nashville: W Publishing Group, 2003). Also see Hank Hanegraaff, "The Search for Jesus Hoax," available at www.equip.org.

LUKE 1:1–4

"Many have undertaken to draw up an account of the things that have been fulfilled among us, just as they were handed down to us by those who from the first were eyewitnesses and servants of the word.

– 6 0 –

DO THE GENEALOGIES OF JESUS IN MATTHEW AND LUKE CONTRADICT ONE ANOTHER?

t first blush the genealogies of Matthew and Luke appear to be contradictory. In reality the genealogies are ingeniously constructed to highlight different aspects of the person and work of Jesus Christ.

Matthew, writing to a primarily Jewish audience, emphasizes that Jesus Christ is the seed of Abraham and the legal heir of David, the long–awaited King of Israel who would ultimately restore his people from exile. As such, Matthew records fourteen generations from Abraham to David, fourteen from David to the exile and fourteen from the exile to the Christ (Matthew 1:17). Matthew, a former tax collector, skillfully organizes the genealogy of Jesus into three groups of fourteen, the numerical equivalent of the Hebrew letters in King David's name (4+6+4 =ד+ו+ד). Thus Matthew's genealogy simultaneously highlights the most significant names in the lineage of Jesus and artistically emphasizes our Lord's identity as Messiah who would forever sit upon the throne of David.

Furthermore, Luke, writing to a primarily Gentile audience, extends his genealogy past Abraham to the first Adam, thus highlighting that Christ, the Second Adam, is the Savior of all humanity. Additionally, calling Adam "the son of God" (3:38) and strategically placing the genealogy between Jesus' baptism and the desert temptation, Luke masterfully reveals Jesus as *Theanthropos*—the God–Man. It is also instructive to note that while Luke's genealogy stretches from the first Adam to the second, only mountain peaks in the lineage are accounted for. Thus, it is impossible to determine how many years elapsed between the creation of Adam and the birth of Jesus.

Matthew, writing to a primarily Jewish audience, emphasizes that Jesus Christ is the seed of Abraham and the legal heir of David, the long–awaited King of Israel who would ultimately restore his people from exile.

Finally, just as there are different emphases in the genealogies, so too there are different explanations for the dissimilarities between them. Matthew traces his genealogy through David's son Solomon, while Luke traces his genealogy through David's son Nathan.

It may be that Matthew's purpose is to provide the legal lineage from Solomon through Joseph, while Luke's purpose is to provide the natural lineage from Nathan through Mary. It could also be that Matthew and Luke are both tracing Joseph's genealogy—Matthew, the legal line, and Luke, the natural line. As such, the legal line diverges from the natural in that Levirate Law stipulated if a man died without an heir his genealogy could legally continue through his brother (Deuteronomy 25:5–6). Obviously, the fact that there are a number of ways to resolve dissimilarities rules out the notion that the genealogies are contradictory.

For further study, see Craig L. Blomberg, *Jesus and the Gospels* (Nashville: Broadman and Holman Publishers, 1997): 199, 207–08.

MATTHEW 1:1

"A record of the genealogy of Jesus Christ the son of David, the son of Abraham."

WAS JESUS REALLY IN THE GRAVE
FOR THREE DAYS AND THREE NIGHTS?

Jesus specifically tells us, "As Jonah was three days and three nights in the belly of a huge fish, so the Son of Man will be three days and three nights in the heart of the earth" (Matthew 12:40). The Gospels also tell us that Jesus died on the day before the Sabbath—Friday—and rose on the day after the Sabbath—Sunday. How do we resolve this apparent contradiction?

First, in Jewish idiom any part of a day counted as a day–night unit. Thus, there is no need to literalistically demand that seventy–two hours be accounted for. This is particularly evident in light of Jesus' own contention that he would rise *on* the third day, not *after* the third day and night had ended (Matthew 16:21; 17:23; 20:19; Luke 24:46; cf. Matthew 26:61; 27:40, 63–64).

Furthermore, the Gospels unanimously declare that Jesus died on the Day of Preparation; that is, Friday, the day leading up to the beginning of the Sabbath at sundown (Matthew 27:62; Mark 15:42;

Luke 23:54; John 19:31, 42). The gospel writers demonstrate similar unanimity regarding the discovery of Jesus' resurrection early in the morning on the day following the Sabbath; that is, Sunday, the first day of the week (Matthew 28:1; Mark 16:1; Luke 24:1; John 20:1). Thus, to suggest as some have that Jesus died on Wednesday and rose on Saturday, or died on Thursday and rose on Sunday directly contradicts the testimony of all four gospel writers.

Jesus' sacrificial death and miraculous resurrection on the third day is the glorious archetypal fulfillment of Old Testament types.

Finally, once knowledge of ancient culturally informed modes of oral and literary expression replaces a naïve literalistic interpretation, the majestic harmony of Scripture shines through. Indeed, Jesus' sacrificial death and miraculous resurrection on the third day is the glorious archetypal fulfillment of Old Testament types including the Passover Lamb (Exodus 12; cf. 1 Corinthians 5:7), Jonah's preservation "for three days and three nights" (Jonah 1:17), and the restoration of Israel "on the third day" prophesied by Hosea (Hosea 6:2).

For further study, see Hank Hanegraaff, *Resurrection* (Nashville: Word Publishing, 2000).

L U K E 24:46

"He told them, 'This is what is written: The Christ will suffer and rise from the dead on the third day.'"

– 6 2 –

IS THE NEW TESTAMENT CANON
AUTHORITATIVE OR AUTHORITARIAN?

R ecently the Bible has come under attack
by liberal scholars who claim that the
New Testament canon was determined by
the winners of a supposed struggle for dominance in
the early centuries of Christianity. As the following
evidence reveals, however, the canon is not arbitrary
or authoritarian, but divinely authoritative.

First, the entire New Testament canon was
recorded *early* and thus was not subject to legendary
contamination. Had any part of the canon been
composed after AD 70 it would most certainly have
mentioned the destruction of the very temple that
had given the ancient Jews their theological and
sociological identity. Additionally, because Matthew
and Luke likely used Mark as a source and Luke
composed his gospel prior to the writing of Acts,
which was completed prior to Paul's martyrdom in
the mid–60s, Mark may have been composed as
early as the AD 40s, just a few years after the events
recorded. Moreover, in 1 Corinthians 15 Paul

reiterates a Christian creed that can be traced to within three to eight years of Christ's crucifixion. By contrast, the Gnostic gospels, including the Gospel of Thomas and the Gospel of Judas, are dated long after the close of the first century.

The entire New Testament canon was recorded *early* and thus was not subject to contamination. . . . The authority of the New Testament is confirmed through the *eyewitness* credentials of its authors. . . . And *extra–biblical* evidence confirms the New Testament canon.

Furthermore, the authority of the New Testament is confirmed through the *eyewitness* credentials of its authors. John writes, "That which was from the beginning, which we have heard, which we have seen with our eyes, which we have looked at and our hands have touched—this we proclaim concerning the Word of life" (1 John 1:1). Likewise, Peter reminded his readers that the disciples "did not follow cleverly invented stories" but "were eyewitnesses of [Jesus'] majesty" (2 Peter 1:16). Moreover, the New Testament contains *embarrassing* details that no authoritarian association bent on dogmatic dominance would have adopted.

For instance, the Gospels present the founding members of the movement as dissident disciples who not only doubted but denied their Master.

The canon was not *determined* by men but *discovered* by the community of early believers based on principles of canonicity.

Finally, *extra–biblical* evidence confirms the New Testament canon and knows nothing of early competing canons. Secular historians—including Josephus (before AD 100), the Roman Tacitus (around AD 120), the Roman Suetonius (AD 110), and the Roman governor Pliny the Younger (AD 110)—confirm the many events, people, places, and customs chronicled in the New Testament. Early church leaders such as Irenaeus, Tertullian, Julius Africanus, and Clement of Rome—all writing before AD 250—also shed light on New Testament historical accuracy. From such sources, we can piece together the highlights of the life of Christ independent of the New Testament canon. Moreover, Eusebius of Caesarea acknowledged the centrality of the canonical Gospels and recorded their widespread use in important Christian centers including Jerusalem, Antioch, Alexandria, and Rome. As such, the canon was not *determined* by men but *discovered* by the community of early believers based on principles of canonicity.

For further study, see Gary R. Habermas and Michael R. Licona, *The Case for the Resurrection of Jesus* (Grand Rapids: Kregel, 2004).

LUKE 1:1–2

"Many have undertaken to draw up an account of the things that have been fulfilled among us, just as they were handed down to us by those who from the first were eyewitnesses and servants of the word."

IS THE NEW TESTAMENT ANTI–SEMITIC?

Liberal scholars today are forwarding the notion that the canonization of the New Testament was driven by anti–Semitic motives. In fact, it has become increasingly popular to assert that the story of Judas's betrayal of Christ was invented because "Judas" allegedly meant "Jew." In reality, anti–Semitism had nothing to do with the canonization of the New Testament. Early dating, eyewitness attestation, and extra–biblical corroboration did!

First, as is obvious to any unbiased person from scholar to schoolchild, the New Testament is anything but anti–Semitic. Jesus, the twelve apostles, and the apostle Paul were all Jewish! In fact, Christians proudly refer to their heritage as the Judeo–Christian tradition. In the book of Hebrews, Christians are reminded of Jews, from David to Daniel, who are members of "the faith hall of fame." Indeed, Christian children grow up with Jews as their heroes!

Furthermore, the New Testament writers clearly proclaimed that salvation through the Jewish Messiah was given first to the Jewish people and then to the rest of the world (Matthew 15:24; Romans 1:16). Additionally, Peter's vision followed by Cornelius's receiving the Holy Spirit (Acts 10) and the subsequent Jerusalem council (Acts 15) clearly demonstrate both the inclusive nature of the church as well as the initial Jewish Christian resistance to Gentile inclusion (see also Galatians 2:11–14). While the early Christians were certainly not anti–Semitic, at least some Jewish believers initially manifested the opposite prejudice. Far from being anti–Semitic, the New Testament simply records the outworking of redemptive history as foretold by the Jewish prophets who prophesied that one of Christ's companions would betray him (Psalm 41:9; John 13:18). There is nothing subtle about the crucifixion narrative. The Jewish gospel writers explicitly state that it was their leaders who condemned Christ of blasphemy. There would be no motive to fabricate a fictional Judas to represent the quintessential Jew.

Far from being anti–Semitic, the New Testament simply records the outworking of redemptive history as foretold by the Jewish prophets who prophesied that one of Christ's companions would betray him.

Finally, the whole of Scripture goes to great lengths to underscore the fact that when it comes to faith in Christ there is no distinction between Jew and Gentile (Galatians 3:28) and that Jewish people throughout the generations are no more responsible for Christ's death than anyone else. As Ezekiel put it, "The son will not share the guilt of the father, nor will the father share the guilt of the son" (Ezekiel 18:20). Truly, liberal scholars owe the world an apology for inventing an idiosyncratic brand of fundamentalism that foments bigotry and hatred by entertaining the absurd notion that the New Testament is anti–Semitic.

For further study, see Hank Hanegraaff, "The Search for Jesus Hoax," *Christian Research Journal* 23, 2 (2000), available through the Christian Research Institute (CRI) at www.equip.org.

ROMANS 1:16
"I am not ashamed of the gospel, because it is the power of God for the salvation of everyone who believes: first for the Jew, then for the Gentile."

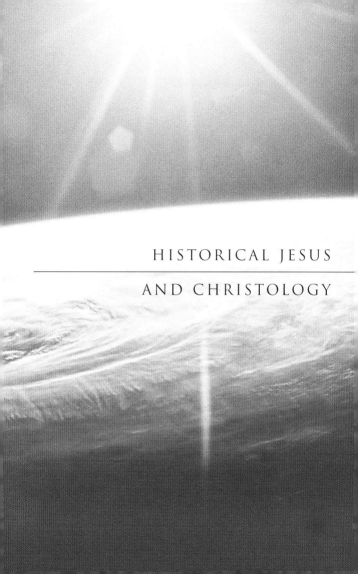

HISTORICAL JESUS

AND CHRISTOLOGY

64

Does the Bible claim Jesus is God?

any biblical texts can be used to demonstrate that Jesus is God. Three, however, stand out above the rest. Not only are they clear and convincing, but their "addresses" are easy to remember as well—John *1*, Colossians *1*, and Hebrews *1*.

First, is *John 1*: "In the beginning was the Word, and the Word was with God, *and the Word was God*" (v.1). Here Jesus not only is in existence before the world began but is differentiated from the Father and explicitly called God, indicating that he shares the same nature as his Father.

Furthermore, *Colossians 1* informs us that *"all things were created by him"* (v. 16); he is *"before all things"* (v. 17); and *"God was pleased to have all his fullness dwell in him"* (v. 19). Only deity has the prerogative of creation, preexists all things, and personifies the full essence and nature of God.

Finally, *Hebrews 1* overtly tells us that according to God the Father himself—Jesus *is* God: *"But about the Son he* [the Father] *says, 'Your throne, O*

God, will last for ever and ever'" (v. 8). Not only is the entirety of Hebrews 1 devoted to demonstrating the absolute deity of Jesus, but in verses 10–12 the inspired writer quotes a passage in Psalm 102 referring to Yahweh and directly applies it to Christ. In doing so, the Scripture specifically declares Jesus ontologically equal with Israel's God.

Many similar texts could be adduced. For example, in *Revelation 1* the Lord God says, "I am the Alpha and the Omega, who is, and who was, and who is to come, the Almighty" (v. 8). In the last chapter of Revelation, Jesus applies these self-same words— "Alpha and Omega"—to himself! Additionally, in *2 Peter 1* Jesus is referred to as "our God and Savior Jesus Christ" (v. 1). In these passages and a host of others, the Bible explicitly claims that Jesus *is* God.

For further study, see Hank Hanegraaff, *Resurrection* (Nashville: Word Publishing, 2000).

TITUS 2:13

"We wait for the blessed hope—the glorious appearing of our great God and Savior, Jesus Christ."

65

DID JESUS CLAIM TO BE GOD?

hen Jesus came to Caesarea Philippi, he asked his disciples the mother of all questions, *"Who do you say that I am?"* (Matthew 16:15; Mark 8:29; Luke 9:20). Mormons answer this question by saying that Jesus is the spirit brother of Lucifer; Jehovah's Witnesses answer by saying that Jesus is the archangel Michael; New Agers say Jesus is an avatar or enlightened messenger. Jesus, however, answered by claiming that he was God.

First, Jesus claimed to be the unique Son of God. As a result, the Jewish leaders tried to kill him because in "calling God his own Father, [Jesus was] making himself equal with God" (John 5:18). In John 8:58 Jesus went so far as to use the very words by which God revealed himself to Moses from the burning bush (Exodus 3:14). To the Jews this was the epitome of blasphemy for they knew that in doing so Jesus was clearly claiming to be God. On yet another occasion, Jesus explicitly told the Jews: "'I and the Father are one.' Again the Jews picked up stones to stone him, but Jesus said to them, 'I have shown you many great miracles from the Father. For which of these do you stone me?' 'We are not stoning you for any of these,' replied the Jews, 'but for blasphemy, because you, a mere man, claim to be God'" (John 10:30–33).

Furthermore, Jesus made an unmistakable claim to deity before the chief priests and the whole Sanhedrin. Caiaphas the high priest asked him: "'Are you the Christ, the Son of the Blessed One?' 'I am,' said Jesus. 'And you will see the Son of Man sitting at the right hand of the Mighty One and coming on the clouds of heaven'" (Mark 14:61–62). A biblically illiterate person might well have missed the import of Jesus' words. Caiaphas and the council, however, did not. They knew that in saying he was "the *Son of Man*" who would come "*on the clouds of heaven*" he was making an overt reference to the *Son of Man* in Daniel's prophecy (Daniel 7:13–14). And in doing so, he was not only claiming to be the preexistent Sovereign of the Universe but prophesying that he would vindicate his claim by judging the very court that was now condemning him. Moreover, by combining Daniel's prophecy with David's proclamation in Psalm 110, Jesus was claiming that he would sit upon the throne of Israel's God and share God's very glory. To students of the Old Testament this was the height of "blasphemy," thus "they all condemned him as worthy of death" (Mark 14:64).

Finally, Jesus claimed to possess the very attributes of God. For example, he claimed *omniscience* by telling Peter, "This very night, before the rooster crows, you will disown me three times" (Matthew 26:34); declared *omnipotence* by not only resurrecting Lazarus (John 11:43) but by raising himself from the dead (John 2:19); and professed *omnipresence* by promising he would be with his disciples "to the very end of the age" (Matthew 28:20). Not only so, but Jesus said to the paralytic in Luke 5:20, "Friend, your sins are forgiven." In doing so, he claimed a prerogative reserved for God alone. In addition, when Thomas worshiped Jesus, saying "My Lord and my God!" (John 20:28), Jesus responded with commendation rather than condemnation.

For further study, see Millard J. Erickson, *The Word Became Flesh: A Contemporary Incarnational Christology* (Grand Rapids: Baker Book House, 1996).

REVELATION 1:17–18
"I am the First and the Last. I am the Living One; I was dead, and behold I am alive for ever and ever!"

– 66 –

WHAT CREDENTIALS BACK UP
JESUS' CLAIM TO DEITY?

 esus not only claimed to be God but also
provided many convincing proofs that
he indeed was divine.

First, Jesus demonstrated that he was God in
human flesh by manifesting the credential of
sinlessness. While the Qur'an exhorts Muhammad
to seek forgiveness for his sins, the Bible exonerates
Messiah saying Jesus "had no sin" (2 Corinthians
5:21). And this is not a singular statement. John
declares, "and in him is no sin" (1 John 3:5), and
Peter says Jesus "committed no sin, and no deceit
was found in his mouth" (1 Peter 2:22). Jesus himself
went so far as to challenge his antagonists asking,
"Can any of you prove me guilty of sin?" (John 8:46).

Furthermore, Jesus demonstrated supernatural
authority over sickness, the forces of nature, fallen
angels, and even death itself. *Matthew 4* records that
Jesus went throughout Galilee teaching, preaching
"and healing every disease and sickness among the
people" (v. 23). *Mark 4* documents Jesus rebuking
the wind and the waves saying, "Quiet! Be still!" (v.

39). In *Luke 4* Jesus encounters a man possessed by an evil spirit and commands the demon to "Come out of him!" (v. 35). And in *John 4*, Jesus tells a royal official whose son was close to death, "Your son will live" (v. 50). In fact, the four Gospels record how Jesus demonstrated ultimate power over death through the immutable fact of his resurrection.

Finally, the credentials of Christ's deity are seen in the lives of countless men, women, and children. Each day, people of every tongue and tribe and nation experience the resurrected Christ by repenting of their sins and receiving Jesus as Lord and Savior of their lives. Thus, they not only come to know about Christ evidentially, but experientially Christ becomes more real to them than the very flesh upon their bones.

ADAPTED FROM *The Third Day*

For further study, see William Lane Craig, *Reasonable Faith: Christian Truth and Apologetics*, rev. ed. (Wheaton, Ill.: Crossway Books, 1994), chapters 7 and 8.

MATTHEW 11:2–5

"When John heard in prison what Christ was doing, he sent his disciples to ask him, 'Are you the one who was to come, or should we expect someone else?' Jesus replied, 'Go back and report to John what you hear and see; The blind receive sight, the lame walk, those who have leprosy are cured, the deaf hear, the dead are raised, and the good news is preached to the poor.'"

How can we be sure
about the resurrection of Christ?

 f devotees of the kingdom of the cults, adherents of world religions, or liberal scholars are correct, the biblical account of the resurrection of Christ is fiction, fantasy, or a gargantuan fraud. If, on the other hand, Christianity is factually reliable, his resurrection is the greatest feat in human history. No middle ground exists. The resurrection is history or hoax, miracle or myth, fact or fantasy.

First, liberal and conservative scholars alike agree that the body of Jesus was buried in the private tomb of Joseph of Arimathea. As a member of the Jewish court that condemned Jesus, Joseph of Arimathea is unlikely to be Christian fiction (Mark 15:43); Jesus' burial in the tomb of Joseph of Arimathea is substantiated by Mark's gospel (15:46) and is, therefore, far too early to have been the subject of legendary corruption; the earliest Jewish response to the resurrection of Christ presupposes the empty tomb (Matthew 28:11–13); and in the centuries following the resurrection, the fact of the empty tomb was forwarded by Jesus' friends and foes alike.

Additionally, as apologist William Lane Craig points out, "when you understand the role of women in first-century Jewish society, what's really extraordinary is that this empty tomb story should feature females as the discoverers of the empty tomb. . . . The fact that women are the first witnesses to the empty tomb is most plausibly explained by the reality that—like it or not—they *were* the discoverers of the empty tomb. This shows that the gospel writers faithfully recorded what happened, even if it was embarrassing." In short, early Christianity could not have survived an identifiable tomb containing the corpse of Christ.

Furthermore, Jesus gave his disciples many convincing proofs that he had risen from the dead. Paul, for example, points out that Christ "appeared to more than five hundred of the brothers at the same time, most of whom are still living, though some have fallen asleep" (1 Corinthians 15:6). It would have been one thing to attribute these supernatural experiences to people who had already died. It was quite another to attribute them to multitudes who were still alive. As the famed New

Testament scholar of Cambridge University C. H. Dodd points out, "There can hardly be any purpose in mentioning the fact that most of the five hundred are still alive, unless Paul is saying in effect, 'The witnesses are there to be questioned.'"

Finally, what happened as a result of the resurrection is unprecedented in human history. In the span of a few hundred years, a small band of seemingly insignificant believers succeeded in turning an entire empire upside down. While it is conceivable that they would have faced torture, vilification, and even cruel deaths for what they fervently believed to be true, it is inconceivable that they would have been willing to die for what they knew to be a lie. As Dr. Simon Greenleaf, the famous Royall Professor of Law at Harvard put it: "If it were morally possible for them to have been deceived in this matter, every human motive operated to lead them to discover and avow their error . . . If then their testimony was not true, there was no possible motive for this fabrication."

ADAPTED FROM The Third Day

For further study, see Hank Hanegraaff, *The Third Day* (Nashville: W Publishing Group, 2003); Lee Strobel, *The Case for Christ* (Zondervan, 1999); and see, especially, William Lane Craig, *Reasonable Faith* (Crossway Books, 1996), chapter 8.

1 CORINTHIANS 15:13–20

"If there is no resurrection of the dead, then not even Christ has been raised. And if Christ has not been raised, our preaching is useless and so is your faith. More than that, we are then found to be false witnesses about God, for we have testified about God that he raised Christ from the dead. But he did not raise him if in fact the dead are not raised. For if the dead are not raised, then Christ has not been raised either. And if Christ has not been raised, your faith is futile; you are still in your sins. Then those also who have fallen asleep in Christ are lost. If only for this life we have hope in Christ, we are to be pitied more than all men. But Christ has indeed been raised from the dead, the firstfruits of those who have fallen asleep."

68

WHAT DOES IT MEAN TO SAY
THAT JESUS ASCENDED INTO HEAVEN?

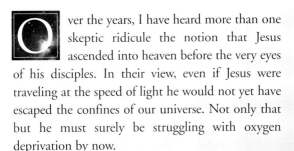

Over the years, I have heard more than one skeptic ridicule the notion that Jesus ascended into heaven before the very eyes of his disciples. In their view, even if Jesus were traveling at the speed of light he would not yet have escaped the confines of our universe. Not only that but he must surely be struggling with oxygen deprivation by now.

In response, let me first point out that to say Jesus ascended into heaven does not imply that he is traveling through space but rather that as the God-man he transcended time and space. Put another way, heaven is not located in time and space; it exists in another dimension.

Furthermore, the physical universe does not exhaust reality. It doesn't take a rocket scientist to understand that an effect such as the universe must have a cause greater than itself. This is self-evident not only to those who are philosophically sophisticated but to thinking people everywhere.

Thus, the notion that the creator of the universe transcended his universe should pose no problem.

Finally, I should note that God often uses physical examples to point to spiritual realities. Thus, the physical fact of Christ's ascension points to the greater truth that he is now glorified in the presence of God and that our glorification is divinely guaranteed as well.

For further study, see Peter Toon, *The Ascension of Our Lord* (Nashville: Thomas Nelson, 1984).

ACTS 1:9–11
*"After he said this, he was taken up
before their very eyes, and a cloud hid him from
their sight. They were looking intently up into the sky
as he was going, when suddenly two men
dressed in white stood beside them. 'Men of Galilee,'
they said, 'why do you stand here looking
into the sky? This same Jesus, who has been taken
from you into heaven, will come back
in the same way you have seen him go into heaven.'"*

69

WAS CHRISTIANITY INFLUENCED
BY ANCIENT PAGAN MYSTERY RELIGIONS?

A common refrain sung by those determined to demolish the biblical Jesus in the court of public opinion is that his life, death, burial, and resurrection are myths borrowed from ancient pagan mystery religions. Once reverberating primarily through the bastions of private academia, this refrain is now also commonly heard in public arenas.

The first prevailing myth widely circulated in this regard is that the similarities between Christianity and the mystery religions are striking. Purveyors of this mythology employ biblical language and then go to great lengths to concoct commonalities. Take, for example, the alleged similarities between Christianity and the cult of Isis. The god Osiris is supposedly murdered by his brother and buried in the Nile. The goddess Isis recovers the cadaver, only to lose it once again to her brother-in-law who cuts the body into fourteen pieces and scatters them around the world. After finding the parts, Isis "baptizes" each piece in the Nile River and Osiris is "resurrected."

The alleged similarities as well as the terminology used to communicate them are greatly exaggerated. Parallels between the "resurrection" of Osiris and the resurrection of Christ are an obvious stretch. And, sadly for the mysteries, this is as good as it gets. Other parallels typically cited by liberal scholars are even more far-fetched. Not only that but liberals have the chronology all wrong—most mysteries flourished long after the closing of the cannon of Scripture. Thus, it would be far more accurate to say that the mysteries were influenced by Christianity than the other way around.

Furthermore, the mystery religions reduced reality to a personal experience of enlightenment. Through secret ceremonies initiates experienced an esoteric transformation of consciousness that led them to believe that they were entering into a higher realm of reality. While followers of Christ were committed to essential Christian doctrines, devotees of the mysteries worked themselves into altered states of consciousness. They were committed to the notion that experience is a better teacher than words. In fact, the reason mystery religions are so named is that they directly involve secret esoteric practices and initiation rites. Far from being rooted in history and evidence, the mysteries reveled in hype and emotionalism.

Finally, the mystery religions were syncretistic in that adherents not only worshiped various pagan deities but also frequently embraced aspects of competing mystery religions while continuing to worship within their own cultic constructs. Not so with Christianity. Converts to Christ singularly placed their faith in the One who said, "I am the way and the truth and the life. No one comes to the Father except through me" (John 14:6).

For further study, see Ronald H. Nash, *The Gospel and the Greeks* (Richardson, Texas: Probe Books, 1992). See also Hank Hanegraaff, "Answering More Prime Time Fallacies," available at www.equip.org.

ACTS 17:29–31

"Therefore since we are God's offspring, we should not think that the divine being is like gold or silver or stone—an image made by man's design and skill. In the past God overlooked such ignorance, but now he commands all people everywhere to repent. For he has set a day when he will judge the world with justice by the man he has appointed. He has given proof of this to all men by raising him from the dead."

IS THE VIRGIN BIRTH MIRACLE OR MYTH?

In an op-ed piece published by the *New York Times* (August 15, 2003), columnist Nicholas Kristof used the virgin conception of Jesus to shamelessly promote the Enlightenment's false dichotomy between faith and reason. In his words, "The faith in the Virgin Birth reflects the way American Christianity is becoming less intellectual and more mystical over time." Kristof ends his piece with the following patronization: "The heart is a wonderful organ, but so is the brain." Those who have a truly open mind, however, should resist rejecting the virgin birth *a priori* (prior to examination).

First, miracles are not only possible but necessary in order to make sense of the universe in which we live. According to modern science, the universe not only had a beginning, but it is unfathomably fine-tuned to support life. Not only so, but the origin of life, information in the genetic code, irreducible complexity in biological systems, and the phenomenon of the human mind pose intractable difficulties for merely natural explanations. Thus, reason forces us to look beyond the natural world to a supernatural Designer who periodically intervenes in the affairs of his created handiwork. In other words, if we are willing to believe that God created the heavens and the earth (Genesis 1:1), we should have no problem accepting the virgin birth.

Reason forces us to look beyond the natural world to a supernatural Designer who periodically intervenes in the affairs of his created handiwork.

Furthermore, we are compelled by reason and evidence to acknowledge that the Bible is divine rather than human in origin. Manuscript evidence, archaeology, predictive prophecy, and the science of statistical probability together provide a persuasive case for the reliability of Scripture. Thus, we may appeal legitimately to the Word of God as evidence for the virgin birth. Moreover, Christ, who demonstrated that he was God in human flesh through the undeniable fact of resurrection, pronounced the Scriptures infallible (John 10:35; 14:24–26; 15:26–27; 16:13; Hebrews 1:1–2). And if Christ concurs with the virgin birth, no one should have the temerity to contradict his claim.

Finally, while it is currently popular to suggest that the gospel writers borrowed the virgin birth motif from pagan mythology, the facts say otherwise. Stories of gods having sexual intercourse with women—such as the sun-god Apollo becoming a snake and impregnating the mother of Augustus Caesar—hardly parallel the virgin birth account. Moreover, given the strict monotheistic worldview of New Testament authors it should stretch credulity beyond the breaking point to suppose they borrowed from pagan mythologies—especially myths extolling the sexual exploits of pagan gods!

It has become all too common for people to buy into what has been well described as "a unique brand of fundamentalism" that values rhetoric and emotional stereotypes over reason and evidential substance. Those who suppose that the virgin birth is mythological would be well served to carefully consider defensible arguments rather than uncritically swallowing dogmatic assertions.

For further study, see R. Douglas Geivett and Gary R. Habermas, eds., *In Defense of Miracles: A Comprehensive Case for God's Action in History* (Downers Grove, Ill.: InterVarsity Press, 1997).

MATTHEW 1:23

"'The virgin will be with child and will give birth to a son, and they will call him Immanuel'—which means, 'God with us.'"

ARE IMAGES OF JESUS IDOLATROUS?

n the fourth-century AD Emperor Leo III ordered the abolition of icons (revered images or sculptures) of Jesus, Mary, angels, and saints. This sparked the great Iconoclastic controversy, so called because those who supported the eradication of icons, often on the grounds that they violated the second commandment's prohibition of "graven images," were known as iconoclasts or "image breakers." The controversy sparked in the fourth century persists to this very day. Do images of Jesus really violate the second commandment?

First, if the second commandment condemns images of Jesus, then it condemns making images of anything at all. Therefore, God would have been guilty of contradicting himself because he commanded the Israelites to adorn the ark of the covenant with the images of cherubim (Exodus 25:18–20).

Furthermore, in context, the commandment is not an injunction against making "graven images," but an injunction against worshiping them. As such, God warns, "You shall not make for yourself an idol in the form of anything in heaven above or on the earth beneath or in the waters below. *You shall not bow down to them or worship them*; for I, the Lord your God, am a jealous God" (Exodus 20:4–5, emphasis added).

The commandment is not an injunction against making "graven images," but an injunction against using these carved images as objects of worship.

Finally, if viewing an image necessarily leads to idolatry, then the incarnation of Christ was the greatest temptation of all. Yet, Jesus thought it appropriate for people to look on him and worship him as God (Matthew 28:9; Luke 24:52). That worship, however, was to be directed to his person, not his appearance. Indeed, idolatry lies not in the making of images, but in the worship of manmade images in place of the "image of the invisible God" (Colossians 1:15).

For further study on a related issue, see Hank Hanegraaff, "Should Christians Celebrate Christmas?" *The Bible Answer Book Volume 1* (Nashville: J Countryman, 2004): 86–88.

GENESIS 1:27

"So God created man in his own image, in the image of God he created him; male and female he created them."

Was Isaiah thinking about Jesus
when he prophesied the virgin birth?

ooking back at the Old Testament through the lens of the New, it is easy to assume that Isaiah understood the Messianic meaning of his prophecy. However, those who believe that the Bible is the infallible repository of redemptive revelation must be willing to test all things in light of Scripture and hold fast to that which is good (1 Thessalonians 5:21).

First, the prophecy in Isaiah chapter seven—"the virgin will be with child and will give birth to a son, and will call him Immanuel"—was fulfilled in Isaiah chapter eight. As Isaiah makes clear, this prophecy was fulfilled when Isaiah "went to the prophetess, and she conceived and gave birth to a son" named Maher–Shalal–Hash–Baz (8:3). In context, Judah "was shaken" as two powerful kingdoms sought the nation's demise (7:1–2). God, however, promised that the birth of Maher–Shalal–Hash–Baz was a sign that Judah would be spared. In the words of Isaiah, "Before the boy knows enough to reject the wrong and choose the right, the land of the two kings you dread will be laid waste" (7:16; cf. 8:4).

Furthermore, though Isaiah's wife, unlike Mary, was not a virgin when she gave birth, she nonetheless was the near–future fulfillment of Isaiah's prophecy. "Virgin" (*almah*) was simply a term used to refer to the prophetess prior to her union with Isaiah, not to indicate that she would give birth to a child as a virgin. By way of analogy, it would have been true in 1999 to say that "the governor of Texas will one day lead this country," but this obviously does not mean that George W. Bush would lead the United States as the governor of Texas.

Finally, while the Holy Spirit may have revealed to Isaiah that his prophecy pointed forward to Jesus (John 12:41), it was not until after the miraculous virginal conception and birth of Jesus more than six hundred years later that it became entirely clear that the near–future fulfillment of Isaiah's prophecy was a type, the archetype of which is Jesus the Messiah (Matthew 1:22–23). While Maher–Shalal–Hash–Baz signified temporal salvation for Judah, Jesus Christ—the literal "Immanuel"—embodied eternal salvation for true Israel.

For further study, see Craig L. Blomberg, *Jesus and the Gospels* (Nashville: Broadman and Holman Publishers, 1997): 199–200.

"All this took place to fulfill what the Lord had said through the prophet: 'The virgin will be with child and will give birth to a son, and they will call him Immanuel—which means, God with us.'"

- 7 3 -

WAS JESUS MARRIED?

In an age of historical and blblical illiteracy it has become increasingly popular to perpetuate the notion that Jesus was married. The role of "Mrs. Jesus" in these fanciful depictions is most often played by Mary Magdalene. Most recently Dan Brown's bestselling novel *The Da Vinci Code* (Doubleday, 2003) has received much attention for its iteration of this tired tale. In contradiction to the claims of sensationalistic scholars, a survey of the evidence demonstrates that the married–Jesus myth is nothing more than radical historical revisionism.

First, there is not a scintilla of evidence in Scripture, in the writings of the early church, or in the extra–biblical accounts of Jesus' life that he was ever married. Contrary to the offhanded mention by Brown's character Teabing of "countless references to Jesus and Magdalene's union" (247), there are absolutely none.

Furthermore, the two documents most often cited in support of the married–Jesus myth—the Gospel of Philip and the Gospel of Mary Magdalene—were not only written too late to be considered reliable, but neither specifies nor implies that Jesus and Mary were actually married.

Finally, while no evidence from the historical record supports the notion that Jesus was married, the New Testament contains powerful evidence that Jesus was not. In 1 Corinthians 9:5 Paul defended his right to have a wife by appealing to the fact that Peter and other apostles had wives: "Don't we have a right to take a believing wife along with us, as do the Lord's brothers and Cephas?" If Jesus had been married it is unthinkable that Paul would have neglected to appeal to Jesus as the ultimate precedent. For this reason Paul Maier, professor of ancient history at Western Michigan University, aptly refers to 1 Corinthians 9:5 as "the graveyard of the married–Jesus fiction."

For further study, see Hank Hanegraaff and Paul L. Maier, *The Da Vinci Code: Fact or Fiction?* (Wheaton, IL: Tyndale House, 2004), 15–21.

MATTHEW 19:11–12
"Jesus replied, 'Not everyone can accept this word, but only those to whom it has been given. For some are eunuchs because they were born that way; others were made that way by men; and others have renounced marriage because of the kingdom of heaven. The one who can accept this should accept it.'"

DID JESUS HAVE ANY SIBLINGS?

The teaching that Jesus did not have any biological brothers or sisters is often championed in an attempt to support belief in the perpetual virginity of Mary. The most popular defense of this position holds that when the New Testament authors speak of Jesus' brothers, the Greek word translated "brother" ought to be interpreted as "cousin" or "distant relative." Proper interpretation, however, precludes this pretext.

First, the Bible explicitly tells us that Jesus Christ had brothers and sisters. Indeed, Matthew's gospel records the rhetorical questions of those acquainted with Jesus' immediate family: "'Isn't this the carpenter's son? Isn't his mother's name Mary, and aren't his brothers James, Joseph, Simon and Judas? Aren't all his sisters with us?'" (Matthew 13:54–56). Numerous other passages can be cited as proof positive that Jesus had siblings (Matthew 12:46–47; Mark 3:31–32; 6:3; Luke 8:19–20; John 2:12; 7:3–5; Acts 1:14; 1 Corinthians 9:5; Galatians 1:19).

Furthermore, there is no biblical precedent for rendering the Greek word *adelphos* (brother) or its feminine form *adelphae* (sister) as cousin. If the New Testament writers had wanted to designate Jesus' siblings as cousins, they would have used the word *anepsios*. In point of fact, this is precisely what Paul does in referring to Mark as the "cousin [*anepsios*] of Barnabas" (Colossians 4:10).

The Bible explicitly tells us that
Jesus Christ had brothers and sisters.

Finally, Matthew tells us that Joseph did not have sexual relations with Mary "until she gave birth to a son" (Matthew 1:25). Thus, we are justified in inferring that Mary *did* have sexual relations with Joseph *after* the birth of Jesus. The notion that having sexual intercourse with her husband after the birth of Jesus would have defiled Mary in some sense is completely inconsistent with a biblical worldview.

For further study, see Eric D. Svendsen, *Who Is My Mother?* (Amityville, NY: Calvary Press, 2001).

"While Jesus was still talking to the crowd, his mother
and brothers stood outside, wanting to speak to him.
Someone told him, 'Your mother and brothers are
standing outside, wanting to speak to you.' He replied
to him, 'Who is my mother, and who are my brothers?'
Pointing to his disciples, he said, 'Here are my mother
and my brothers. For whoever does the will of my
Father in heaven is my brother and sister and mother.'"

IS THE INCARNATION INCOHERENT?

ike the Trinity, the incarnation is often considered to be logically incoherent. While the Incarnation may transcend our human understanding, it does not transgress the laws of logic.

First, because God created humanity in his own image (Genesis 1:27), the essential properties of human nature (rationality, will, moral character, and the like) are not inconsistent with his divine nature. Though the notion of God becoming a clam would be absurd, the reality that God became a man is not.

Furthermore, it is crucial to point out that though the God–Man is *fully* human, he is not *merely* human. Though he took on all the essential properties of human nature, he did not take on that which is nonessential (e.g., sinful inclinations). Indeed, as Adam was created without a proclivity toward sin, so the Second Adam was untainted by original sin. As with his moral perfection, Jesus' other divine attributes (omniscience, omnipotence, omnipresence, and so forth) were not undermined in the incarnation.

Finally, while Jesus Christ voluntarily refrained from exercising certain attributes of deity, he did not divest himself of a single divine attribute (John 1:14; Philippians 2:1–11; Colossians 1:15–20; Hebrew 2:14–18). With respect to his omniscience, for example, his human nature may have served as a filter limiting his knowledge as a man (e.g., Mark 13:32). Nonetheless, Jesus' divine omniscience was ever accessible at the will of the Father. In sum, there is no incoherence in the biblical teaching that Jesus became and will forever remain one person with two distinct natures neither commingling his natures nor becoming two persons.

For further study, see Ronald H. Nash, *Is Jesus the Only Savior?* (Grand Rapids: Zondervan, 1994): pages 84–91; for the definitive philosophical work on this topic, see Thomas V. Morris, *The Logic of God Incarnate* (Ithaca, NY: Cornell University Press, 1986).

JOHN 1:14

"The Word became flesh and made his dwelling among us. We have seen his glory, the glory of the One and Only, who came from the Father, full of grace and truth."

IF GOD CANNOT BE TEMPTED, HOW COULD JESUS BE TEMPTED?

n the one hand Scripture tells us that "God cannot be tempted by evil" (James 1:13). On the other, it informs us that during his wilderness sojourn, Jesus *was* tempted by the evil one (Matthew 4:1–11). Could Jesus be tempted or couldn't he?

First, for sin to take place there must be a sinful inner response to a seductive suggestion to sin. Though Satan appealed to Jesus' natural human desires (e.g., hunger), our Lord did not fantasize over Satan's suggestion. To mull over Satan's suggestion even for a moment would have constituted sin. And, had Jesus sinned, he could not have been our Savior.

Furthermore, although Christ did not have any sinful proclivities that inclined him toward evil, Satan's temptations were nonetheless as real as the very flesh upon his bones. Even those who are born into sin can identify with being tempted to do something they are utterly disinclined to do. By way of analogy, most mothers would never consider killing their children—even if offered a life free from suffering. Nonetheless, the natural desire to avoid suffering would render such a temptation genuine.

Finally, in saying "God cannot be tempted by evil," James focuses on God as the self–sufficient sovereign of the universe. As such, he has no unmet needs. Conversely, the accounts of the temptation focus on God–Incarnate who experienced all the essential physical and psychological needs commensurate with humanity—including hunger, fatigue, and the desire for self–preservation. Thus, the biblical truths that God cannot be tempted and yet Christ *was* tempted are complementary, not contradictory.

For further study, see Adam Pelser, "Genuine Temptation and the Character of Christ," *Christian Research Journal* 30, 2 (2007), available through the Christian Research Institute (CRI) at www.equip.org.

HEBREWS 4:15

"For we do not have a high priest who is unable
to sympathize with our weaknesses, but we
have one who has been tempted in every way,
just as we are—yet was without sin."

HOW CAN THE ETERNAL SON OF GOD BE "THE FIRSTBORN OVER ALL CREATION"?

n his letter to the Colossians, Paul calls Jesus Christ the "firstborn over all creation" (Colossians 1:15). How can Christ be both the eternal Creator of all things and yet himself be the *firstborn*?

First, in referring to Christ as the *firstborn*, Paul has in mind preeminence. This usage is firmly established in the Old Testament. For example, Ephraim is referred to as the Lord's "firstborn" (Jeremiah 31:9) even though Manasseh was born first (Genesis 41:51). Likewise, David is appointed the Lord's "firstborn, the most exalted of the kings of the earth" (Psalm 89:27), despite being the youngest of Jesse's sons (1 Samuel 16:10–13). While neither Ephraim nor David was the first one born in his family, both were firstborn in the sense of preeminence or "prime position."

Furthermore, Paul refers to Jesus as the firstborn *over* all creation not the firstborn *in* creation. As such, "He is before *all things* and in him *all things* hold together" (Colossians 1:17, emphasis added). The force of Paul's language is such that the cult of the Jehovah's Witnesses, who ascribe to the ancient Arian heresy that the Son is not preexistent and co-eternal with the Father, have been forced to insert the word "other" (e.g., "all other things") in their deeply flawed New World Translation of the Bible in order to demote Christ to the status of a created being.

Finally, as the panoply of Scripture makes plain, Jesus is the eternal Creator who spoke and the limitless galaxies leapt into existence. In John 1 he is overtly called "God" (v. 1), and in Hebrews 1 he is said to be the one who "laid the foundations of the earth" (v. 10). And in the very last chapter of the Bible, Christ refers to himself as "the Alpha and the Omega, the First and the Last, the Beginning and the End" (Revelation 22:13). Indeed, the whole of Scripture precludes the possibility that Christ could be anything other than the preexistent sovereign of the universe.

For further study, see Robert L. Reymond, *Jesus, Divine Messiah* (Tain, Ross–shire, Scotland: Christian Focus Publications, 2003) at www.equip.org.

"He is the image of the invisible God, the firstborn over all creation. For by him all things were created: things in heaven and on earth, visible and invisible, whether thrones or powers or rulers or authorities; all things were created by him and for him."

RELIGIONS AND CULTS

What distinguishes Christianity from other religions?

Christianity is unique among the religions of the world for several reasons.

First, unlike other religions, Christianity is rooted in history and evidence. Jesus of Nazareth was born in Bethlehem in Judea during the reign of Caesar Augustus and was put to death by Pontius Pilate, a first-century Roman governor. The testimony of his life, death, and resurrection is validated both by credible eyewitness testimony and by credible extra-biblical evidence as well. No other religion can legitimately claim this kind of support from history and evidence.

Furthermore, of all the influential religious leaders of the world (Buddha, Moses, Zoroaster, Krishna, Lao Tzu, Muhammad, Baha'u'llah), only Jesus claimed to be God in human flesh (Mark 14:62). And this was not an empty boast. For through the historically verifiable fact of the resurrection, Christ vindicated his claim to deity (Romans 1:4; 1 Corinthians 15:3–8). Other religions, such as

Buddhism and Islam, claim miracles in support of their faith; however, unlike Christianity, such miracles lack historical validation.

Finally, Christianity is unique in that it is a coherent belief structure. Some Christian doctrines may transcend comprehension; however, unlike the claims of other religions, they are never irrational or contradictory. Christianity is also unique in that it cogently accounts for the vast array of phenomena we encounter in everyday life: the human mind, laws of science, laws of logic, ethical norms, justice, love, meaning in life, the problem of evil and suffering, and truth. In other words, Christianity corresponds with the reality of our present condition.

For further study, see James W. Sire, *The Universe Next Door*, 3rd edition (Downers Grove, Ill.: InterVarsity Press, 1997); and Lee Strobel, *The Case for Christ* (Grand Rapids: Zondervan Publishing House, 1998).

2 PETER 1:16

"We did not follow cleverly invented stories when we told you about the power and coming of our Lord Jesus Christ, but we were eyewitnesses of his majesty."

DON'T ALL RELIGIONS LEAD TO GOD?

Before answering this question, a word of warning is in order: Anyone who answers in the negative may well be ostracized for being narrow-minded and intolerant. That being said, my answer is, "No, not all religions lead to God, and it is incorrect and illogical to maintain that they do."

First, when you begin to examine world religions such as Judaism, Hinduism, and Buddhism, you will immediately recognize that they directly contradict one another. For example, Moses taught that there was only one God; Krishna believed in many gods; and Buddha was agnostic. Logically, they can all be wrong but they can't all be right.

Furthermore, the road of religion leads steeply uphill, while the road of Christianity descends downward. Put another way, Religion is fallen humanity's attempt to reach up and become acceptable to God through what we *do*; Christianity, on the other hand, is a divine gift based on what Christ has *done*. He lived the perfect life that we could never live and offers us his perfection as an absolutely free gift.

Finally, Jesus taught that there was only one way to God. "I am *the way* and *the truth* and *the life*," said Jesus, "No one comes to the Father except through me" (John 14:6, emphasis added). Moreover, Jesus validated his claim through the immutable fact of his resurrection. The opinions of all other religious leaders are equally valid in that they are equally worthless. They died and are still dead. Only Jesus had the power to lay down his life and to take it up again. Thus, his opinion is infinitely more valid than theirs.

For further study, see John MacArthur, *Why One Way? Defending an Exclusive Claim in an Inclusive World* (Nashville: W Publishing Group, 2002); and Ronald Nash, *Is Jesus the Only Savior?* (Grand Rapids: Zondervan, 1994).

ACTS 4:12
"Salvation is found in no one else,
for there is no other name under heaven given to men
by which we must be saved."

WHAT HAPPENS TO A PERSON
WHO HAS NEVER HEARD OF JESUS?

One of the most frequently asked questions on the *Bible Answer Man* broadcast is "What happens to those who have never heard of Jesus?" Will God condemn people to hell for not believing in someone they have never heard of?

First, people are not condemned to hell for not believing in Jesus. Rather they are *already* condemned because of their *sin*. Thus, the real question is not how can God send someone to hell, but how can God condescend to save any one of us?

Furthermore, if ignorance were a ticket to heaven, the greatest evangelistic enterprise would not be a Billy Graham crusade but a concerted cover-up campaign. Such a campaign would focus on ending evangelism, burning Bibles, and closing churches. Soon no one will have heard of Christ and everyone will be on their way to heaven.

Finally, it should be emphasized that everyone has the light of both creation and conscience. God is not capricious! If we respond to the light we have,

God will give us more light. In the words of the apostle Paul: "From one man he made every nation of men, that they should inhabit the whole earth; and he determined the times set for them and the exact places where they should live. God did this so that men would seek him and perhaps reach out for him and find him, though he is not far from each one of us" (Acts 17:26–27).

For further study, see Ronald H. Nash, *Is Jesus the Only Savior?* (Grand Rapids: Zondervan, 1994). See also Hank Hanegraaf, "Is Jesus the Only Way," available at www.equip.org.

JOHN 14:6

"I am the way and the truth and the life.
No one comes to the Father except through me."

HOW WERE PEOPLE WHO LIVED
BEFORE THE TIME OF CHRIST SAVED?

ome say that those who lived before the time of Christ were saved by keeping the law. The Scriptures, however, say otherwise.

First, the Bible from first to last demonstrates that the saved throughout history come to faith in exactly the same way—*by grace alone through faith alone on account of Christ alone.* The apostle Paul quotes the Old Testament extensively to drive home the reality that no one has been, or ever will be, declared righteous by observing the law (Romans 3:20).

Furthermore, Paul points to Abraham, the father of the Jews, to prove that salvation comes through faith apart from works that we perform. In his words, "If, in fact, Abraham was justified by works, he had something to boast about—but not before God. What does the Scripture say? 'Abraham believed God, and it was credited to him as righteousness'" (Romans 4:3; Genesis 15:6; Galatians 3:6–9).

Finally, Jesus Christ is the substance that fulfills the types and shadows in the Old Testament (Luke 24:44; Romans 3:21–22; Hebrews 1:1–3). Each year the Jews celebrated the Passover to keep them focused on the One who was to come to die for their sins (1 Corinthians 5:7; Hebrews 11:28, 39–40). As Hebrews says, "The law is only a shadow of the good things that are coming, not the realities themselves" (Hebrews 10:1).

The Bible from first to last demonstrates that the saved throughout history come to faith in exactly the same way—by grace alone through faith alone on account of Christ alone.

Jesus Christ stands at the apex of history. Just as people today look back in history to Christ's sacrifice on the cross, so too people who lived before the time of Christ looked forward to his sacrifice for them.

For further study see Bruce Milne, *Know the Truth* (Downer's Grove: InterVarsity Press: 1998), pages 189–191.

WHAT IS A CULT?

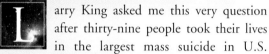

Larry King asked me this very question after thirty-nine people took their lives in the largest mass suicide in U.S. history. He went on to ask whether Christianity might legitimately be referred to as a cult. As I explained on *Larry King Live* the word "cult" has various connotations.

First, a cult may be defined *sociologically*. From this perspective, a cult is a religious or semi-religious sect whose followers are controlled by strong leadership in virtually every dimension of their lives. Devotees characteristically display a displaced loyalty for the guru and the group and are galvanized together through physical and/or psychological intimidation tactics. This kind of cultist more often than not displays a "we/they" siege mentality and has been cut off from all former associations including their immediate families.

Furthermore, a cult may be defined *theologically*. In this sense a cult can be a pseudo-Christian organization that claims to be Christian but compromises, confuses, or contradicts essential Christian doctrine. Such cults operate under the guise of Christianity but deviate from the orthodox teachings of the historic Christian faith as codified in the ancient ecumenical creeds. Typically, devotees become masters at taking texts out of context to develop pretexts for their theological perversions.

Finally, I should note that although the media-driven culture has given the term "cult" an exclusively pejorative connotation, denotatively the word "cult" can be broadly defined as a group of people centered around a religious belief structure. As such, Christianity might rightly be referred to as a cult of Old Testament Judaism. In fact, the Latin verb *cultus* from which we derive the word "cult" simply means to worship a deity. Thus, in dealing with cults it is crucial to be diligent in defining terms.

For further study, see Hank Hanegraaff, *Counterfeit Revival*, rev. ed. (Nashville: Word Publishing Group, 2001), part 5; and Ron Rhodes, *The Challenge of the Cults and New Religions* (Grand Rapids: Zondervan, 2001).

2 CORINTHIANS 11:3–4
"But I am afraid that just as Eve was deceived by the serpent's cunning, your minds may somehow be led astray from your sincere and pure devotion to

*Christ. For if someone comes to you and preaches a
Jesus other than the Jesus we preached, or if you receive
a different spirit from the one you received,
or a different gospel from the one you accepted, you put
up with it easily enough."*

L
ike Mormons, Jehovah's Witnesses believe
that Christianity died with the last of the
apostles. They believe Christianity was
not resurrected until their founder, Charles Taze
Russell, began organizing the Watchtower Society in
the 1870s. In their view the cross is a pagan symbol
adopted by an apostate church and salvation is
impossible apart from the Watchtower. While the
Witnesses on your doorstep consider themselves to
be the only authentic expression of Christianity,
the Society they serve compromises, confuses, or
contradicts essential Christian doctrine.

First, the Watchtower Society compromises the
nature of God. They teach their devotees that the
Trinity is a "freakish-looking, three headed God"
invented by Satan and that Jesus is merely a god. In
Watchtower theology Jesus was created by God as
the archangel Michael, during his earthly sojourn
became merely human, and after his crucifixion was
re-created an immaterial spirit creature. JWs also
deny the physical resurrection of Jesus. According to

Russell, the body that hung on a torture stake either "dissolved into gasses" or is "preserved somewhere as the grand memorial of God's love."

Furthermore, while Christians believe all believers will spend eternity with Christ in "a new heaven and a new earth" (Revelation 21:1; 22:17) the Watchtower teaches that only 144,000 people will make it to heaven while the rest of the faithful will live apart from Christ on earth. Thus in Watchtower lore there is a "little flock" of 144,000 who get to go to heaven and a "great crowd" of others who are relegated to earth. The heavenly class are born again, receive the baptism of the Holy Spirit, and partake of communion; the earthly class do not. To substantiate the notion that heaven's door was closed irrevocably in 1935, JWs point to "flashes of prophetic light" received by Joseph F. Rutherford at a JW convention in Washington D.C. Other false "flashes of prophetic light" include Watchtower predictions of end-time cataclysms that were to occur in 1914 . . . 1918 . . . 1925 . . . 1975.

Finally, under the threat of being "disfellowshipped," Jehovah's Witnesses are barred from celebrating Christmas, birthdays, or holidays such as Thanksgiving and Good Friday. Even more troubling are Watchtower regulations regarding vaccinations, organ transplants, and blood transfusions. In 1931, JWs were instructed to refuse vaccinations—by 1952, this regulation was rescinded. In 1967, organ transplants were ruled a forbidden form of cannibalism—by 1980, this edict was erased. In 1909, the Watchtower produced a prohibition against blood transfusions. No doubt, this too will one day become a relic of the past. In the meantime, tens of thousands have not only been ravished spiritually by the Watchtower Society but have paid the ultimate physical price as well.

While Watchtower adherents are often willing to do more for a lie than Christians are willing to do for the truth, these and a host of other doctrinal perversions keep JWs from rightly being considered Christian.

For further study, see Ron Rhodes, *Reasoning from the Scriptures with the Jehovah's Witnesses* (Eugene, Ore.: Harvest House Publishers, 1993).

DEUTERONOMY 18:22

"If what a prophet proclaims in the name of the Lord does not take place or come true, that is a message the Lord has not spoken. That prophet has spoken presumptuously. Do not be afraid of him."

IS THE NEW WORLD TRANSLATION
OF THE BIBLE CREDIBLE?

J ehovah's Witnesses claim that the *New World Translation* (*NWT*) is the "work of competent scholars." Conversely, they contend that other Bible translations are corrupted by religious traditions that are rooted in paganism. In reality, the *NWT* is the work of a Bible Translation Committee with no working knowledge of biblical languages. Their bias is so blatant that Dr. Bruce Metzger, professor of New Testament at Princeton, not only characterized the *NWT* as a "frightful mistranslation" but as "erroneous," "pernicious," and "reprehensible."

First, the *NWT* mistranslates the Greek Scriptures in order to expunge the deity of Jesus Christ. Against all credible scholarship, Jesus is downgraded from God to *"a"* god in John 1 and demoted from the Creator of all things to a mere creature who created all *other* things in Colossians 1. According to the translation committee of the Watchtower Society, Jesus was created by God as the archangel Michael, during his earthly sojourn was merely human, and after his crucifixion was re-created an immaterial spirit creature.

Furthermore, the Translation Committee has sought to conform the *NWT* to their religious traditions by replacing the *cross* of Christ with a *torture stake*. Matthew 10:38, for example, has been altered to read, "And whoever does not accept his *torture stake* and follow after me is not worthy of me." In Watchtower lore, the cross is a pagan symbol adopted by an apostate Christianity when Satan took control of the early church. Jehovah's Witnesses view wearing a cross as a blatant act of idolatry. Conversely, Christians wear crosses as a reminder of what was at once the most brutal and beautiful act in redemptive history.

Finally, the Watchtower Society claims that the Christian Scriptures have "been tampered with" in order to eliminate the name *Jehovah* from the text. In reality, it is the Translation Committee of the *NWT* that can rightly be accused of tampering. In well over two hundred cases the name Jehovah has been gratuitously inserted into the New Testament text. In passages such as Romans 10:13 this is done to obscure the unique deity of Christ. In other passages, it is done under the pretext that referring to God as

Lord rather than Jehovah is patently pagan. Ironically, in *The Kingdom Interlinear Translation of the Greek Scriptures*, Watchtower translators themselves fall into this "pagan" practice by translating the Greek word *kurios* as Lord even in cases where it specifically refers to the Father.

For these and a host of other reasons, Greek scholars across the board denounce the *NWT*. Dr. Julius Mantey, author of *A Manual Grammar of the Greek New Testament*, called the *NWT* a "shocking mistranslation," and Dr. William Barclay characterized the translators themselves as "intellectually dishonest."

For further study, see David A. Reed, *Answering Jehovah's Witnesses: Subject by Subject* (Grand Rapids: Baker Book House, 1996).

REVELATION 22:18–19

"I warn everyone who hears the words of the prophecy
of this book: If anyone adds anything to them, God
will add to him the plagues described in this book.
And if anyone takes words away from this book
of prophecy, God will take away from him
his share in the tree of life and in the holy city,
which are described in this book."
(SEE ALSO DEUTERONOMY 4:2)

Is Mormonism Christian?

The Church of Jesus Christ of Latter-day
Saints was birthed in 1820 by an alleged
vision in which two celestial personages
appeared to Joseph Smith claiming *all* existing
churches were wrong, *all* their creeds were an
abomination, and *all* their professors were corrupt.
According to these personages, Smith had been
chosen to *restore*—not *reform*—a church that had
disappeared from the face of the earth. The Mormon
doctrines that evolved from this vision compromise,
confuse, or contradict the nature of God, the
authority of Scripture, and the way of salvation.

First, while Christians believe that God is spirit
(John 4:24), Joseph Smith taught, "God Himself was
once as we are now, and is an exalted man, and sits
enthroned in yonder heavens!" Mormonism also
holds to a plurality of gods and contends that "as
man is, God once was; as God is, man may become."
Additionally, the Latter-day Saints compromise the
nature of the God-man, Jesus Christ. In Christianity,
Jesus is the self-existent creator of all things

(Colossians 1:15–20). In Mormonism, he is the spirit brother of Lucifer who was conceived in heaven by a celestial Mother and came in flesh as the result of the Father having sex with the Virgin Mary.

Doctrinal perversions exclude
Mormonism from rightly being called Christian.

Furthermore, in sharp distinction to orthodox Christian theology, Mormons do not believe that the Bible is the *infallible* repository for redemptive revelation (2 Timothy 3:16). In their view, the *Book of Mormon* is "the most correct of any book on earth, and the keystone of our religion." Two further revelations complete the Mormon quad, namely *Doctrine and Covenants* and *The Pearl of Great Price*. *Doctrine and Covenants* is a compilation of divine revelations that includes the doctrine of polygamy. Not until threatened by the Federal government did Mormon president Wilford Woodruff receive a revelation relegating polygamy to the afterlife. *The Pearl of Great Price* is no less troubling; this extra-biblical revelation was used by Mormonism to prevent African-Americans from entering the priesthood and from being exalted to godhood.

Finally, while Christians believe that they will stand before God dressed in the spotless robes of Christ's righteousness (Romans 3:21–22; Philippians 3:9), Mormons contend that they will appear before Heavenly Father dressed in fig-leaf aprons holding good works in their hands. According to the Latter-day Saints, virtually everyone qualifies for heaven. Murderers, unrepentant whoremongers, and the world's vilest people make it into the *Telestial heaven*; lukewarm Mormons, religious people, and those who accept the Mormon gospel in the spirit world typically enter the *Terrestrial heaven*; and temple Mormons make it to the *Celestial heaven*. Only those who are sealed in secret temple rituals, however, will make it to the third level of the Celestial kingdom and become gods of their own planets.

These and many other doctrinal perversions exclude Mormonism from rightly being called Christian.

For further study, see Richard Abanes, *One Nation Under Gods* (New York: Four Walls Eight Windows, 2003); and James R. White, *Is the Mormon My Brother?* (Minneapolis: Bethany House, 1997).

"You are my witnesses," declares the LORD,
"and my servant whom I have chosen,
so that you may know and believe me and understand
that I am he. Before me no god was formed,
nor will there be one after me."

IS THE BOOK OF MORMON CREDIBLE?

In 1823, the angel Moroni allegedly visited Mormon prophet Joseph Smith and divulged the location of some golden plates containing the "fullness of the everlasting gospel." These plates—abridged by Moroni and his father, Mormon, fourteen hundred years earlier— were written in "reformed Egyptian hieroglyphics." Along with the plates, Smith found a pair of magical eyeglasses that he used to translate the cryptic writing into English. The result was a new revelation called the *Book of Mormon* and a new religion called *Mormonism*. How millions can take the *Book of Mormon* seriously is almost beyond comprehension.

First, while Smith referred to the *Book of Mormon* as "the most correct of any book on earth and the keystone of our religion" its flaws run the gamut from the serious to the silly. In the category of serious, the *Book of Mormon* contains modalistic language that militates against the biblical doctrine of the Trinity (Ether 3:14). In the category of silly, a man struggles to catch his breath after having his head cut off (Ether 15:31).

Furthermore, while archeology is a powerful testimony to the accuracy of the Bible the same cannot be said for the *Book of Mormon*. Not only is there no archeological evidence for a language such as "reformed Egyptian hieroglyphics," there is no archeological support for lands such as the "land of Moron" (Ether 7:6). Nor is there any archeological evidence to buttress the notion that the Jaredites, Nephites, and Lamanites migrated from Israel to the Americas. On the contrary, both archeology and anthropology demonstrate conclusively that the people and places chronicled in the *Book of Mormon* are little more than the product of a fertile imagination.

Finally, Joseph Smith asserted that the golden plates were translated "by the power of God" and produced "the most correct of any book on earth." Joseph F. Smith, the sixth president of the Mormon church, went so far as to say that the words were not only correct but "every letter was given to [Smith] by the gift and power of God." In reality however, the *Book of Mormon* has had to be corrected thousands of times to compensate for Smith's poor grammar and spelling. The *Book of Mormon* is fraught with other errors as well. For example, "Benjamin" was changed to "Mosiah" when Mormon leaders realized that in the chronology of the *Book of Mormon* King

Benjamin had already died—thus he would have been hard pressed to "interpret" the engravings mentioned in Mosiah 21:28. Perhaps the greatest crack in the credibility of the *Book of Mormon* is that whole sections were derived directly from the King James Version of the Bible—this despite the fact that according to Mormon chronology, the *Book of Mormon* predates the King James Version by more than a thousand years.

Little wonder that Mormons accept the *Book of Mormon* based on a "burning in the bosom" rather than on history and evidence.

For further study, see Jerald and Sandra Tanner, *The Changing World of Mormonism* (Chicago: Moody Press, 1980).

GALATIANS 1:6–9

"I am astonished that you are so quickly deserting the one who called you by the grace of Christ and are turning to a different gospel—which is really no gospel at all. Evidently some people are throwing you into confusion and are trying to pervert the gospel of Christ. But even if we or an angel from heaven should preach a gospel other than the one we preached to you, let him be eternally condemned! As we have already said, so now I say again: If anybody is preaching to you a gospel other than what you accepted, let him be eternally condemned!"

DOES MORMONISM *REALLY* TEACH THAT
JESUS IS THE SPIRIT BROTHER OF SATAN?

o begin with, according to official Mormon teaching, Jesus Christ is the first spirit child conceived and begotten by Heavenly Father and one of Heavenly Father's many wives (commonly referred to as "Heavenly Mother"). Just as Heavenly Father before him progressed to godhood, so Jesus progressed through obedience to the status of a god (prior to his incarnation on earth). In the words of the late Mormon Apostle and General Authority Bruce McConkie, Jesus Christ through obedience and devotion "attained that pinnacle of intelligence which ranked him as a God." As such, according to LDS authorities, Jesus is not to be worshiped or prayed to as one would worship or pray to Heavenly Father.

Furthermore, Mormons teach that Heavenly Father subsequently had other spirit children. We ourselves are thought to be spirit children of Father God and Mother God. As such, Mormons refer to Jesus as our "Elder brother." As the official LDS teacher's manual *Gospel Principles* explains, "We needed a Savior to pay for our sins and teach us how to return to our Heavenly Father. Our Father said, 'Whom shall I send?' (Abraham 3:27). Two of *our* brothers offered to help. *Our* oldest brother, Jesus Christ, who was then called Jehovah, said, 'Here am I, send me'" (emphasis added).

Finally, it stands to reason that if Jesus is the first spirit child conceived and begotten by Heavenly Father; and if Heavenly Father and Mother subsequently conceived other spirit children including Satan; then Jesus and Satan logically are spirit brothers. While LDS spokespersons sometimes obfuscate this fundamental Mormon teaching, apostles of the Mormon Church and current official LDS publications clearly affirm it. As explained by the Mormon publication *Ensign*, "On first hearing, the doctrine that Lucifer and our Lord, Jesus Christ, are brothers may seem surprising to some—especially to those unacquainted with latter-day revelations. But both the scriptures and the prophets affirm that Jesus Christ and Lucifer are indeed offspring of our Heavenly Father and, therefore, spirit brothers."

In sharp contrast to Mormon Christology, the biblical witness is clear and convincing: Jesus Christ is the eternal Creator God (John 1; Colossians 1; Hebrews 1; Revelation 1). Paul explicitly teaches that Jesus is the creator of all, including the angelic realm to which Satan belongs (Colossians 1:15–16; cf. John 1:3). *Jesus is thus Satan's creator, not his spirit brother.*

For further study, see "Is Mormonism Christian?" p. 253; and "Is the Book of Mormon credible?" p. 257; and Hank Hanegraaff, "The Mormon Mirage: Seeing Through the Illusion of Mainstream Mormonism" (Charlotte: Christian Research Institute, 2008).

COLOSSIANS 1:15–16

"He is the image of the invisible God, the firstborn over creation. For by him all things were created: things in heaven and on earth, visible and invisible, whether thrones or powers or rulers or authorities; all things were created by him and for him."

Is Oneness Pentecostalism biblical?

According to the *Dictionary of Pentecostal and Charismatic Movements* (DPCM), "Oneness Pentecostalism (OP) is a religious movement that emerged in 1914 within the Assemblies of God (AG) of the early American Pentecostal movement, challenging the traditional Trinitarian doctrine, and baptismal practice with a modalistic view of God, a revelational theory of the name of Jesus, and an insistence on rebaptism in the name of the Lord Jesus Christ."

First, Oneness Pentecostals believe that unless you are baptized using the correct formula you are not truly saved. In their view the formula is, "I baptize you in the name of Jesus" not "I baptize you in the name of the Father, Son, and Holy Spirit." Conversely, when Peter says we are to be baptized "in the name of Jesus" (Acts 2:38) or when Jesus says we are to baptize "in the name of the Father and of the Son and of the Holy Spirit" (Matthew 28:19), they were not prescribing different formulas. Rather, they were saying that we are baptized by the authority vested in the one true God revealed in

Scripture. Thus to be baptized in the name of Jesus is to be baptized on the basis of our belief in his death, burial, and resurrection.

By way of analogy, when a police officer commands someone to "stop in the name of the law" the power is not in the phrase, but in the authority it signifies. Likewise, when a physician provides someone who is sick with a prescription, their trust is not in the paper on which it is penned, but rather the potion to which it points. So it is with baptism. The power is not in a prescribed formula but in the heavenly physician to whom the act of baptism points. Baptism is not essential for salvation; it is, however, essential to obedience.

Furthermore, error begets error; thus the belief that one must be baptized only in the name of Jesus has led Oneness Pentecostalism to the further error that Jesus is himself the Father, the Son, and the Holy Spirit. They do not hold to one God revealed in three persons who are eternally distinct but to three manifestations of one God revealed in Jesus. Indeed, according to Oneness, the doctrine of the Trinity is pagan polytheistic philosophy.

In truth, the Trinity is neither pagan polytheism nor pagan philosophy. Rather it is biblically based. Scripture plainly reveals personal self–distinctions within the Godhead. As such, the Father says of the Son, "Your throne, O God will last for ever and ever" (Hebrews 1:8); and the Son says of the Father, "I am one who testifies for myself; my other witness is the father, who sent me" (John 8:18). Moreover, the very fact that Jesus prays to the Father demonstrates that Jesus cannot be the Father. While I am frequently told by Oneness adherents that this is explained by the notion that Jesus' human nature prays to his divine nature this is clearly not the case—natures can't pray, only persons can.

Finally, Oneness Pentecostalism holds to a litany of legalistic proscriptions including the test of rebaptism by their formula with evidence of speaking in tongues. No tongues, no salvation. As one can imagine, this has placed tremendous socio–psychological pressure on adherents to conjure up the gift of tongues. Those who do not speak in tongues are thought to be lacking in faith or even to be entirely unrepentant.

In sharp distinction, the Bible relates baptism in the Spirit to empowering for service (Acts 1:5–8) rather than evidence for salvation. In the words of Jesus to his disciples, "You will receive power when the Holy Spirit comes on you; and you will be my witnesses in Jerusalem, and in all Judea and

Samaria, and to the ends of the earth" (Acts 1:8). The disciples were not still awaiting salvation; rather, they awaited a special anointing of the Holy Spirit that would serve as evidence that their evangelistic message was not of men, but of God (cf. Acts 2:14–21; 1 Corinthians 14:22).

For further study, see Gregory A. Boyd, *Oneness Pentecostals and the Trinity* (Grand Rapids: Baker Books, 1992).

MATTHEW 28:18–20

"Then Jesus came to them and said, 'All authority in heaven and on earth has been given to me. Therefore, go make disciples of all nations, baptizing them in the name of the Father and of the Son and of the Holy Spirit, and teaching them to obey everything I have commanded you. And surely I am with you always, to the very end of the age.'"

– 8 9 –

WHAT IS JUDAISM?

While Judaism finds its genesis in Abraham, Isaac, and Jacob, its modern-day expression is largely a function of the destruction of the temple in AD 70. As such, Judaism now finds expression in Torah study rather than temple sacrifice. The three main branches of Judaism are Orthodox, Reform, and Conservative.

First, Orthodox Judaism (Torah Judaism) is best known for its strict dedication to the eternal and unalterable Mosaic Law as reinterpreted by rabbis subsequent to the fall of Jerusalem. Only through devotion to the complex code of Jewish law (*Halakhah*) can one experience nearness to God. Orthodox Jews await a rebuilt temple, a Jewish Messiah who will restore the kingdom to Israel, and the physical resurrection of the dead. Ironically, it is possible to be an Orthodox Jew and yet not believe in the God of Abraham, Isaac, and Jacob.

Furthermore, unlike Orthodox Judaism, which teaches that observance of the Law leads to freedom, Reform Judaism (Liberal) begins with the freedom to decide what Law to observe. In other words, human autonomy trumps the authority of *Halakhah*. As a movement arising in the eighteenth century, Reform Judaism seeks to adapt to the modern world in order to preserve Jewish identity amidst pressures of assimilation. Thus, Reform Judaism is reformed and always reforming.

Finally, Conservative Judaism (Historical) is a late–nineteenth-century reaction to the liberal tendencies inherent in Reform Judaism. As such, Conservative Judaism forges a middle way between Orthodox and Reform Judaism. On the one hand, adherents embrace modern culture. On the other, they observe Jewish laws and customs without the fundamentalistic fervor of the Orthodox.

Regardless of the religious affiliation of those to whom we are witnessing, our duty is to demonstrate the reality of Jesus Christ through the testimony of our love, our life, and our lips. For as the apostle Paul explains, the gospel of Jesus Christ "is the power of God for the salvation of everyone who believes: first for the Jew, then for the Gentile. For in the gospel a righteousness from God is revealed, a righteousness that is by faith from first to last, just as it is written: 'The righteous will live by faith'" (Romans 1:16–17).

For further study, see Richard Robinson, "Understanding Judaism: How to Share the Gospel with Your Jewish Friends," *Christian Research Journal*, 19, 4, (1997), available through the Christian Research Institute (CRI) at www.equip.org.

LUKE 24:44

"He said to them, 'This is what I told you
while I was still with you: Everything must be fulfilled
that is written about me in the Law of Moses,
the Prophets and the Psalms.'"

IS KABBALAH CONSISTENT
WITH CHRISTIANITY?

K abbalah is a form of Jewish mysticism that
is being packaged and popularized for
Western consumption. Leading the "red
string" craze are such celebrities as Madonna and
Demi Moore. In the final analysis Kabbalah is just
one more dish in a smorgasbord of popular religions
that distort the true meaning of Scripture and
oppose the gospel of Christ.

First, Kabbalists search for mystical meanings
and messages in the Torah that allegedly have power
to remedy personal and social ills. Indeed, Kabbalists
believe that through Kabbalah the unfettered
communion with God experienced in Eden can be
regained. As such, Kabbalism has more in common
with the esotericism of Gnostic cults than with
orthodox Christianity.

Furthermore, "Ein Sof"—the dualistic and
ultimately unknowable deity of Kabbalah—bears
little resemblance to the God of the Bible. Unlike
Ein Sof, the Everlasting Sovereign is perfect in unity

and simplicity and has ultimately revealed himself through Jesus Christ (cf. John 1; Colossians 1; Hebrews 1).

Kabbalah is just one more dish in a smorgasbord of popular religions that distort the true meaning of Scripture and oppose the gospel of Christ.

Finally, Kabbalah holds to reincarnation, which can never be reconciled with the Christian hope of resurrection. The biblical teaching of *one body* per person alone demonstrates that the gulf between reincarnation and resurrection can never be bridged. Far from the *transmigration* of our soul into another body, Christianity holds that Christ will *transform* our body like unto his resurrected body (cf. 1 Corinthians 15).

For further study, see Marcia Montenegro, "Kabbalah: Getting Back to the Garden," *Christian Research Journal*, 28, 2 (2005): 12–21.

JOHN 1:18
"No one has ever seen God, but God the One and Only, who is at the Father's side, has made him known."

Is the Allah of Islam
the God of the Bible?

ong before Muhammad was born, Arabic Christians already were referring to God as Allah—and millions continue do so today. The Allah of Islam, however, is definitely not the God of the Bible. For while Muslims passionately defend the unity of God, they patently deny his triunity. Thus, they recoil at the notion of God as Father, reject the unique deity of Jesus Christ the Son, and renounce the divine identity of the Holy Spirit.

First, while the Master taught his disciples to pray "Our Father in heaven," devotees of Muhammad find the very notion offensive. To their way of thinking, calling God, "Father" and Jesus Christ, "Son" suggests sexual procreation. According to the Qur'an, "It is not befitting to [the majesty of] Allah that He should beget a son" (Sura 19:35), Allah "begetteth not, nor is he begotten"(Sura 112:3). The Bible however does not use the term "begotten" with respect to the Father and the Son in the sense of sexual reproduction but rather in the sense of special relationship. Thus, when the apostle John speaks of Jesus as "the only *begotten* of the Father" (John 1:14 NKJV, emphasis added), he is underscoring the unique deity of Christ. Likewise, when the apostle Paul refers to Jesus as "the *firstborn* over all creation" (Colossians 1:15, emphasis added) he is emphasizing Christ's preeminence or prime position as the Creator of *all* things (Colossians 1:16–19). Christians are sons of God through adoption; Jesus is God the Son from all eternity.

Furthermore, Muslims dogmatically denounce the Christian declaration of Christ's unique deity as the unforgivable sin of *shirk*. As the Qur'an puts it, "God forgiveth not the sin of joining other gods with Him; but He forgiveth whom He pleaseth other sins than this" (Sura 4:116). While Muslims readily affirm the sinlessness of Christ, they adamantly deny his sacrifice upon the cross and subsequent resurrection. In doing so, they deny the singular historic fact which demonstrates that Jesus does not stand in a long line of peers from Abraham to Muhammad, but is God in human flesh. The Qur'anic phrase "Allah raised him up" (Sura 4:158) is taken to mean that Jesus was supernaturally raptured rather than resurrected from the dead. In Islamic lore, God made someone look like Jesus, and this look-alike was crucified in his place. In recent years, the myth that Judas was crucified in place of Jesus has been popularized in Muslim circles by a late medieval invention titled *The Gospel of Barnabas*. Against the weight of history and evidence the Qur'an exudes, "they killed him not, nor crucified him, but so it was made to appear to them" (Sura 4:157).

Finally, in addition to rejecting the divinity of Jesus, Islam also renounces the divine identity of the Holy Spirit. Far from being the third person of the Triune God who inspired the text of the Bible, Islam teaches that the Holy Spirit is the archangel Gabriel who dictated the Qur'an to Muhammad over a period of twenty-three years. Ironically, while the Holy Spirit who dictated the Qur'an is said to be the archangel Gabriel, Islam identifies the Holy Spirit promised by Jesus in John 14 as Muhammad. The Bible, however, roundly rejects such corruptions and misrepresentation. Biblically the Holy Spirit is neither an angel nor a mere mortal; rather he is the very God who redeems us from our sins and will one day resurrect us to life eternal (Acts 5:3–4; Romans 8:11).

For further study, see Timothy George, *Is the Father of Jesus the God of Muhammad?* (Grand Rapids: Zondervan, 2002).

1 JOHN 2:23
"No one who denies the Son has the Father;
whoever acknowledges the Son has the Father also."

IS THE QUR'AN CREDIBLE?

According to Islam, the Qur'an is not only credible; it is God's *only* uncorrupted revelation. Thus, according to Muslim scholars, if it is to be compared with anything in Christianity it is to be compared with Christ rather than the Bible. In truth, however, the Bible can be demonstrated to be divine rather than human in origin. The same cannot be said for the Qur'an. Moreover, unlike the Bible the Qur'an is replete with faulty ethics and factual errors.

First, unlike the Qur'an, the Bible is replete with prophecies that could not have been fulfilled through chance, good guessing, or deliberate deceit. Surprisingly, the predictive nature of many Bible passages was once a popular argument among liberals against the reliability of the Bible. Critics argued that various passages were written later than the biblical texts indicated because they recounted events that happened sometimes hundreds of years after they supposedly were written. They concluded that subsequent to the events, literary editors went back and "doctored" the original nonpredictive texts. But this is simply wrong. Careful research *affirms* the predictive accuracy of the Scriptures. Since Christ is the culminating theme of the Old Testament and the Living Word of the New Testament, it should not surprise us that prophecies regarding him outnumber all others. Many of these prophesies would have been impossible for Jesus to deliberately conspire to fulfill—such as his descent from Abraham, Isaac, and Jacob (Genesis 12:3; 17:19; Matthew 1:1–2; Acts 3:25); his birth in Bethlehem (Micah 5:2; Matthew 2:1–6); his crucifixion with criminals (Isaiah 53:12; Matthew 27:38; Luke 22:37); the piercing of his hands and feet on the cross (Psalm 22:16; John 20:25); the soldiers gambling for his clothes (Psalm 22:18; Matthew 27:35); the piercing of his side (Zechariah 12:10; John 19:34); the fact that his bones were not broken at his death (Psalm 34:20; John 19:33–37); and his burial among the rich (Isaiah 53:9; Matthew 27:57–60).

In sharp contrast, predictive prophecies demonstrating the divine origin of the Qur'an are conspicuous by their absence. While the Qur'an contains a number of self-fulfilling prophecies such as Muhammad's prediction that he would return to Mecca (Sura 48:27), this is very different from the kinds of prophecies outlined above. Other prophecies such as Muhammad's prediction that the Romans would defeat the Persians at Issus (Sura 30:2–4) are equally underwhelming. Unlike the biblical examples presented above, this prophecy is not fulfilled in the far future and thus can be easily explained through good guessing or an accurate apprehension of prevailing military conditions.

Furthermore, the Qur'an is replete with questionable ethics—particularly when it comes to the equality of women. For example, in Sura 4:3 Muhammad allegedly received a revelation from God allowing men to "marry women of your choice, two, three, or four." Ironically, in Sura 33:50 Muhammad receives a divine sanction to marry "any believing woman who dedicates her soul to the Prophet if the Prophet wishes to wed her." Thus while other men were only permitted to marry up to four wives, Allah provided Muhammad with a divine exception for his marriage to at least twelve women—including Aishah, whom he married at the tender age of eleven (see the *Life of Muhammad* by Muhammad Husayn Haykal). Also troubling is the fact that the Qur'an allows men to "beat" (lightly) their wives in order that they might "return to obedience" (Sura 4:34). When we compare the personal morality of Muhammad in the Qur'an with that of Jesus in the Bible, the difference is remarkable. The Qur'an exorts Muhammad to ask "forgiveness for thy fault" (Sura 40:55). Conversely, Christ's ethics with regard to every aspect of life—including his treatment of women—was so unimpeachable that he could rightly ask: "Can any of you prove me guilty of sin?" (John 8:46; 2 Corinthians 5:21; 1 John 3:5)

Finally, unlike the Bible the Qur'an is riddled with factual errors. A classic case in point involves the Qur'an's denial of Christ's crucifixion. This denial chronicled in Sura 4:157 is explicit and emphatic: "They killed him not, nor crucified him, but so it was made to appear to them … for of a surety they killed him not." In reality, however, the fatal suffering of Jesus Christ as recounted in the New Testament is one of the most well-established facts of ancient history. Even in today's modern age of scientific enlightenment, there is a virtual consensus among New Testament scholars, both conservative and liberal, that Jesus died on a Roman cross.

Recent archaeological discoveries not only dramatically corroborate the Bible's description of Roman crucifixion but authenticate the biblical details surrounding the trail that led to the fatal torment of Jesus Christ—including the Pilate Stone and the burial grounds of Caiaphas, the high priest who presided over the religious trials of Christ. These discoveries have been widely acclaimed as a compelling affirmation of biblical history. Not only so but the earliest Jewish response to the death and burial of Jesus Christ presuppose the reality of the empty tomb. Instead of denying that the tomb was empty, the antagonists of Christ accused his disciples of stealing the body.

One final point should be made. The Qur'anic denial of Christ's crucifixion has led to a host of other errors as well. From a Muslim perspective, Jesus was never crucified and, thus, never resurrected. Instead, in Islam, God made someone look like Jesus and the look-alike was mistakenly crucified in his place. The notion that Judas was made to look like Jesus has recently been popularized in Muslim circles by a late medieval invention titled *The Gospel of Barnabas.*

In short, the distance between the Muslim Qur'an and the Christian Scriptures is the distance of infinity. Not only does the prophetic prowess of the Bible elevate it far above the holy books of other religions, but as new archeological nuggets are uncovered the trustworthiness of Scripture as well as the unreliability of pretenders are further highlighted. Faulty ethics and factual errors demonstrate that the Qur'an is devoid of divine sanction. In sharp distinction, ethics and factual evidence demonstrate that the Bible is divine rather than human in origin.

For further study, see Norman L. Geisler and Abdul Saleeb, *Answering Islam* (Grand Rapids: Baker Books, 2002).

HEBREWS 1:1–3

"In the past God spoke to our forefathers through the prophets at many times and in various ways, but in these last days he has spoken to us by his Son, whom he appointed heir of all things, and through whom he made the universe. The Son is the radiance of God's glory and the exact representation of his being, sustaining all things by his powerful word. After he had provided purification for sins, he sat down at the right hand of the Majesty in heaven."

WHAT'S WRONG WITH BAHA'I?

n the way that John the Baptist prepared the way for Jesus, so a Persian prophet known as the Báb (the Gate) (1819–1850) prepared the way for Bahá'u'lláh (glory of God) the founder of Baha'i. While Bahá'u'lláh (1817–1892) believed his messianic mandate was the unification of the world's religions, his message was fatally flawed.

First, Baha'is believe that Bahá'u'lláh is a greater manifestation of God than Moses, Muhammad, or the Christian Messiah. Thus the Baha'i thrust toward the unification of all religions is primed for failure. Islam, the mother religion of Baha'i would not and could not consider Bahá'u'lláh as a prophet of God greater than Muhammad. Likewise, Christianity is committed to Christ as "*the way* and *the truth* and *the life*" (John 14:6, emphasis added; cf. Acts 4:12).

Furthermore, Baha'i teaches that every few hundred years the spirit and attributes of divinity are mirrored in a new messenger and manifestation of God. Each revelator reveals as much revelation as the faithful are ready to receive. As such, Moses,

Buddha, Zoroaster, Confucius, Christ, Muhammad, and Krishna all paved the way toward the ultimate revelations personified in the Báb and Bahá'u'lláh. The fallacy, of course, is that the revelators and their revelations directly conflict with one another. For example, Moses was fiercely monotheistic whereas Zoroaster and Krishna were polytheistic. Likewise, the Qur'an condemns Christ's claim to be the Son of God as the unforgivable sin of *shirk*. Logically, the messengers and manifestations can all be wrong but they can't all be right.

Finally, Baha'i explicitly denies objective truth claims of Christianity such as the Trinity, virgin birth, incarnation, resurrection, and second coming of Christ. Moreover, while the Báb said that Bahá'u'lláh was the quintessential messenger and manifestation of God—the "Best-beloved" and "the Desire of the World"—the Bible states that Christ is "the exact representation of God" (Hebrews 1:3) in whom "all the fullness of the Deity lives in bodily form" (Colossians 2:9).

For further study, see Francis J. Beckwith, "Baha'i–Christian Dialogue: Some Key Issues Considered," *Christian Research Journal* (1989) 11, 3, available through the Christian Research Institute (CRI) at www.equip.org.

*"In the past God spoke to our forefathers through
the prophets at many times and in various ways,
but in these last days he has spoken to us by his Son,
whom he appointed heir of all things,
and through whom he made the universe."*

WHAT ARE THE BASIC BELIEFS OF BUDDHISM?

he year was 1893. The place was Chicago. Buddhists had arrived from the East to attend the inaugural World's Parliament of Religions. While their contingent was sizable, they were vastly outnumbered by Bible believers from the West. One hundred years later, at the centennial celebration of the original Parliament, Buddhists outnumbered Baptists and saffron robes were more common than Christian clerical clothing. Given its growing impact, it is important to grasp basic Buddhist beliefs and use them as springboards for sharing the liberating truth of the gospel.

First, Buddhism, a historical offshoot of Hinduism, teaches adherents to seek refuge in the Three Jewels: *Buddha*, *Dharma*, and *Sangha*. Embracing the triple gem is to find refuge in Buddha who became the "enlightened one" for this age during a deep state of meditation under a bodhi tree; to find refuge in the Buddha's teaching—*dharma*; and to find refuge in the community of Buddhist priests—*sangha*—who guide devotees along the path to enlightenment.

Furthermore, the essence of Buddhism is summed up in the Four Noble Truths: 1) all life is suffering (*dukkha*); 2) the source of suffering is desire and attachment because all is impermanent; 3) liberation from suffering is found in the elimination of desire; 4) desire is eliminated by following the eightfold path.

In sharp contrast to the Buddhist teaching that we must eliminate desire, the Bible teaches that we must exercise disciplines in order to transform our desires.

Finally, the eightfold path consists of right understanding, right thought, right speech, right action, right livelihood, right effort, right awareness, and right meditation. By following this path through many reincarnations, Buddhists hope to erase karmic debt and achieve the *nirvanic* realization of "no self," thus attaining liberation from suffering and escaping the endless cycle of life, death, and rebirth (*samsara*).

In sharp contrast to the Buddhist teaching that we must eliminate desire, the Bible teaches that we must exercise disciplines in order to transform our desires (Romans 6:17–19). Ultimately, suffering is not overcome through stamping out the self, but through the selfless sacrifice of a sinless Savior.

For further study, see J. Isamu Yamamoto's four-part *Christian Research Journal* series on Buddhism in North America, available through the Christian Research Institute (CRI) at www.equip.org.

ROMANS 5:1–5

"Therefore, since we have been justified through faith, we have peace with God through our Lord Jesus Christ, through whom we have gained access by faith into this grace in which we now stand. And we rejoice in the hope of the glory of God. Not only so, but we also rejoice in our sufferings, because we know that suffering produces perseverance; perseverance, character; and character, hope. And hope does not disappoint us, because God has poured out his love into our hearts by the Holy Spirit, whom he has given us."

WHAT IS ZEN BUDDHISM?

Though Zen Buddhism did not catch on in the West until the 1950s, it has now virtually cornered the meditation market. Phil Jackson even used Zen to prepare his teams to win nine NBA championships. Because of its growing popularity I've developed the acronym Z–E–N to help us understand it.

First, the dominant discipline of Zen Buddhism is *zazen*. Through *zazen* (literally, "sitting in meditation") Zenists seek to stamp out the self and become one with the impersonal cosmic consciousness of the universe (the only mind). Postures, breathing techniques, and chants are variously utilized in an attempt to free the mind from meaningful thought and achieve a state of absolute emptiness.

Furthermore, the stated objective of Zen is *enlightenment*—the inner perception that all of reality is one and duality is an unenlightened illusion (*satori*). Enlightenment is said to be the key to extinguishing individual identity and the doorway to *nirvana* ("blown out"). As the golf mantra goes: "Be the ball."

Finally, enlightenment is achieved through *nonsensical riddles*. Nonsensical riddles or *koans* are used to attack reason and logic in order to achieve the alternate reality that the universe is an interdependent whole and that each individual is that whole. Zen literally utilizes hundreds of nonsensical riddles to dismantle the mind—the most famous of which is, *"What is the sound of one hand clapping?"*

Zenists seek to stamp out the self and become one with the impersonal cosmic consciousness of the universe . . . by freeing the mind from meaningful thought and achieving a state of absolute emptiness.

In sharp distinction to Zen, biblical meditation seeks to center one's self on the personal Creator of the universe. And it does so through a singular focus on Scripture. Far from emptying our minds, Christians are called to be filled with the Holy Spirit and to be transformed by the renewing of our minds (Ephesians 5:18; Romans 12:1–2).

The basics of Zen Buddhism are:

Zazen—"sitting in meditation" to achieve emptiness

Enlightenment—inner perception that all reality is one

Nonsensical riddles—for rejecting reason and
dismantling the mind

For further study, see J. Isamu Yamamoto, "Zest for Zen: North Americans Embrace a Contemplative School of Buddhism" *Christian Research Journal* 17, 3 (1995): 8–15, available through the Christian Research Institute (CRI) at www.equip.org.

ROMANS 12:2

"Do not conform any longer to the pattern of this world, but be transformed by the renewing of your mind. Then you will be able to test and approve what God's will is—his good, pleasing and perfect will."

WHAT SETS CHRISTIANITY APART
FROM AN EASTERN WORLDVIEW?

W hile it has become increasingly popular to merge Eastern spirituality with biblical Christianity, the chasm that separates these worldviews is an unbridgeable gulf.

First, in an Eastern worldview God is an impersonal force or principle. In sharp distinction, the God of Christianity is a personal being who manifests such communicable attributes as spirituality, rationality, and morality (John 4:24; Colossians 3:10; Ephesians 4:24).

Furthermore, in an Eastern worldview humanity's goal is to become one with nature because nature is God. In this sense, the Eastern worldview is pantheistic—in other words, "God is all and all is God." Conversely, Christianity teaches that man is created in the image and likeness of his Creator and as such is distinct from both nature and God (Genesis 1:26–27).

Finally, in an Eastern worldview truth is realized through intuition rather than through the cognitive thinking process. In contrast, Christianity teaches that truth is realized through revelation (Hebrews 1:1–2), which is apprehended by the intellect (Luke 1:1–4), and then embraced by the heart (Mark 12:29–31).

For further study, see James W. Sire, *The Universe Next Door: A Basic Worldview Catalog*, third ed. (Downers Grove, Ill.: InterVarsity Press, 1997); Charles Strohmer, *The Gospel and the New Spirituality* (Nashville: Thomas Nelson, 1996).

ROMANS 1:25

"They exchanged the truth of God for a lie,
and worshiped and
served created things rather than the Creator."

WHAT DO HINDUS BELIEVE?

hile Hinduism is multifaceted rather than monolithic, its basic tenets with respect to God, humanity, and salvation can be summed up as follows.

First, Hindus suppose that ultimate reality (*Brahman*) is an impersonal oneness that transcends all distinctions including personal and propositional differentiations. Put another way, all of reality is a continuum or simplified whole. As such, there is no distinction between morals and mice.

Furthermore, Hindus hold that humans, in concert with the rest of the universe, are a continuous extension of *Brahman*. Thus, our illusory individuated selves (*atman*) are one with the impersonal cosmic consciousness of the universe—"*atman* is *Brahman* and *Brahman* is *atman*."

Finally, the Hindu scriptures (*Vedas* and *Upanishads*) teach the goal of humanity as liberation from an endless cycle of death and reincarnation (*samsara*). Liberation (*moksha*) from *samsara* is attained when we realize that our individual selves are an illusion and all is one. Until such enlightenment is achieved, the law of *karma* dictates that our deeds in previous lives determine whether we are reborn as man, monkey, or mosquito; woman, walrus, or wasp.

The solution to the fear of karmic reincarnation is faith in our Kinsman Redeemer.

While the Hindu scriptures tout the hell of reincarnation, the Holy Scriptures teach the hope of resurrection. The solution to the fear of karmic reincarnation is faith in our Kinsman Redeemer.

For further study, see Dean Halverson, *The Illustrated Guide to World Religions* (Minneapolis: Bethany House Publishers, 2003).

ISAIAH 44:24–25
*"This is what the LORD says—your Redeemer,
who formed you in the womb: I am the LORD,
who has made all things, who alone stretched out the
heavens, who spread out the earth by myself,
who foils the signs of false prophets and makes fools of
diviners, who overthrows the learning of the
wise and turns it into nonsense."*

WHAT IS YOGA?

Since Swami Vivekananda first introduced yoga to the West more than a hundred years ago, yoga has become as American as apple pie. According to the *Columbia Journalism Review,*

> Everybody loves yoga; sixteen and a half million Americans practice it regularly, and twenty-five million more say they will try it this year. If you've been awake and breathing air in the twenty-first century, you already know that this Hindu practice of health and spirituality has long ago moved on from the toe-ring set. Yoga is American; it has graced the cover of *Time* twice, acquired the approval of A-list celebrities like Madonna, Sting, and Jennifer Aniston, and is still the go-to trend story for editors and reporters, who produce an average of eight yoga stories a day in the English-speaking world. . . . Consumers drop $3 billion every year on

yoga classes, books, videos, CDs, DVDs, mats, clothing, and other necessities.

As noted by New Age expert Elliot Miller, "Yoga is rapidly becoming integrated into such traditionally secular institutions as public education, health care, and the workplace. It has been widely embraced by Roman Catholics and mainline Protestants, and over the past several years a Christian yoga movement has been thriving among evangelicals." Because of its rock-star status, I've developed the acronym Y-O-G-A to give you a memorable overview on what this practice entails.

"Y" reminds us that the word "yoga" comes from the Sanskrit word "*yogah*," which means "to yoke or to unite." Indeed, the goal of yoga is to uncouple oneself from the material world and to unite oneself with the God of Hinduism, commonly understood to be *Brahman*, the impersonal cosmic consciousness of the universe. Put another way, yoga is the means by which the user's mind is merged into the universal mind.

"O" represents the Hindu mantra "*Om*"—a sacred Sanskrit syllable cherished by Hindu yogis as the spoken quintessence of the universe. Repeating such mantras as "*Om*" over and over is a principal means by which yoga practitioners work their way into altered states of consciousness. The objective of achieving an altered state of consciousness is always the same: to dull the critical-thinking process because the mind is seen to be the obstacle to enlightenment. As noted by the late Indian guru Bhagwan Shree Rajneesh, "the goal is to create a new man, one who is happily mindless." Shockingly, what was once relegated to the kingdom of the cults is now being replicated in churches. In the ashrams of the cults there is no pretense. Despite such dangers as possession or insanity, Hindu gurus openly encourage trance states through which devotees tap into realms of the demonic and discover their "higher selves." Whether experiencing involuntary movements or encountering illusory monsters, all is written off as progress on the road to enlightenment.

"G" is reminiscent of the gurus who developed and disseminated yoga for the express purpose of achieving oneness with the impersonal God of Hinduism. Most noteworthy among the gurus is Patanjali—the Hindu sage who founded yoga around the second-century BC Of particular significance in the West is the aforementioned guru Swami Vivekananda, a disciple of the self-proclaimed "god-man" Sri Ramakrishna. In 1893

Vivekananda used the Parliament of World Religions to skillfully sow the seeds for a new global spirituality. Second only to Vivekananda in the Westernization of yoga was Yogananda—proudly hailed as "Father of Yoga in the West." In 1920 he founded the L.A.-based Self-Realization Fellowship, a principal means of disseminating yoga to multiplied millions of Americans. Finally, of special note is Swami Muktananda, popularizer of *kundalini yoga*, a method by which divine energy thought to reside as a coiled serpent at the base of the spine is aroused; ascends through six *chakras*; and aims for union with the Hindu deity Shiva in a seventh center allegedly located in the crown of the head. Such Hindu gurus have been so successful in exporting yoga to the West that today it is common fare in classrooms, corporations, and even churches.

Finally, the "A" in Y-O-G-A will serve to remind you of the Hindu word *asana*. As repetition of the word "*Om*" is used to work devotees into altered states of consciousness, so too a regiment of *asanas*—or body postures—are used to achieve a feeling of oneness with the cosmic energy flow of the universe. Coupled with breathing exercises and meditation practices, *asana* positions are the pathway to serenity and spirituality. According to *Yoga Journal*, "asanas are their own type of meditation; to perform difficult postures you have to focus on your body and breath and relax into the pose." While multitudes are being seduced into believing that *asanas* are spiritually neutral, nothing could be farther from the truth. Indeed, as pointed out by Swami Param of the Dharma Yoga Ashram in New Jersey, to think of *asanas* as mere body positions or stretching exercises is analogous to believing "baptism is just an underwater exercise."

In sum, while an alarming number of Western Christians suppose they can achieve physical and spiritual well-being through a form of yoga divorced from its Eastern worldview, in reality attempts to Christianize Hinduism only Hinduize Christianity.

For further study, see Elliot Miller's three-part article series, entitled, "The Yoga Boom: A Call for Christian Discernment," which was published in *Christian Research Journal*, Volume 21 / Numbers 2, 3, and 4; available through Christian Research Institute at www.equip.org.

"Do not be yoked together with unbelievers.
For what do righteousness and wickedness have in
common? Or what fellowship can light have
with darkness? What harmony is there between Christ
and Belial? What does a believer have in common with
an unbeliever? What agreement is there between
the temple of God and idols?"

Yogah

Om

Gurus

Asana

DOES THE BIBLE *REALLY* TEACH
REINCARNATION?

eincarnation, literally, "rebirth in another body," has long been considered to be a universal law of life in the Eastern world. Tragically, today in the West, it is now also believed to be backed by the Bible. The words of Jeremiah, John, and Jesus are typically cited as irrefutable evidence. A quick look at the context of these Scripture passages, however, reveals that they have nothing whatsoever to do with reincarnation.

First, in Jeremiah, God allegedly tells his prophet that he knew him as the result of a prior incarnation—"Before I formed you in the womb, I knew you, before you were born, I set you apart; I appointed you as a prophet to the nations" (Jeremiah 1:5). In reality, far from suggesting that his prophet had existed in a prior incarnation, Jeremiah underscores the reality that the One who exists from all eternity pre-ordained Jeremiah as "a prophet to the nations."

Furthermore, in John's gospel, the disciples allegedly wonder whether a man born blind is paying off karmic debt for himself or for his parents (cf. John 9:1-2). The gospel of John dispels this notion by overtly stating that the man's blindness had nothing to do with either his sin or that of his parents (John 9:3). If indeed the man was suffering for past indiscretions, Jesus would have violated the law of karma by healing him.

Finally, Jesus himself is cited as suggesting that Elijah was reincarnated as John the Baptist (cf. Matthew 11:14). This tired tale is explicitly dismissed by Scripture itself. When the priests and the Levites asked John if he was Elijah, he replied, "I am not" (John 1:21). In context, Elijah and John are not said to be two incarnations of the same *person*, but rather two separate people who function in a strikingly similar *prophetic* role. Or as Luke puts it, John came "in the spirit and power of Elijah" (1:17).

One thing is certain! Reincarnation is completely foreign to the teachings of Scripture.

For further study, see "Can reincarnation and resurrection be reconciled?" p. 303.

*"Do not be amazed at this, for a time is
coming when all who are in their graves will hear
his voice and come out—those who have done
good will rise to live, and those who have done evil
will rise to be condemned."*

Can reincarnation
and resurrection be reconciled?

n ever-growing number of people in both the church and the culture have come to believe that reincarnation and resurrection can be reconciled. In fact, multitudes have embraced the odd predilection that Scripture actually promotes reincarnation. In reality, however, the Bible makes it crystal clear that reincarnation and resurrection are mutually exclusive.

To begin with, the resurrectionist view of *one death* per person is mutually exclusive from the reincarnationist view of an ongoing cycle of death and rebirth. The writer of Hebrews emphatically states that human beings are "destined to die *once*, and after that to face judgment" (Hebrews 9:27, emphasis added). In sharp contrast to a worldview in which humanity perfects itself through an endless cycle of birth and rebirth, the Christian worldview maintains that we are vicariously perfected by the righteousness of Christ (Philippians 3:9).

Furthermore, the biblical teaching of *one body* per person demonstrates that the gulf between reincarnation and resurrection can never be bridged. Rather than the *transmigration* of our souls into different bodies, the apostle Paul explains that Christ "will *transform* our lowly bodies" (Philippians 3:21, emphasis added). He explicitly says that the body that dies is the very body that rises (1 Corinthians 15:42–44).

Finally, the Christian belief that there is only *one way* to God categorically demonstrates that resurrection and reincarnation can never be reconciled. As Christ himself put it, "I am *the* way and *the* truth and *the* life. No one comes to the Father except through me" (John 14:6, emphasis added). If Christ is truly God, his claim to be the only way has to be taken seriously. If, on the other hand, he is merely one more person in a pantheon of pretenders, his proclamations can be pushed aside easily. That is precisely why the resurrection is axiomatic to Christianity. Through his resurrection Christ demonstrated that he does not stand in a line of peers with Buddha, Baha'u'llah, Krishna, or any other founder of a world religion. They died and are *still* dead, but Christ is risen.

Ultimately, resurrection and reincarnation can never be reconciled because the former is a historical fact while the latter is but a Hindu fantasy.

ADAPTED FROM *Resurrection*

For further study, see Hank Hanegraaff, *Resurrection* (Nashville: Word Publishing, 2000), Chapter 14.

HEBREWS 9:27–29

"Just as man is destined to die once, and after that to face judgment, so Christ was sacrificed once to take away the sins of many people; and he will appear a second time, not to bear sin, but to bring salvation to those who are waiting for him."

101

What is the New Age movement?

 ot everyone who wears a cross is a Christian. Likewise, not everyone who owns a crystal is a New Ager. To accurately identify New Agers we must move beyond superficial symbols such as crystals, unicorns, and rainbows to identify their beliefs and practices.

First, New Agers hold to pantheistic monism. Thus, in their view, God is all, all is God, and all is one. Additionally, they believe that the universe operates under the law of karma and its corollary, the doctrine of reincarnation.

Furthermore, the goal of New Agers is to spiritually evolve and tap into their human potential through the help of "ascended masters" or spirit guides. To attain such enlightenment New Agers engage in occult practices such as astrology, magic, psychic healing, out-of-body experiences, and meditation. In New Age meditation, for example, the goal is to stamp out the self—and to become one with the impersonal cosmic consciousness of the universe. In sharp contrast, biblical meditation seeks to center one's self on the personal Creator of the universe—and does so through a singular focus on Scripture (Joshua 1:8).

Finally, New Agers share the vision of a coming "age of Aquarius" that is marked by global peace, prosperity, and planetary transformation. Their ultimate goal is encapsulated in such catchphrases as "global village" and "planetary consciousness." Far from being a monolith, however, the New Age movement is a multifaceted amorphous network of organizations such as *Planetary Initiative for the World*, *Divine Light Mission*, and *Self-Realization Fellowship*, loosely linked yet autonomous.

For further study, see Douglas R. Groothuis, *Unmasking the New Age* (Downers Grove, Ill.: InterVarsity Press, 1986); for a comprehensive work, see Elliot Miller, *A Crash Course on The New Age Movement* (Grand Rapids: Baker Book House, 1989).

DEUTERONOMY 18:9–13

"When you enter the land the LORD your God is giving you, do not learn to imitate the detestable ways of the nations there. Let no one be found among you who sacrifices his son or daughter in the fire, who practices divination or sorcery, interprets omens, engages in witchcraft, or casts spells, or who is a medium or spiritist or who consults the dead. Anyone who does these things is detestable to the LORD."

102

What is wrong with astrology?

As Charles Strohmer has well said, "Astrology has been debunked more than the tooth fairy and cheered more than the Pope." Despite the fact that it is denounced by Scripture, debunked by science, and demonstrably superstitious, humankind's fascination with astrology continues unabated. While multitudes view astrology as a harmless pastime, in reality it is a rigged "game" replete with self-validating prophecies and a dangerous form of divination.

First, Scripture clearly condemns astrology as a practice that is "detestable to the Lord" (Deuteronomy 18:10–12). Isaiah goes so far as to say that the counsel of the "astrologers" and "stargazers who make predictions month by month" not only wore out the Babylonians but could not save them from their future ruin (Isaiah 47:13–14). Despite the clear condemnation of Scripture, there are those who maintain that there is a biblical precedent for using stars to chart the future. As a case in point, they cite the star guiding the Magi to the Messiah. However, a quick look at context reveals that this star was not used to *foretell* the future but to *forth tell* the future. In other words, the star of Bethlehem did not *prophesy* the birth of Christ; it *pronounced* the birth of Christ (Matthew 2:9–10).

Furthermore, science has debunked astrology as a pseudoscience based on the odd predilection that *galaxies* rather than *genes* determine inherited human characteristics. Not only so, astrology cannot account for the problem posed by mass tragedies and twins. People with a wide variety of horoscopes all perished on 9/11/2001. And twins born under the same sign of the zodiac frequently end up with widely diverse futures. Even King Nebuchadnezzar's astrologers recognized the impotence of their craft. When Nebuchadnezzar asked them to remind him of his dream and then interpret it, they responded in terror, saying, "No man on earth can do what the king asks!" (Daniel 2:10)

Finally, astrology subverts the natural use of the stars, which God ordains, for a superstitious use, which he disdains. Genesis 1:14 points to the natural use of the stars to separate the day from the night, to serve as signs that mark seasons, days, and years, and to illuminate the earth. They also can rightly be used for varied purposes ranging from navigation to natural revelation. Thus, sailors may use astronavigation to chart their course; however, saints may not use astrology to chart their careers.

For further study, see Charles R. Strohmer, *America's Fascination with Astrology: Is it Healthy?* (Greenville, South Carolina: Emerald House, 1998).

ISAIAH 47:13–15

"Let your astrologers come forward, those stargazers
who make predictions month by month,
let them save you from what is coming upon you.
Surely, they are like stubble; the fire will burn them up.
They cannot even save themselves from the power
of the flame. . . . Each of them goes on in his error;
there is not one that can save you."

WHAT IS SCIENTOLOGY?

he Church of Scientology was founded in the 1950s by science-fiction author Lafayette Ronald (L. Ron) Hubbard. Although the church claims to be compatible with Christianity, the two belief structures—one rooted in science fiction, the other in soteriological fact—are contradictory and cannot be harmonized.

First, Scientology teaches that humans are immortal *thetans* trapped in a physical universe of their own mental construction. Thus, humans are not sinners in need of a savior, but immortal beings who can overcome enslaving *engrams*—the accumulation of trillions of years of painful subconscious memories—through the pseudo–psychology of *auditing*—the counseling process through which devotees can locate and resolve past traumatic experiences and experience spiritual enlightenment. As such, Scientology is a rejection of the biblical doctrines of creation, original sin, and exclusive salvation through Jesus Christ (cf. Genesis 1–3; John 14:6; Romans 3:23; 6:23).

Furthermore, Scientology holds that, apart from auditing, a continuous cycle of *reincarnation* (or "rebirth") awaits each one of us. In order to escape this vicious cycle we must become self–actualized through the pseudo–psychology of Scientology. No religion that teaches self–actualization by escape from the body can be reconciled with the Christian belief of perfection, purification, and preservation through resurrection (1 Corinthians 15).

Scientology's philosophy leaves a trail of tears:

Thetans—immortal state of humans

Engrams—accumulation of painful subconscious memories

Auditing—counseling process for identifying and overcoming engrams and achieving enlightenment

Reincarnation—cycle of rebirth to be repeated until self-actualization

Supreme Being—a god remarkably like the Brahman of Hinduism

Finally, despite allowing its adherents to believe in a god of their own choosing, Scientology champions a *Supreme Being* that bears a remarkable resemblance to the Brahman of Hinduism. While L. Ron Hubbard's Supreme Being is science fiction and ultimately cannot heal our pain, the Supreme Being of the Bible can both stem Scientology's trail of tears—*Thetans, Engrams, Auditing, Reincarnation, Supreme Being*—and meet our deepest needs.

While L. Ron Hubbard's Supreme Being is science fiction and ultimately cannot heal our pain, the Supreme Being of the Bible can meet our deepest needs.

For further study, see John Weldon, "Scientology: From Science Fiction to Space-Age Religion," *Christian Research Journal*, 16, 1 (1993) available through the Christian Research Institute (CRI) at www.equip.org.

ACTS 20:30–31

*"Even from your own number men will arise
and distort the truth to draw away disciples after them.
So be on your guard! Remember that
for three years I never stopped warning each
of you night and day with tears."*

IS SEVENTH DAY ADVENTISM ORTHODOX?

ver the years I have encountered many Seventh Day Adventists who have told me that to worship on Sunday is to take the mark of the Beast. Far from being monolithic, however, Seventh Day Adventism is multifaceted.

First, there are Adventists who are thoroughly orthodox. As such, they embrace the essentials of the historic Christian faith. While we may vigorously debate secondary issues, we are unified around the essentials for which the martyrs shed their blood.

Furthermore, there are Adventists who are thoroughly liberal. They not only compromise and confuse but consistently contradict essentials of the faith such as the virgin birth, the bodily resurrection, and the infallibility of Scripture.

Finally, there are traditionalists who major on aberrant Adventist doctrines including soul sleep, Sabbatarianism, and the seer status of Ellen G. White. In sharp distinction to soul sleep the Bible provides ample evidence that the soul continues to exist apart from the body (Philippians 1:23–24).

Likewise, God himself provided early Christians with a new pattern of worship through Christ's resurrection on the first day of the week as well as the Spirit's descent on Pentecost Sunday. Additionally, while Ellen White (1827–1915) claimed divine authority for her prophecies, she was obviously wrong when she prophesied that she would be alive at the second coming of Christ.

For further study, see Hank Hanegraaff, "Why do Christians worship on Sunday rather than on the Sabbath day?" and "Is there evidence for life after death?" *The Bible Answer Book* Volume 1 (Nashville: J Countryman, 2004), 70–72, 165–169.

HEBREWS 4:9–10

"There remains then, a Sabbath–rest for the people of God; for anyone who enters God's rest also rests from his own work, just as God did from his."

WHAT IS THE OCCULT?

While the word "occult" (from the Latin *occultus*) literally means "hidden" or "secret," the world of the occult is clearly out of the closet. It has been glamorized as New Age, but its genesis is as old age as the hiss of the serpent: "Your eyes will be opened, and you will be like God, knowing good and evil" (Genesis 3:5). The objective of occultism is self–deification through sorcery, spiritism, and soothsaying.

First, through sorcery (magick), occultists seek to harness paranormal powers for private purposes. Using ritualistic formulas, spells, and incantations, occultists seek to harness what they perceive to be the natural and spiritual powers of the universe in order to satisfy their own desires. God warned the ancient Israelites that these very practices would inevitably lead to their downfall (Deuteronomy 18:9–14; cf. 2 Kings 17:16–18). Likewise, he rebuked the ancient Babylonians for supposing that they could bypass his power through their "many sorceries" and "potent spells" (Isaiah 47:8–15).

Furthermore, occultists employ spiritualistic practices (mediumship) in order to contact non–physical entities including the souls of the dead. These spirits are believed to be capable of providing cosmic insights into this world and the next. As such, spiritists employ Ouija boards, crystal balls, and the belongings of the dead to conjure up the departed. God's warning against those who practice spiritism could not be more ominous or direct: "I will set my face against the person who turns to mediums and spiritists to prostitute himself by following them, and I will cut him off from his people" (Leviticus 20:6; cf. 19:31; 1 Chronicles 10:13–14; Isaiah 8:19).

The objective of occultism is self–deification through sorcery, spiritism, and soothsaying.

Finally, occultists seek to access secret or hidden information about the future through soothsaying (divination). Among the most common tools of the soothsayer are Tarot cards, astrological charts, horoscopes, and tea leaves. The Lord's command is emphatic and explicit: "Do not practice divination" (Leviticus 19:26). Indeed, a tremendous insult to the power and providence of the Almighty is to seek guidance through the occult. Thus, when the Israelites were about to enter the land of Promise, the Lord warned them not to imitate the detestable ways of the nations there: "Let no one be found among you who sacrifices his son or daughter in the fire, who practices divination or sorcery, interprets omens, engages in witchcraft, or casts spells, or who is a medium or spiritist or who consults the dead. Anyone who does these things is detestable to the LORD" (Deuteronomy 18:10–12; cf. Acts 13:6–11; 16:16–18; Galatians 5:19–21).

For further study, see Elliot Miller, *A Crash Course on the New Age Movement* (Grand Rapids: Baker, 1989, out of print but available used online through many outlets).

ACTS 19:18–20

"Many of those who believed now came and openly confessed their evil deeds. A number who had practiced sorcery brought their scrolls together and burned them publicly. When they calculated the value of the scrolls, the total came to fifty thousand drachmas. In this way the word of the Lord spread widely and grew in power."

WHAT'S WRONG WITH WICCA?

Wicca is a neo–pagan, earth–centered religion that has its modern origins in the teaching and practice of the original English Wiccan, Gerald Gardner (1884–1964). Today, Wicca is experiencing dramatic growth as teens reject what they perceive as Christian paternalism, homophobia, and insensitivity to the environment. While stereotypes of Wiccans as Satanists or sinister spell–casters are spurious, the worldviews of Christianity and Wicca are nonetheless worlds apart.

First, Wicca, also known as "The Craft" or "The Old Religion," holds that all reality is divine. Thus, Wiccans revere the natural world as a living, breathing organism, and they revere people as "gods" and "goddesses." As Wicca is a distinctively feminist form of neo–paganism, however, Wiccans often consider the supreme manifestation of deity to be a nature goddess (such as the Triple Goddess of the Moon). In sharp contrast to the Christian worldview, Wiccans worship creation rather than the Creator (cf. Romans 1:25). While the Bible does teach that people should care for the environment (Genesis 2:15; Deuteronomy 20:19–20; Psalm 115:16) and appreciate its magnificence (Psalm 19; Matthew 6:28–30), our worship belongs only to the Creator whose glory is reflected in creation (Job 38–41; Psalm 148; Romans 1).

Furthermore, the supreme ethical rule of Wicca is the Wiccan Rede: "If it harms none, do as ye Will." Despite this proscription against harming others, Wiccans hold that moral and religious truths are ultimately relative. Thus, while the Wiccan Rede sets the Craft apart from the malevolent activities of Satanists, the Wiccan worldview stands in direct opposition to the biblical notions of absolute moral truth and exclusive salvation through Jesus Christ who alone is "the way and the truth and the life" (John 14:6).

Finally, Wiccans practice magick (spelled with a *k* to differentiate it from conjuring for entertainment) in an attempt to manipulate the natural world and alter mental and material conditions. As such, Wicca is an esoteric occult practice designed to manipulate reality in concert with the Wiccan's will. Tools of the Craft include swords and spell books, as well as chalices, censers, cords, and crystals. Regardless of whether the motivation is benevolent or malevolent, Scripture unequivocally condemns all occult practices as detestable to the Lord (Deuteronomy 18:10–12; Acts 13:6–11; 16:16–18; Galatians 5:19–21).

For further study, see Richard G. Howe, "Modern Witchcraft: It may not be what you think," *Christian Research Journal* 28, 1 (2005): 12–21, available through the Christian Research Institute (CRI) at www.equip.org.

DEUTERONOMY 18:10–11

"Let no one be found among you who sacrifices his son or daughter in the fire, who practices divination or sorcery, interprets omens, engages in witchcraft, or casts spells, or who is a medium or spiritist or who consults the dead."

DISCERNMENT AND

ABERRANT TEACHINGS

SHOULD CHRISTIANS JUDGE
THE TEACHINGS OF THEIR LEADERS?

Not only is judging permissible, it is our responsibility. Nobody's teachings are above sound judgment—especially those of influential leaders! Biblically, authority and accountability go hand in hand (cf. Luke 12:48). The greater the responsibility one holds, the greater the accountability (cf. James 3:1).

First, the precedent for making right judgments comes from Scripture itself. In the Old Testament the Israelites were commanded to practice sound judgment by thoroughly testing the teachings of their leaders (Deuteronomy 13). Similarly, in the New Testament, the apostle Paul commands the Thessalonians to test all things and to hold fast to that which is good (1 Thessalonians 5:21–22). Moreover, Paul lauds the Bereans for testing his teachings (Acts 17:11).

Furthermore, while our Lord cautioned followers not to judge self–righteously (Matthew 7:1–5), he also counseled them to make judgments based on right standards (John 7:24). In the context of his oft–misquoted command "Judge not, or you too will be judged," Jesus exhorts us to judge false prophets, whose teachings and behavior lead people astray (Matthew 7:15–20). Thus while we are commanded to not judge hypocritically, we are nevertheless called to judge.

Finally, common sense should be sufficient to alert us to the importance of making public as well as private judgments regarding false doctrine. During the infamous Tylenol scare in 1982, public warnings were issued by the media and the medical community regarding the physical danger of ingesting Tylenol capsules that someone had laced with cyanide. In similar fashion, when spiritual cyanide is dispensed within the Christian community, we are duty–bound to warn the public. As such, Paul publicly rebuked Hymenaeus and Philetus whose teachings "spread like gangrene" (2 Timothy 2:17–18; cf. Galatians 2:11–14).

For further study, see Hank Hanegraaff, "The Untouchables: Are 'God's Anointed' Beyond Criticism?" and Bob and Gretchen Passantino, "Christians Criticizing Christians: Can It Be Biblical?" both available through the Christian Research Institute (CRI) at www.equip.org.

JOHN 7:24
"Stop judging by mere appearances,
and make a right judgment."

IS THE GOSPEL OF PEACE A PROMISE
OF EASE AND PROSPERITY?

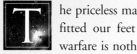he priceless material with which God has
fitted our feet for readiness in spiritual
warfare is nothing less than the gospel of
peace (Ephesians 6:15). However, the promise of peace
is not grounds for an expectation of easy existence.

First, when the Bible speaks of the gospel of
peace, the emphasis is not prosperity but peace
with God. "Once you were alienated from God and
were enemies in your minds because of your evil
behavior" (Colossians 1:21). Your heart once
entertained contemptible thoughts about God. You
had an inbred disgust for his principles and
precepts. "But now he has reconciled you by
Christ's physical body through death to present you
holy in his sight, without blemish and free from
accusation" (Colossians 1:22). Thus, as soldiers of
the cross we can march through life's battles with a
song in our hearts and with our "feet fitted with
the readiness that comes from the gospel of peace"
(Ephesians 6:15). God does not promise us a

panacea, but he does promise us peace in the midst of life's storms.

Furthermore, to "stand firm with your feet fitted with the readiness that comes from the gospel of peace" is to have peace with others. While we cannot make everyone love us, we can love everyone. The gospel of peace enables us to tread confidently through canyons of conflict and controversy with others. In the words of Solomon, "When a man's ways are pleasing to the LORD, he makes even his enemies to live at peace with him" (Proverbs 16:7).

Finally, the gospel of peace is a preview of perfect peace in paradise. In the present, peace is yet an unperfected process. One day, however, we will step over the threshold into perfect peace. The bottom line is this: pilgrims who stand firm with their "feet fitted with the readiness that comes from the gospel of peace" are only a step away from perfect peace.

For further study, see Hank Hanegraaff, *The Covering* (Nashville: W Publishing Group, 2002).

JOHN 16:33

"I have told you these things, so that in me you may have peace. In this world you will have trouble. But take heart! I have overcome the world."

Is being "slain in the spirit" consistent with a biblical worldview?

oday thousands of people are routinely being "slain in the spirit" in the name of a fashionable and palpable demonstration of Holy Ghost power. Practitioners claim ample validation for this phenomenon in Scripture, church history, and experience. However, the phenomenon not only is conspicuous by its absence in the ministry of Jesus and the apostles but is generally inconsistent with a biblical worldview.

First, as aptly noted by pro-Pentecostal sources such as the *Dictionary of Pentecostal and Charismatic Movements (DPCM)* (Grand Rapids: Zondervan, 1988), "An entire battalion of Scripture proof texts is enlisted to support the legitimacy of the phenomenon, although Scripture plainly offers no support for the phenomenon as something to be expected in the normal Christian life" (p. 790).

Furthermore, the experience of being "slain in the spirit" can be attributed to mere human manipulation. According to the *DPCM*, "in addition to God, the source of the experience can be a purely human response to autosuggestion, group 'peer pressure,' or simply a desire to experience the phenomenon" (p. 789). Cynics may write off the use of altered states of consciousness, peer pressure, expectations, and suggestive powers as mere socio-psychological manipulation, but Christians must perceive an even more significant threat—these techniques are fertile soil for satanic and spiritual deception.

Finally, the "slain in the spirit" phenomenon has more in common with occultism than with a biblical worldview. As popular "slain in the spirit" practitioner Francis MacNutt candidly confesses in his book *Overcome by the Spirit*, the phenomenon is externally similar to "manifestations of voodoo and other magic rites" and is "found today among different sects in the Orient as well as among primitive tribes of Africa and Latin America." In sharp contrast, Scripture makes it clear that as Christians we must be "self-controlled and alert" (1 Peter 5:8) rather than being in an altered state of consciousness or "slain in the spirit."

ADAPTED FROM *Counterfeit Revival*

For further study, see Hank Hanegraaff, *Counterfeit Revival: Looking for God in All the Wrong Places*, rev. ed. (Nashville: Word Publishing, 2001).

1 PETER 5:8–9

"Be self-controlled and alert. Your enemy the devil prowls around like a roaring lion looking for someone to devour. Resist him, standing firm in the faith."

ARE THERE APOSTLES
AND PROPHETS TODAY?

hile it has become increasingly popular to believe in the restoration of "end-time" apostles and prophets, the Bible clearly does not support this notion.

First, to address this question we must first learn to scale the language barrier. In other words, the issue is not so much the words "prophet" or "apostle" but the meaning that is ascribed to these words. For example, *apostle* may be used in the sense of a church planter, a missionary, or a pastor of pastors. Likewise, *prophet* may be used in the sense of a leader who inspires the church with vision for its mission or who challenges the church to deeper commitment to Christ. However, the words "apostle" and "prophet" must not be used in a synonymous sense with the first-century apostle John or the Old Testament prophet Jeremiah. People whose authority cannot be questioned or who receive new doctrinal revelations simply do not exist today.

Furthermore, the Bible teaches that apostles and prophets were commissioned by God to be his personal spokesmen. Moreover, Ephesians 2:20 tells us that the church is "built on the foundation of the apostles and prophets, with Christ Jesus himself as the chief cornerstone." Clearly, then, those who claim to be that kind of apostle and prophet today have taken upon themselves authority that was not given to them by God.

Finally, the prophetic words of Scripture expose today's pretenders. Not only do they fail the biblical tests given in Deuteronomy 13 and 18, as well as Acts 1:21–22, but "they mouth empty, boastful words and, by appealing to the lustful desires of sinful human nature, they entice people who are just escaping from those who live in error. They promise freedom, while they themselves are slaves of depravity" (2 Peter 2:18–19).

For further study, see Hank Hanegraaff, *Counterfeit Revival: Looking for God in All the Wrong Places*, rev. ed. (Nashville: Word Publishing, 2001).

"'How can we know when a message has not been spoken by the LORD?' If what a prophet proclaims in the name of the LORD does not take place or come true, that is a message the LORD has not spoken.
That prophet has spoken presumptuously.
Do not be afraid of him."

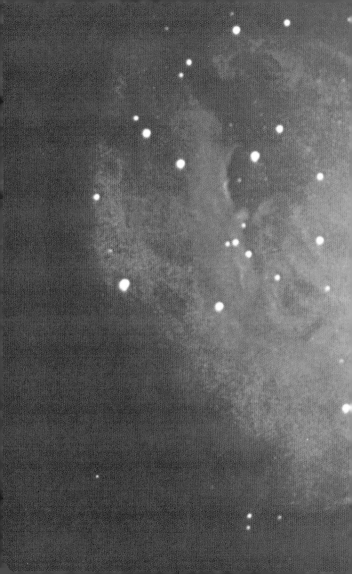

SPIRITUAL WARFARE

Over the years, I have read a wide variety of stories that claim to support the notion that Christians can be demonized. In the end, they all have one thing in common: they greatly overestimate the power and province of Satan. Some deliverance ministers make a more valiant attempt than others to provide a biblical basis for the contention that a Christian can be inhabited by a demon. Inevitably, however, Scripture itself undermines their stories.

First, Christ himself precludes the possibility that a Christian could be inhabited by demons. Using the illustration of a house, Jesus asks, "How can anyone enter a strong man's house and carry off his possessions unless he first ties up the strong man?" (Matthew 12:29). In the case of a demon-possessed person, the strong man is obviously the devil. In a Spirit-indwelt believer, however, the strong man is God. The force of Christ's argument leads inexorably to the conclusion that, in order for demons to possess believers, they would first have to bind the one who occupies them—namely God himself!

Furthermore, I discovered an equally airtight argument against Christian demonization in the gospel of John. The Jews once again were accusing Jesus of being demon-possessed. Rather than circumvent their accusations, Jesus condescends to reach out to his accusers with reason. The essence of his argument is "I am not possessed by a demon" because "I honor my Father" (John 8:49). The point is impossible to miss: Being demon-possessed and honoring God are mutually exclusive categories.

Finally, Scripture does not contain a single credible example of a demonized believer. Instead, the consistent teaching of the Bible is that Christians cannot be controlled against their wills through demonic inhabitation. The principle is foolproof. If you are a follower of Christ, the King himself indwells you. And you can rest assured that "the one who is in you is greater than the one who is in the world" (1 John 4:4).

ADAPTED FROM *The Covering*

For further study, see Hank Hanegraaff, *The Covering: God's Plan to Protect You from Evil* (Nashville: W Publishing, 2002).

1 JOHN 4:4
"You, dear children, are from God and have overcome them, because the one who is in you is greater than the one who is in the world."

112

Is the "binding and loosing" of demons biblical?

ne of the most common expressions in contemporary Christianity is "I bind you, Satan, in the name of Jesus." Biblically however, the phrase "binding and loosing" has nothing whatsoever to do with demons.

First, when Jesus told the disciples, "Whatever you bind on earth will be bound in heaven, and whatever you loose on earth will be loosed in heaven" (Matthew 16:19), he was not talking about demons but discipline. In other words, in the context of church discipline, those who repent are to be "loosed" (i.e., restored to fellowship). Those who persist in sin are to be "bound" (i.e., removed from fellowship). Demons are totally foreign to the context.

Furthermore, humans are not authorized anywhere in Scripture to "bind or loose" Satan. Even the archangel Michael did not tackle Satan on his own. Despite his wisdom and power, he called on God to rebuke Satan. Christians should never suppose that they are smart enough to engage Satan on their own. Rather they, like Michael, should pray, "The Lord rebuke you" (Jude 9).

Finally, while it makes sense to ask the Lord to "bind" the power of demons in the sense of thwarting their plans to undo us, to "loose" Satan and his minions makes no sense at all. Thus, common sense alone should be enough to convince us that biblically "binding and loosing" has nothing whatsoever to do with demons.

For further study on biblical spiritual warfare, see Hank Hanegraaff, *The Covering: God's Plan to Protect You from Evil* (Nashville: W Publishing, 2002).

MATTHEW 18:15–20

"If your brother sins against you, go and show him his fault, just between the two of you. If he listens to you, you have won your brother over. But if he will not listen, take one or two others along, so that 'every matter may be established by the testimony of two or three witnesses.' If he refuses to listen to them, tell it to the church; and if he refuses to listen even to the church, treat him as you would a pagan or a tax collector.
"I tell you the truth, whatever you bind on earth will be bound in heaven, and whatever you loose on earth will be loosed in heaven.

*"Again, I tell you that if two of you
on earth agree about anything you ask for,
it will be done for you by my Father in heaven.
For where two or three come
together in my name, there am I with them."*

113

DOES SATAN HAVE ACCESS TO OUR MINDS?

hile we would greatly overestimate Satan's power by supposing that he can interact directly with us in a physical sense, an equal and opposite error would be to suppose that he does not have access to our minds.

First, while Satan cannot read our minds he can influence our thoughts. Thus, the Bible instructs us to "put on the full armor of God so that you can take your stand against the devil's schemes" (Ephesians 6:11). Without it, you are a guaranteed casualty in the invisible war; with it, you are invincible. Spiritual warfare is waged against invisible beings that personify the extremities of evil. And their weapons are spiritual, not physical. While they cannot bite us physically, violate us sexually, or cause us to levitate, they can tempt us to cheat, steal, and lie.

Furthermore, it is crucial to note that if we open the door to Satan by failing to put on the full armor of God, he does, as it were, sit on our shoulders and whisper into our ears. The whisper cannot be discerned with the physical ear; it can, however, penetrate "the ear" of the mind. We cannot explain how such communication takes place any more than we can explain how our immaterial minds can cause the physical synapses of the brain to fire. But that such mind-to-mind communication takes place is indisputable. If it were not so, the devil could not have tempted Judas to betray his Master, seduced Ananias and Sapphira to deceive Peter, or incited David to take a census.

Finally, while fallen angels are not material beings and thus cannot interact with us directly in the physical sense, they are as real as the very flesh upon our bones. No doubt much to the devil's delight we often depict him as either a cartoonish clown, with an elongated tail, red tights, and a pitchfork—or as a cultural caricature. Far from silly or stupid, however, Satan appears as a cosmopolitan angel of enlightenment. He knows full well that without our spiritual armor we are but pawns in a devil's game.

In the final analysis, the whole of Scripture informs us that spiritual warfare is the battle for the mind.

ADAPTED FROM *The Covering*

For further study, see Hank Hanegraaff, *The Covering: God's Plan to Protect You from Evil* (Nashville: W Publishing Group, 2002); and C. S. Lewis, *The Screwtape Letters* (New York: Macmillan, 1982).

EPHESIANS 6:12–13

"For our struggle is not against flesh and blood, but against the rulers, against the authorities, against the powers of this dark world and against the spiritual forces of evil in the heavenly realms. Therefore put on the full armor of God, so that when the day of evil comes, you may be able to stand your ground, and after you have done everything, to stand."

SATAN HAS ACCESS TO OUR MINDS THROUGH
WHAT WE PUT INTO OUR MINDS.

"Do not be anxious about anything, but in
everything, by prayer and petition, with
thanksgiving, present your requests to God.
And the peace of God, which transcends all
understanding, will guard your hearts and
your minds in Christ Jesus.

"Finally, brothers, whatever is true,
whatever is noble, whatever is right,
whatever is pure, whatever is lovely,
whatever is admirable—if anything is
excellent or praiseworthy—think about such
things. Whatever you have learned
or received or heard from me, or seen in
me—put it into practice. And the God
of peace will be with you."

—PHILIPPIANS 4:6–9

Is Satan always the cause of sickness?

If you tune into Christian television on virtually any given day you can hear faith healers screaming at satanic spirits of sicknesses ranging from asthma to arthritis. But is Satan really behind every sickness?

First, while Scripture makes it clear that Satan is often the *agent* of sickness, he is not always the *author* of sickness. Sometimes God is. For example, in Exodus 4:11 God himself asks the rhetorical question "Who gave man his mouth? Who makes him deaf or dumb? Who gives him sight or makes him blind? Is it not I, the LORD?" In 2 Kings 15:5 we read the well-known story of the Lord striking King Azariah with a skin disease from which he suffered till the day he died. And in Luke, the angel of the Lord came directly from God's presence to strike Zechariah with an affliction because he doubted God's word regarding the birth of John the Baptist (Luke 1:19–20).

Furthermore, we live in a cursed creation in which aging is the primary sickness of humanity.

Thus, humanity's fall into a life of constant sin terminated by death, rather than Satan, is by far the primary cause of sickness. As we get older we all get wrinkles, some of us need glasses, our muscles get shorter, and eventually we all die. Since the fall of humankind, both the righteous and the unrighteous have been subject to sickness and disease. Job, who is affirmed by Scripture as a great man of faith, was covered with painful sores from the soles of his feet to the top of his head (Job 2:7). Paul confessed to the Galatians that he preached the gospel to them for the first time because of a "bodily illness" (Galatians 4:13). Timothy was called Paul's "son in the faith" (1 Timothy 1:2) yet he suffered from frequent stomach problems (1 Timothy 5:23). And Elisha was blessed with a "double-portion anointing," yet he suffered and died a sick man (2 Kings 13:14).

Finally, it is crucial to note that this world is under the sovereign control of God, not Satan. Thus, we can rest assured that even in sickness and suffering all things work together for good to those who love God and are called according to his purpose (Romans 8:28). For the child of God, the hope is not perfect health in this lifetime but a resurrected body in the life to come. As John the apostle so beautifully put it, "'There will be no more death or mourning or crying or pain, for the old order of things has passed away' He who was seated on the throne said, 'I am making everything new!'" (Revelation 21:4–5).

IN PART ADAPTED FROM *Christianity in Crisis*

For further study, see Hank Hanegraaff, *Christianity in Crisis* (Eugene, Ore.: Harvest House Publishers, 1993).

EXODUS 4:11 NASB
"The LORD said to him, 'Who has made man's mouth? Or who makes him mute or deaf, or seeing or blind? Is it not I, the LORD?'"

DID DEMONS HAVE SEXUAL RELATIONS
WITH WOMEN IN GENESIS 6:4?

enesis 6:4 is one of the most controversial
passages in the Bible. As with any difficult
section of Scripture, it has been open to a
wide variety of interpretations. It is my conviction
however, that those who hold consistently to a
biblical worldview must reject the notion that
women and demons can engage in sexual relations.
I reject this interjection of pagan superstition into
the Scriptures for the following reasons.

First and foremost, the notion that demons
can "produce" real bodies and have real sex with
real women would invalidate Jesus' argument for
the authenticity of his resurrection. Jesus assured
his disciples that "a spirit does not have flesh and
bones, as you see I have" (Luke 24:39 NKJV).
If indeed a demon could produce flesh and bones
Jesus' argument would be not only flawed but also
misleading. In fact, it might be logically argued that
the disciples did not see the postresurrection

appearances of Christ but rather a demon masquerading as the resurrected Christ.

Furthermore, demons are nonsexual, nonphysical beings and as such are incapable of having sexual relations and producing physical offspring. To say that demons can create bodies with DNA and fertile sperm is to say that demons have creative power—which is an exclusively divine prerogative. If demons could have sex with women in ancient times, we would have no assurance they could not do so in modern times. Nor would we have any guarantee that the people we encounter every day are fully human. While a biblical worldview does allow for fallen angels to *possess* unsaved human beings, it does not support the notion that a demon-possessed person can produce offspring that are part-demon, part-human. Genesis 1 makes it clear that all of God's living creations are designed to reproduce "according to their own kinds."

Finally, the mutant theory creates serious questions pertaining to the spiritual accountability of hypothetical demon-humans and their relation to humanity's redemption. Angels rebelled individually, are judged individually, and are offered no plan of redemption in Scripture. On the other hand, humans fell corporately in Adam, are judged corporately in

Adam, and are redeemed corporately through Jesus Christ. We have no biblical way of determining what category the demon-humans would fit into—whether they would be judged as angels or as men, or more significantly, whether they might even be among those for whom Christ died.

I believe the better interpretation is that "sons of God" simply refers to the godly descendants of Seth, and "daughters of men" to the ungodly descendants of Cain. Their cohabitation caused humanity to fall into such utter depravity that God said: "I will wipe mankind, whom I have created, from the face of the earth—men and animals, and creatures that move along the ground, and birds of the air—for I am grieved that I have made them. But Noah found favor in the eyes of the Lord" (Genesis 6:7–8).

For further study, see Hank Hanegraaff, "Questions and Answers: Genesis 6:4," available from CRI at www.equip.org; see also Gleason L. Archer, *New International Encyclopedia of Bible Difficulties* (Grand Rapids: Zondervan, 1982), 79–80.

GENESIS 6:4

"The Nephilim were on the earth in those days—and also afterward—when the sons of God went to the daughters of men and had children by them. They were the heroes of old, men of renown."

WHY IS SATAN CALLED
"THE GOD OF THIS AGE"?

n the Bible Satan is called "the god of this age" (2 Corinthians 4:4) and "the prince of this world" (John 12:31; 16:11), which begs the question: In what sense is Satan a god and a prince?

First, Satan is not God's equal. Rather, according to Scripture, Satan is a finite, created being (Colossians 1:16). He was the first sinner (1 John 3:8; Revelation 12:7–9) and will one day be cast into the lake of burning sulfur for all eternity (Matthew 25:41; Revelation 20:10; cf. 2 Peter 2:4; Jude 6). Thus, Christians need not fear the god of this age, for "the one who is in you is greater than the one who is in the world" (1 John 4:4).

Furthermore, Satan, whose name means "adversary," is the god of this age in that he is the supreme exemplar of evil. In the words of Jesus, "He was a murderer from the beginning, not holding to the truth, for there is no truth in him. When he lies, he speaks his native language, for he is a liar and the father of lies" (John 8:44). Indeed, all the sin of the world is patterned after Satan: "He who does what is sinful is of the devil, because the devil has been sinning from the beginning" (1 John 3:8). It is he "who leads the whole world astray" (Revelation 12:9).

Satan, whose name means "adversary," is the . . . *de facto* ruler of all who willingly subject themselves to his masterful deceit.

Finally, Satan is the *de facto* ruler of all who willingly subject themselves to his masterful deceit (2 Corinthians 4:4; 11:3). If we do not belong to the God of the ages, then we are of Satan—the god of this age.

For further study, see Hank Hanegraaff, *The Covering: God's Plan to Protect You from Evil* (Nashville: W Publishing, 2002).

ISAIAH 44:6

"This is what the LORD says—Israel's King and Redeemer, the LORD Almighty: I am the first and I am the last; apart from me there is no God."

ARE GENERATIONAL CURSES BIBLICAL?

Based on texts taken out of context and used as pretexts, it has become increasingly common for Christians to suppose that they are victims of generational curses. As such, they suppose they have inherited demons ranging from anger to alcoholism, from laziness to lust. Closer examination, however, demonstrates this notion to be seriously flawed.

First, Scripture clearly communicates that consequences—not curses—are passed on through the generations. In this sense, the Bible says that children are punished for the sins of their fathers "to the third and fourth generation" (Exodus 20:5). The children of alcoholic fathers frequently suffer neglect and abuse as a direct consequence of their father's sinful behavior. Moreover, the descendants of those who hate God are likely to follow in the footsteps of their forefathers.

Furthermore, Scripture explicitly tells us that "the son will not share the guilt of the father, nor will the father share the guilt of the son" (Ezekiel 18:20). Indeed, when ancient Israel quoted the proverb,

"The fathers eat sour grapes, and the children's teeth are set on edge" (Ezekiel 18:2), God responded in no uncertain terms: "As surely as I live, declares the Sovereign LORD, you will no longer quote this proverb in Israel . . . *The soul who sins is the one who will die*" (vv. 3–4, emphasis added).

Consequences—not curses—
are passed on through the generations.

Finally, while the notion of generational curses is foreign to Scripture, there is a sense in which the curse of sin has been passed on from generation to generation. Through the first Adam, "all have sinned and fall short of the glory of God" (Romans 3:23). Through the Second Adam—Jesus Christ—atonement is offered to all. Says Paul, "Just as the result of one trespass was condemnation for all men, so also the result of one act of righteousness was justification that brings life for all men" (Romans 5:18). Through no act of our own we are condemned; likewise, through no act of our own we are saved (Romans 5:12–21).

For further study, see Hank Hanegraaff, *The Covering: God's Plan to Protect You from Evil* (Nashville: W Publishing, 2002).

"The soul who sins is the one who will die.
The son will not share the guilt of the father, nor will
the father share the guilt of the son.
The righteousness of the righteous man will be
credited to him, and the wickedness of the wicked
will be charged against him."

PSEUDOSCIENTIFIC

APOLOGETICS

ARE BIBLE CODES CREDIBLE?

 significant number of Christian leaders today hail Bible Codes as important evidence for the inspiration of Scripture. While they claim post–prophecies such as Israeli prime minister Yitzhak Rabin's assassination in 1995 are encoded in the biblical text, Bible Codes, in reality, are little more than a fringe variety of Jewish mysticism repackaged for Christian consumption.

First, like its older permutation, Bible Numerics, Bible Codes are at best a pseudoscience. Codes are "discovered" by searching for equidistant letter sequences (ELS) that can be compiled into intelligible messages pertaining to past events. One can search left to right, right to left, top to bottom, bottom to top, or in diagonal directions. Although sequencing can vary from word to word, none of the prophecies can be known *beforehand*. Like Monday–morning quarterbacking, hindsight is always perfect.

Furthermore, Bible Codes are a rigged game complete with after–the–fact prophecies and self–validating messages. While ELS practitioners contend such historical events as the assassination of Rabin are encoded in the Torah, nothing could be farther from the truth. Because Old Testament Hebrew does not contain vowels, an alleged code such as "Rabin Bang Bang" could just as easily refer to Christopher Robin's shooting his pop gun at the balloons Winnie the Pooh was holding when he floated over the Hundred Acre Wood ("Robin Bang Bang"). For that matter, the self–validating message could refer to the tire blowout that Batman's sidekick Robin experienced while riding in the Batmobile. It could even refer to a Mafia hitman named Robino who had two successful kills—bang, bang.

Bible Codes shift the focus of biblical apologetics from the essential core of the gospel to esoteric speculations.

Finally, though the message of the *autographa* (original texts of the Bible) is unaltered in the best available manuscript copies, minor differences in spelling and style make it impossible to validate the divine inspiration of equidistant letter sequencing. Such minor divergences leave the meaning unaltered but completely undermine all attempts to find equidistant letter sequences by altering the distance between letters. Moreover, the coincidences of equidistant letter sequences that do occur in the Torah are not unique. They occur in every other work of literature from Homer to Hobbes and from Tolkien to Tolstoy.

Bible Codes shift the focus of biblical apologetics from the essential core of the gospel to esoteric speculations. Those who deny the incontrovertible evidence that Jesus rose from the dead are not likely to be persuaded by the pseudo–apologetic of Bible Codes.

For further study, see Hank Hanegraaff, "Magic Apologetics," *Christian Research Journal* 20, 1 (1997), available through the Christian Research Institute (CRI) at www.equip.org.

LUKE 16:31

"If they do not listen to Moses and the Prophets, they will not be convinced even if someone rises from the dead."

IS THERE A GOSPEL IN THE STARS?

O ver the years I have observed an alarming trend toward what I call "magic apologetics." In place of an emphasis on such great apologetic verities as the creation of the cosmos, the resurrection of Christ, and the inspiration of Scripture, we are being bombarded with host of apologetic pretenders. One of the more curious brands of magic apologetics circulating through the Christian community is called the gospel in the stars (GIS). This apologetic posits that God from the beginning wrote the unique message of the gospel in the signs of the zodiac. At first blush this magic apologetic may appear to have merit; closer examination, however, exposes it as a counterfeit.

First, GIS compromises the formal principle of the Reformation, namely, *sola Scriptura*. While *sola Scriptura* does not claim that the Bible is the sole source of revelation, it does hold that the Bible is the only infallible rule of faith and practice, the sole infallible repository of redemptive revelation. Nowhere in the Bible is there any indication that

God has given us two infallible sources of special revelation—the gospel in the stars and the gospel in the Scriptures. Nor was GIS used by the prophets, the apostles, Jesus Christ, or the early church as an apologetic for the gospel.

Furthermore, GIS confuses special revelation with general revelation. The church has always understood the Bible to make a distinction between general and special revelation. General revelation proclaims the glory of God through order and design (Psalm 19:1). Special revelation is found in the "law of the Lord" inscribed in the pages of Scripture (Psalm 19:7). From the *lights* we gain an unspoken knowledge of the Creator; from the *Law* we find salvation for our souls. Common sense should suffice to tell us that while the heavens declare the glory of God, they do not provide us with specific salvific content. A common person looking at the night sky would be hard–pressed to see the gospel in the zodiac.

Finally, GIS subverts the natural use of the stars for a superstitious use. The natural use of the stars is to "separate the day from the night," "serve as signs to mark seasons and days and years," and "give light on the earth" (Genesis 1:14–15). Stars can also be rightly used for varied purposes ranging from natural revelation to navigation. Indeed, "The heavens declare the glory of God; the skies proclaim the work of his hands. Day after day they pour forth speech; night after night they display knowledge. There is no speech or language where their voice is not heard. Their voice goes out into all the earth, their words to the ends of the world" (Psalm 19:1–4).

Common sense should suffice to tell us that while the heavens declare the glory of God, they do not provide us with specific salvific content.

In light of the fact that GIS compromises *sola Scriptura*, confuses special revelation with general revelation, and promotes superstition, it would behoove Christians to reject it and return to mastering genuine apologetic arguments. Every Christian should be equipped to communicate the evidence that God created the universe, that Jesus Christ demonstrated that he was God through the immutable fact of the resurrection, and that the Bible is divine rather than merely human in origin.

For further study, see Hank Hanegraaff, "What is Wrong with Astrology," *The Bible Answer Book Volume 1* (Nashville: J Countryman, 2004): 262–265; see also Charles Strohmer, "Is there a Christian Zodiac, a Gospel in the Stars?" *Christian Research Journal* 22, 4 (2000), available through the Christian Research Institute (CRI) at www.equip.org.

Genesis 1:14–15

"And God said, 'Let there be lights in the expanse of the sky to separate the day from the night, and let them serve as signs to mark seasons and days and years, and let them be lights in the expanse of the sky to give light on the earth.' And it was so."

CHRISTIANITY AND SCIENCE

120

Is the Big Bang biblical?

he Big Bang postulates that billions of years ago the universe began as an infinitely dense point called a singularity and has been expanding ever since. Though the Big Bang is not taught in the Bible, the theory does lend scientific support to the scriptural teaching that God created the universe *ex nihilo* (out of nothing).

First, like the Bible, the Big Bang postulates that the universe had a beginning. As such, it stands in stark opposition to the scientifically silly suggestion that the universe eternally existed, not to the biblical account of origins.

Furthermore, if the universe had a beginning, it had to have a cause. Indeed, according to empirical science, whatever begins to exist must have a cause equal to or greater than itself. Thus, the Big Bang flies in the face of the philosophically preposterous proposition that the universe sprang from nothing apart from an uncaused First Cause.

Finally, though evolutionists hold to Big Bang cosmology, the Big Bang itself does not entail biological evolution. In other words, the Big Bang theory answers questions concerning the origin of the space–time universe, as opposed to questions concerning the origin of biological life on earth.

The Big Bang itself does not entail biological evolution. In other words, the Big Bang theory answers questions concerning the origin of the space–time universe, as opposed to questions concerning the origin of biological life on earth.

While we must not stake our faith on Big Bang cosmology, we can be absolutely confident that as human understanding of the universe progresses it will ultimately point to the One who spoke before the universe lept into existence.

For further study, see Paul Copan and William Lane Craig, *Creation out of Nothing: A Biblical, Philosophical, and Scientific Exploration* (Grand Rapids: Baker Academic, 2004): 17–19; see also J. P. Moreland, *Scaling the Secular City: A Defense of Christianity* (Grand Rapids: Baker Book House, 1987): 33–34, and Lee Strobel, *The Case for a Creator* (Grand Rapids: Zondervan, 2004), especially chapter 5.

PSALM 19:1
"The heavens declare the glory of God;
the skies proclaim the work of his hands."

121

CAN WE BE CERTAIN
THAT EVOLUTION IS A MYTH?

D
r. Louis Bounoure, former director of research at the French National Center for Scientific Research, calls evolution "a fairy tale for grown-ups." I call it a cruel hoax! In fact, the arguments that support evolutionary theory are astonishingly weak.

First, the fossil record is an embarrassment to evolutionists. No verifiable transitions from one kind to another have as yet been found. Charles Darwin had an excuse; in his day fossil finds were relatively scarce. Today, however, we have an abundance of fossils. Still, we have yet to find even one legitimate transition from one kind to another.

Furthermore, in Darwin's day such enormously complex structures as a human egg were thought to be quite simple—for all practical purposes, little more than a microscopic blob of gelatin. Today, we know that a fertilized human egg is among the most organized, complex structures in the universe. In an age of scientific enlightenment, it is incredible to think people are willing to maintain that something so vastly complex arose by chance. Like an egg or the human eye, the universe is a masterpiece of precision and design that could not have come into existence by chance.

In an age of scientific enlightenment,
it is incredible to think people are willing to maintain that
something so vastly complex arose by chance.

Finally, while chance is a blow to the theory of evolution, the laws of science are a bullet to its head. The basic laws of science, including the laws of *effects* and their causes—*energy conservation* and *entropy*—undergird the creation model for origins and undermine the evolutionary hypothesis. While I would fight for a person's right to have faith in science fiction, we must resist evolutionists who attempt to brainwash people into thinking that evolution is science.

ADAPTED FROM *Fatal Flaws*

For further study, see Hank Hanegraaff, *Fatal Flaws: What Evolutionists Don't Want You to Know* (Nashville: W Publishing, 2003); Phillip E. Johnson, *Darwin on Trial,* second edition (Downers Grove, Ill.: InterVarsity Press, 1993).

"*The heavens declare the glory of God;*
the skies proclaim the work of his hands.
Day after day they pour forth speech;
night after night they display knowledge.
There is no speech or language
where their voice is not heard.
Their voice goes out into all the earth,
their words to the ends of the world."

Did humans evolve from hominids?

In the television premiere of *Ape Man: The Story of Human Evolution*, former CBS anchor Walter Cronkite declared that monkeys were his "newfound cousins." Cronkite went on to say: "If you go back far enough, we and the chimps share a common ancestor. My father's father's father's father, going back maybe a half million generations—about five million years—was an ape." Is Cronkite right? Do we and the chimps share a common ancestor? Or is this an illustration of the antiknowledge surrounding ape–men?

First, whether in *Ape Man*, *National Geographic*, or *Time*, the ape–to–man icon has itself become the argument. Put another way, the illustration of a knuckle–dragging ape evolving through a series of imaginary transitional forms into modern man has appeared so many times in so many places that the picture has evolved into the proof. In light of the fanfare attending the most recent proof-candidates nominated by evolutionists to flesh out the icons of evolution, we would do well to remember that past candidates such as Lucy have bestowed fame on their finders but have done little to distinguish themselves as prime exemplars of human evolution.

Furthermore, as the corpus of hominid fossil specimens continues to grow, it has become increasingly evident that there is an unbridgeable chasm between hominids and humans in both composition and culture. Moreover, homologous structures (similar structures on different species) do not provide sufficient proof of genealogical relationships—common descent is simply an evolutionary assumption used to explain the similarities. To assume that hominids and humans are closely related because both can walk upright is tantamount to saying hummingbirds and helicopters are closely related because both can fly. Indeed, the distance between an ape, who cannot read or write, and a descendant of Adam, who can compose a musical masterpiece or send a man to the moon, is the distance of infinity.

Finally, evolution cannot satisfactorily account for the genesis of life, the genetic code, or the ingenious synchronization process needed to produce life from a single fertilized human egg. Nor can evolution satisfactorily explain how physical processes can produce metaphysical realities such as consciousness and spirituality. The insatiable drive to produce a "missing link" has substituted selling, sensationalism, and subjectivism for solid science. William Fix said it best: "When it comes to finding a new trooper to star as our animal ancestor, there's no business like bone business."

For further study, see Jonathan Wells, *Icons of Evolution: Science or Myth?* (Washington, D.C.: Regnery Publishing, 2000).

GENESIS 1:25–27

"God made the wild animals according to their kinds, the livestock according to their kinds, and all the creatures that move along the ground according to their kinds. And God saw that is was good. Then God said, 'Let us make man in our image, in our likeness, and let them rule over the fish of the sea and the birds of the air, over the livestock, over all the earth, and over all the creatures that move along the ground.' So God created man in his own image, in the image of God he created him; male and female he created them."

IS *ARCHAEOPTERYX* THE MISSING LINK
BETWEEN DINOSAURS AND BIRDS?

henever I say that there are no transitions from one species to another, someone inevitably brings up *Archaeopteryx*. This happens so frequently that I've decided to coin a word for the experience: *pseudosaur*. *Pseudo* means false and *saur* refers to a dinosaur or a reptile (literally lizard). Thus, a pseudosaur is a false link between reptiles (such as dinosaurs) and birds. Myriad evidences demonstrate conclusively that *Archaeopteryx* is a full-fledged bird; not a missing link.

First, fossils of both *Archaeopteryx* and the kinds of dinosaurs *Archaeopteryx* supposedly descended from have been found in a fine-grained German limestone formation said to be Late Jurassic (the Jurassic period is said to have begun 190 million years ago, lasting 54 million years). Thus, *Archaeopteryx* is not a likely candidate as the missing link, since birds and their alleged ancestral dinosaurs thrived during the same period.

Furthermore, initial *Archaeopteryx* fossil finds gave no evidence of a bony sternum, which led paleontologists to conclude that *Archaeopteryx* could not fly or was a poor flyer. However, in April 1993 a seventh specimen was reported that included a bony sternum. Thus, there is no further doubt that *Archaeopteryx* was as suited for power flying as any modern bird.

Finally, to say that *Archaeopteryx* is a missing link between reptiles and birds, one must believe that scales evolved into feathers for flight. Air friction acting on genetic mutation supposedly frayed the outer edges of reptilian scales. Thus, in the course of millions of years, scales became increasingly like feathers until, one day, the perfect feather emerged. To say the least, this idea must stretch the credulity of even the most ardent evolutionists.

These and myriad other factors overwhelmingly exclude *Archaeopteryx* as a missing link between birds and dinosaurs. The sober fact is that *Archaeopteryx* appears abruptly in the fossil record, with masterfully engineered wings and feathers common in the birds observable today. Even the late Stephen Jay Gould of Harvard and Niles Eldridge of the American Museum of Natural History, both militant evolutionists, have concluded that *Archaeopteryx* cannot be viewed as a transitional form.

ADAPTED FROM *Fatal Flaws*

For further study, see Duane T. Gish, Evolution: *The Fossils Still Say No!* (El Cajon, Calif.: Institute for Creation Research, 1995); and Jonathan Wells, *Icons of Evolution: Science or Myth?* (Washington D.C.: Regnery, 2000).

GENESIS 1:25

"God made the wild animals according to their kinds, the livestock according to their kinds, and all the creatures that move along the ground according to their kinds. And God saw that it was good."

HOW SERIOUS ARE THE CONSEQUENCES
OF BELIEVING IN EVOLUTION?

ore consequences for society hinge on the cosmogenic myth of evolution than on any other. Among them are the sovereignty of self, the sexual revolution, and survival of the fittest.

First, the supposed death of God in the nineteenth century ushered in an era in which humans proclaimed themselves sovereigns of the universe. Humanity's perception of autonomy led to sacrificing truth on the altar of subjectivism. Ethics and morals were no longer determined on the basis of objective standards but rather by the size and strength of the latest lobbying group. With no enduring reference point, societal norms were reduced to mere matters of preference.

Furthermore, the evolutionary dogma saddled society with the devastating consequences of the sexual revolution. We got rid of the Almighty and in return got adultery, abortion, and AIDS. Adultery has become commonplace as evolutionary man fixates on feelings rather than fidelity. Abortion has become epidemic as people embrace expediency over ethics. And AIDS has become pandemic as people clamor for condoms apart from commitment. Tragically, more people have died of AIDS than America has lost in all its wars combined. Despite the consequences, promiscuous sex continues to be glorified in the media, in movies, through music, and by Madison Avenue. Only one rule seems to endure: life has no rules.

Finally, evolutionism has popularized such racist clichés as "survival of the fittest." In *The Descent of Man*, Darwin speculated "at some future period, not very distant as measured by centuries, the civilized races of man will almost certainly exterminate, and replace, the savage races throughout the world." In addition, Darwin subtitled his magnum opus *The Preservation of Favored Races in the Struggle for Life*. Indeed, for evolution to succeed, it is as crucial that the unfit die as that the fittest survive. Nowhere were the far-reaching consequences of such cosmogenic mythology more evident than in the pseudoscience of eugenics. Eugenics hypothesized that the gene pool was being corrupted by the less fit genes of inferior people. As a result, segments of our society—including Jews and blacks—were subjected to state–sanctioned sterilization. Thankfully, eugenics has faded into the shadowy recesses of history for now. The tragic consequences of the evolutionary dogma that birthed it, however, are yet with us today.

For further study, see Hank Hanegraaff, *Fatal Flaws* (Nashville: W Publishing Group, 2003).

ROMANS 1:28

"Since they did not think it worthwhile to retain the knowledge of God, he gave them over to a depraved mind, to do what ought not to be done."

IS EVOLUTIONISM RACIST?

irst, while not all evolutionists are racists, the theory of evolution is racist in the extreme. In his book *The Descent of Man* Charles Darwin speculated, "At some future period, not very distant as measured by centuries, the civilized races of man will almost certainly exterminate, and replace, the savage races throughout the world." In addition, he subtitled his magnum opus *The Preservation of Favored Races in the Struggle for Life*." Thomas Huxley, who coined the term *agnostic* and was the man most responsible for advancing Darwinian doctrine, went so far as to say, "No rational man cognizant of the facts, believes that the average Negro is the equal, still less the superior, of the white man." Huxley was not only militantly racist but also lectured frequently against the resurrection of Jesus Christ in whom "[we] are all one" (Galatians 3:28).

Furthermore, for evolution to succeed, it is as crucial that the unfit die as that the fittest survive. Marvin Lubenow graphically portrays the ghastly consequences of such beliefs in his book *Bones of Contention*: "If the unfit survived indefinitely, they would continue to 'infect' the fit with their less fit genes. The result is that the more fit genes would be diluted and compromised by the less fit genes, and evolution could not take place." Adolf Hitler's philosophy that Jews were subhuman and that Aryans were supermen led to the extermination of six million Jews. In the words of Sir Arthur Keith, a militant anti-Christian physical anthropologist: "The German Fuhrer, as I have consistently maintained, is an evolutionist; he has consistently sought to make the practices of Germany conform to the theory of evolution." It is significant to note that crusaders who used force to further their creeds in the name of God were acting in direct opposition to the teachings of Christ, while the worldview of Hitler, however, was completely consistent with the teachings of Darwin. Indeed, social Darwinism has provided the scientific substructure for some of the most significant atrocities in human history.

Finally, while the evolutionary racism of Darwin's day is politically incorrect today, current biology textbooks still promote vestiges of racism. For example, the inherently racist recapitulation theory* not only is common fare in science curricula but has been championed in our generation by such luminaries as Carl Sagan. This despite the fact that modern studies in molecular genetics have demonstrated the utter falsity of the recapitulation theory. The fact that recapitulation is inherently racist is underscored by no less an evolutionary authority than Stephen Jay Gould who lamented that "recapitulation provided a convenient focus for the pervasive racism of white scientists" in the modern era.

ADAPTED FROM *Fatal Flaws*

For further study, see Hank Hanegraaff, *Fatal Flaws: What Evolutionists Don't Want You to Know* (Nashville: W Publishing, 2003).

GENESIS 1:27

"God created man in his own image,
in the image of God he created them; male and
female he created them."

*Recapitulation theory, better known by the popular evolutionary phrase, "Ontogeny recapitulates phylogeny," is the odd predilection that in the course of an embryo's development the embryo repeats or recapitulates the evolutionary history of its species.

—126—

WHAT ABOUT "THEISTIC EVOLUTION"?

U nder the banner of "theistic evolution," a growing number of Christians maintain that God used evolution as his method for creation. This, in my estimation, is the worst of all possibilities. It is one thing to believe in evolution; it is quite another to blame God for it. Not only is *theistic evolution* a contradiction in terms—like the phrase *flaming snowflakes*—but in the words of the Nobel prize-winning evolutionist Jacques Monod:

"[Natural] selection is the blindest, and most cruel way of evolving new species. . . . The struggle for life and elimination of the weakest is a horrible process, against which our whole modern ethic revolts. . . . I am surprised that a Christian would defend the idea that this is the process which God more or less set up in order to have evolution."

First, the biblical account of creation specifically states that God created living creatures according to their own "kinds" (Genesis 1:24–25) As confirmed by science, the DNA for a fetus is not the DNA for a frog, and the DNA for a frog is not the DNA for a fish. Rather the DNA of a fetus, frog, or fish is uniquely programmed for reproduction after its own kind. Thus while the Bible allows for *micro*evolution (transitions within "the kinds") it does not allow for *macro*evolution (amoebas evolving into apes or apes evolving into astronauts).

Furthermore, evolutionary biology cannot account for metaphysical realities such as ego and ethos. Without data demonstrating that physical processes can produce metaphysical realities, there is no warrant for dogmatically declaring that humans evolved from hominids.

Finally, an omnipotent, omniscient God does not have to painfully plod through millions of mistakes, misfits, and mutations in order to have fellowship with humans. As the biblical account of creation confirms he can create humans instantaneously (Genesis 2:7).

Evolutionism is fighting for its very life. Rather than prop it up with theories like theistic evolution, thinking people everywhere must be on the vanguard of demonstrating its demise.

ADAPTED FROM Fatal Flaws

For further study, see J. P. Moreland and John Mark Reynolds, eds., *Three Views on Creation and Evolution* (Grand Rapids: Zondervan Publishing House, 1999).

"The God who made the world and everything in it is the Lord of heaven and earth and does not live in temples built by hands. And he is not served by human hands, as if he needed anything, because he himself gives all men life and breath and everything else. From one man he made every nation of men, that they should inhabit the whole earth; and he determined the times set for them and the exact places where they should live. God did this so that men would seek him and perhaps reach out for him and find him, though he is not far from each one of us."

–127–

Did Darwin have a deathbed conversion?

In order to demonstrate the falsity of evolution, Bible-believing Christians for more than a century have passed on the story of Charles Darwin's deathbed conversion. Evolutionists have attempted to counter them by loudly protesting that Darwin died believing that Christianity was a fraud and that chance was the creator.

In response, it should first be noted that whether Darwin did or did not renounce evolution does *not* speak to the issue of whether or not evolution is true or false. Maybe Darwin renounced evolution because he was senile or he had taken a mind-altering drug. He may have even just hedged his bets with some "eternal fire insurance."

Furthermore, as followers of the One who proclaimed himself to be not only "the way" and "the life" but also "the truth" (John 14:6) we must set the standard for the evolutionist, *not* vice versa. James Fegan was correct in calling the Darwin legend "an

illustration of the recklessness with which the Protestant Controversialists seek to support any cause they are advocating."

Finally, in *The Darwin Legend*, James Moore painstakingly documents the fact that there is *no* substantial evidence that Darwin ever repented, but there is abundant evidence that he consistently held to his evolutionary paradigm.

For further study, see James Moore, *The Darwin Legend* (Grand Rapids: Baker Books, 1994).

EXODUS 20:16
*"You shall not give
false testimony against your neighbor."*

Is intelligent design really science?

Richard Dawkins, professor of the public understanding of science at Oxford and arguably the best-known Darwinist on the planet, claims those who do not believe in evolution are "ignorant, stupid or insane." But in place of rhetoric and emotional stereotypes, intelligent design (ID) proponents actually propose reason and empirical science.

First, ID proponents are willing to follow scientific evidence wherever it leads. ID theorists neither presuppose nor preclude supernatural explanations for the phenomena they encounter in an information-rich universe. As such, the ID movement rightly practices open-minded science.

Furthermore, ID begins with the common scientific principle that intelligent design is detectable wherever there is specified, organized complexity (i.e., "information"). This design principle is central to many scientific fields, including archaeology, forensic pathology, crime scene investigation, cryptology, and the search for extra–terrestrial intelligence (SETI). When applied to information–rich DNA, irreducibly complex biochemical systems, the Cambrian Explosion in the fossil record, as well as the fact that earth is perfectly situated in the Milky Way for both life and scientific discovery, the existence of an intelligent designer is the most plausible scientific explanation.

When applied to information–rich DNA, irreducibly complex biochemical systems, the Cambrian Explosion in the fossil record, as well as the fact that earth is perfectly situated in the Milky Way for both life and scientific discovery, the existence of an intelligent designer is the most plausible scientific explanation.

Finally, although its conclusions are not worldview–neutral, ID lends no more support to Christian theism than Darwinian evolution lends to atheism. Thus, the appropriateness of ID for public education ought to be judged on the basis of the theory's explanatory power, not on its metaphysical implications.

For further study, see William Dembski, *The Design Revolution* (Grand Rapids: IVP, 2004); see also Francis J. Beckwith, "Intelligent Design in the Schools: Is It Constitutional?" *Christian*

Research Journal 25, 4 (2003) available through the Christian Research Institute (CRI) at www.equip.org.

ROMANS 1:20

"For since the creation of the world God's invisible qualities—his eternal power and divine nature—have been clearly seen, being understood from what has been made, so that men are without excuse."

ETHICS

IS IT EVER MORALLY PERMISSIBLE TO LIE?

n the interest of truth, I should first disclose the fact that Christian theologians are divided on this subject. Some—like Saint Augustine—believed that it is never permissible to lie. Others—like Dietrich Bonhoeffer, who had ample time to contemplate this issue from the perspective of a Nazi prison cell—held that under certain circumstances lying was not only morally permissible but morally mandated. Thus, Bonhoeffer advocated deceiving the enemy in circumstances of war, and he had no compunction about lying in order to facilitate escape for Jews facing extermination.

Furthermore, while the Bible never condones lying *qua* lying (lying for the sake of lying), it does condone lying in order to preserve a higher moral imperative. For example, Rahab purposed to deceive (the lesser moral law) in order to preserve the lives of two Jewish spies (the higher moral law). Likewise, a Christian father today should not hesitate to lie in order to protect his wife and daughters from the imminent threat of rape or murder.

Finally, there is a difference between *lying* and *not telling the truth*. This is not merely a matter of semantics; it is a matter of substance. By way of analogy, there is a difference between unjustified and justified homicide. Murder is unjustified homicide and is always wrong. Not every instance of killing a person, however, is murder. Capital punishment and self-defense occasion justified homicide. Similarly, in the case of a lie (Annanias and Sapphira, Acts 5) there is an unjustified discrepancy between what you believe and what you say, and so *lying* is always wrong. But *not telling the truth* in order to preserve a higher moral law (Rahab, Joshua 2) may well be the right thing to do and thus is not actually a lie.

For further study, see Norman L. Geisler, *Christian Ethics: Options and Issues* (Grand Rapids: Baker Book House, 1989), chapter 7.

JOSHUA 2:3–6

"The king of Jericho sent this message to Rahab: 'Bring out the men who came to you and entered your house, because they have come to spy out the whole land.' But the woman had taken the two men and

hidden them. She said, 'Yes, the men came to me,
but I did not know where they had come from.
At dusk, when it was time to close the city gate, the
men left. I don't know which way they went. Go after
them quickly. You may catch up with them.' (But she
had taken them up to the roof and hidden them under
the stalks of flax she had laid out on the roof.)"

IS CAPITAL PUNISHMENT BIBLICAL?

Christians who believe in capital punishment and those who do not both use the Bible to buttress their beliefs. So, what does the Bible really teach regarding capital punishment?

To begin with, it should be noted that in the very first book of the Bible God clearly communicates his position with respect to capital punishment: "Whoever sheds the blood of man, by man shall his blood be shed; for in the image of God has God made man" (Genesis 9:6). It is instructive to note that this passage not only predates the Mosaic Law, but it demands universal adherence to the sanctity of life.

Furthermore, in Exodus 21 and Deuteronomy 19 the Bible reaffirms God's perspective on capital punishment by underscoring the principle of "life for life." To murder a person who is made in the image of God is not only to show contempt for the apex of God's creation but also to show contempt for the Creator himself. Thus, while capital punishment may be reprehensible from a secular perspective, it is basic to a biblical worldview.

Finally, capital punishment is implicitly validated in the New Testament. Jesus acknowledged the legitimacy of capital punishment before Pilate (John 19:11), as did the apostle Paul before the Roman governor Festus (Acts 25:11). Not only so, but one of the thieves crucified with Christ had the candor to confess, "We are punished justly, for we are getting what our deeds deserve" (Luke 23:41). Moreover, Romans 13 implies that the failure of the governing authorities to apply the "sword"—the Roman symbol for capital punishment—exalts evil and eradicates equity.

In short, God instituted capital punishment in the earliest stages of human civilization before the Mosaic Law, and capital punishment is never abrogated by Jesus or the apostles. Thus, capital punishment appears to be an enduring moral principle undergirding the sanctity of life.

For further study, see Hank Hanegraaff "Karla Faye Tucker and Capital Punishment," available from CRI at www.equip.org; See also J. Daryl Charles, "Sentiments as Social Justice: The Ethics of Capital Punishment," *Christian Research Journal,* Spring/Summer 1994.

*"And from each man too, I will demand an accounting
for the life of his fellow man. Whoever sheds the
blood of man, by man shall his blood be shed; for in
the image of God has God made man."*

Is suicide an unforgivable sin?

n a society of stressed–out people, suicide is not a singularly secular problem. Nor is it relegated to any particular segment of society. Indeed, according to the Centers for Disease Control, suicide is the third leading cause of death among young people ages fifteen to twenty–four. As the incidence of suicide continues to skyrocket, I am frequently asked whether suicide is an unforgivable sin.

First, no single act is unforgivable. The unforgivable sin is a *continuous, ongoing* rejection of forgiveness. Those who refuse forgiveness through Christ will spend eternity separated from his love and grace. Conversely, those who sincerely desire forgiveness can be absolutely certain that God will never spurn them.

Furthermore, while suicide is not an unforgivable sin, those who take the sacred name of Christ upon their lips dare not contemplate it. Our lives belong to God and he alone has the prerogative to bring them to an end. In the words of the Almighty, "See now that I myself am He! There is no god beside me. *I put to death and bring to life*, I have wounded and I heal, and no one can deliver out of my hand" (Deuteronomy 32:39, emphasis added).

No single act is unforgivable. The unforgivable sin is a continuous, ongoing rejection of forgiveness.

Finally, suicide is the murder of oneself. As such it is a direct violation of the sixth commandment— "you shall not murder" (Exodus 20:13; cf. Genesis 9:6). Indeed, suicide is a direct attack on the sovereignty of the very One who knit us together in our mothers' wombs (Psalm 139:13).

For further study, see Hank Hanegraaff, "How can I be certain I've not committed the unforgivable sin?" *The Bible Answer Book Volume 1* (Nashville: J Countryman, 2004): 22–25.

REVELATION 21:8

"But the cowardly, the unbelieving, the vile,
the murderers, the sexually immoral, those who
practice magic arts, the idolaters and all liars—
their place will be in the fiery lake of burning sulfur.
This is the second death."

IS EUTHANASIA EVER PERMISSIBLE?

rganizations such as the Hemlock Society are aggressively seeking to legalize euthanasia (Greek: *eu* = good; *thanatos* = death). In their view "mercy murders" for the diseased, disabled, and dying is a step into the light. From a Christian perspective it is a step into the dark.

First, in Christian theology the timing and terms of death are the province of God alone (Deuteronomy 32:39). As such, a doctor is never permitted to usurp the prerogative of deity. Hastening death based on subjective judgments concerning one's quality of life is a direct violation of Scripture (cf. Genesis 9:6; Exodus 20:13). While passive euthanasia is morally permissible in that it allows the process of dying to run its natural course, active euthanasia is morally prohibited because it directly involves the taking of human life.

Furthermore, from a biblical perspective suffering "produces perseverance; perseverance, character; and character, hope" (Romans 5:3–4). Like suffering for our faith, physical suffering has redemptive value. It may be likened unto a furnace that rids us of the dross and fashions us more and more like unto our Lord. In the words of Charles Haddon Spurgeon, "I am certain that I never grew in grace one half as much anywhere as I have on the bed of pain." Or as C. S. Lewis put it, "God whispers to us in our pleasures, speaks in our conscience, but shouts in our pains: it is his megaphone to rouse a deaf world." This, of course, is not to say that there is virtue in needless suffering. To mitigate suffering through the modern medical miracle of pain management is consistent with both the Hippocratic Oath and biblical morality.

We are not called to come to peaceful terms with death; we are called to overcome death through resurrection.

Finally, permitting voluntary active euthanasia opens the door to the greater evil of non–voluntary euthanasia. It is not difficult to imagine financial pressures coercing the diseased, disabled, and dying to surrender to doctor–assisted suicide so as not to burden their families. Worse still, doctors and nursing-home directors may take it upon themselves to euthanize patients without their consent and without the family's knowledge (*crypthanasia* =

"hidden death"). There is ample evidence that this is already occurring at an alarming rate in places like the Netherlands where euthanasia has slid down the slippery slope into crypthanasia.

Cultural thanatologists may urge us to accept death as a friend, but Christian theology sees death as the enemy. We are not called to come to peaceful terms with death; we are called to overcome death through resurrection. As my father told me in the final stages of his life, "Hank, though painful, every moment is precious."

For further study, see J. P. Moreland's two-part *Christian Research Journal* series on "The Euthanasia Debate" available through the Christian Research Institute (CRI) at www.equip.org; see also Scott B. Rae, *Moral Choices*, 2nd ed. (Grand Rapids: Zondervan, 2000).

DEUTERONOMY 32:39

"See now that I myself am He! There is no God beside me. I put to death and I bring to life, I have wounded and I will heal, and no one can deliver out of my hand."

IS CREMATION CONSISTENT
WITH THE CHRISTIAN WORLDVIEW?

remation has become an increasingly popular means for disposing of the dead. In fact, by the year 2010, it is estimated that one-third of all Americans will cremate their loved ones. While those who opt for cremation often do so on the basis of emotional, economical, or ecological considerations, there are compelling reasons for Christians to choose burial.

First, Scripture clearly favors burial over cremation. The Old Testament pattern was always burial except in highly unusual circumstances. Likewise, in the New Testament Paul equates baptism with both burial and resurrection (Romans 6:4).

Furthermore, burial symbolizes the promise of resurrection by anticipating the preservation of the body. Cremation, however, better symbolizes the pagan worldview of reincarnation. While resurrectionists look forward to the restoration of the body, reincarnationists look forward to being relieved from their bodies.

Finally, burial highlights the sanctity of the body. In the Christian worldview, the body is significant in that it has numerical identity to the resurrected body. Thus, while God has no problem resurrecting the cremated, cremation does not point to the resurrection of God.

Adapted from Resurrection

For further study, see Hank Hanegraaff, *Resurrection* (Nashville: Word Publishing, 2000), chapter 15; and Norman L. Geisler and Douglas E. Potter, "From Ashes to Ashes: Is Burial the Only Christian Option?" Available from CRI at www.equip.org.

ROMANS 6:4

"We were therefore buried with him through baptism into death in order that, just as Christ was raised from the dead through the glory of the Father, we too may live a new life."

Today tolerance is being redefined to mean that all views are equally valid and all lifestyles equally appropriate. As such, the notion that Jesus is the only way is vilified as the epitome of intolerance. Rather than capitulating to culture, Christians must be equipped to expose the flaws of today's tolerance, while simultaneously exemplifying true tolerance.

First, to say all views are equally valid sounds tolerant but in reality is a contradiction in terms. If indeed all views are equally valid, then the Christian view must be valid. The Christian view, however, holds that not all views are equally valid. Thus, the redefinition of tolerance in our culture is a self–refuting proposition. Moreover, we do not tolerate people with whom we agree; we tolerate people with whom we disagree. If all views were equally valid, there would be no need for tolerance.

Furthermore, today's redefinition of tolerance leaves no room for objective moral judgments. A modern terrorist could be deemed as virtuous as a

Mother Teresa. With no enduring reference point, societal norms are being reduced to mere matters of preference. As such, the moral basis for resolving international disputes and condemning such intuitively evil practices as genocide, oppression of women, and child prostitution is being seriously compromised.

Christians must be equipped to expose the flaws of today's tolerance, while simultaneously exemplifying true tolerance.... True tolerance entails that, despite our differences, we treat every person we meet with the dignity and respect due them as those created in the image of God. True tolerance does not preclude proclaiming the truth, but it does mandate that we do so with gentleness and with respect.... Tolerance when it comes to personal relationships is a virtue, but tolerance when it comes to truth is a travesty.

Finally, in light of its philosophically fatal features, Christians must reject today's tolerance and revive true tolerance. True tolerance entails that, despite our differences, we treat every person we meet with the dignity and respect due them as those created in the image of God. True tolerance does not preclude proclaiming the truth, but it does mandate that we do so with gentleness and with respect (cf. 1 Peter 3:15–16). In a world that is increasingly intolerant of Christianity, Christians must exemplify tolerance without sacrificing truth. Indeed, tolerance when it comes to personal relationships is a virtue, but tolerance when it comes to truth is a travesty.

For further study, see Paul Copan, "*True for You, but not for Me*": *Deflating the Slogans That Leave Christians Speechless* (Minneapolis: Bethany House Publishers, 1998); see also Josh McDowell and Bob Hostetler, *The New Tolerance* (Wheaton, IL: Tyndale House Publishers, 1998).

JUDE 1:22–23

"Be merciful to those who doubt; snatch others from the fire and save them; to others show mercy, mixed with fear—hating even the clothing stained by corrupted flesh."

HOW DO BIBLICAL ETHICS APPLY
TO HERMAPHRODITES?

he term "hermaphrodite" is derived from conjoining the name of the Greek god Hermes with the Greek goddess Aphrodite. Today, hermaphroditism is appropriately referred to as "intersex" or as a "disorder of sex development" (DSD). Regardless of the term used, confusion reigns on how to respond to this disorder.

First, intersex refers to the rare condition of individuals who are born with both male and female reproductive organs and sex glands, and in even rarer cases both XX and XY chromosomes. The medical treatment for this disorder involves the surgical and hormonal "assignment" of gender, which ideally should be made on the basis of all the relevant factors (e.g., chromosomal, neural, psychological, behavioral, and the like). If there is reasonable certainty that a medical mistake was made in the assignment of gender, it would not be beyond biblical bounds to prayerfully consider reassignment. As with the treatment of any rare disorder, gender assignment is complex and subject to human error; thus, it is crucial to seek the most competent biblical and medical counsel.

Being born with genetic, psychological, or hormonal abnormalities is no more license for sexual sin than being born with violent tendencies is license for violence. Thus, if a same—sex attraction develops, celibacy and singleness, as opposed to homosexual licentiousness, is the proper response.

Furthermore, being born with genetic, psychological, or hormonal abnormalities is no more license for sexual sin than being born with violent tendencies is license for violence. Thus, if a same—sex attraction develops, celibacy and singleness, as opposed to homosexual licentiousness, is the proper response (cf. 1 Corinthians 7:8). Indeed, anyone suffering from gender confusion should not pursue marriage until the confusion has been biblically resolved. Though this may seem harsh, it is no different than the requirement placed on all believers to die to sin and live for righteousness through the power of Christ with the help of the Holy Spirit (Romans 6).

Finally, it is crucial to recognize that all disorders, diseases, deformities, decay, and death ultimately result from the Fall. While sin, suffering, and sickness are present realities, we have the certain promise that "in all things God works for the good of those who love him, who have been called according to his purpose" (Romans 8:28).

For further study, see Scott B. Rae, *Moral Choices*, 2nd ed. (Grand Rapids: Zondervan, 2000).

JOHN 9:1–3

"As he went along, he saw a man blind from birth. His disciples asked him, 'Rabbi, who sinned, this man or his parents, that he was born blind?' 'Neither this man nor his parents sinned,' said Jesus, 'but this happened so that the work of God might be displayed in his life.'"

WHAT'S THE PROBLEM WITH PORNOGRAPHY?

exually explicit images are as near as the click of a mouse. Consequently, pornography has become pandemic. As Joe Dallas has aptly noted, pornography is not only an enslaving addiction and a violation of marriage vows but a precursor to increasingly dangerous and degrading sexual practices.

First, pornography is an addictive behavior that enslaves the mind and conditions users to view others as mere objects of self-gratification. As such, our Lord warns us to guard our gaze: "The eye is the lamp of the body. If your eyes are good, your whole body will be full of light. But if your eyes are bad, your whole body will be full of darkness. If then the light within you is darkness, how great is that darkness!" (Matthew 6:22–23).

Furthermore, pornography breaks the sacred bond of marriage and, as such, tears apart the very fabric of society. Moreover, when pornographic images are used to satisfy sexual desire, a marriage partner is defrauded. In the Sermon on the Mount,

Jesus rendered lustful visual encounters the moral equivalent of extramarital sexual relations (Matthew 5:28).

Finally, just as marijuana is a precursor to experimenting with ever more dangerous substances, so pornography often leads to increasingly degrading sexual behaviors. Says James: "Each one is tempted when, by his own evil desire, he is dragged away and enticed. Then, after desire has conceived, it gives birth to sin; and sin, when it is full–grown, gives birth to death" (James 1:14–15).

Pornography is an addictive behavior that enslaves the mind and conditions users to view others as mere objects of self–gratification. . . . Pornography breaks the sacred bond of marriage. . . . Pornography often leads to increasingly degrading sexual behaviors.

Thankfully, even the strongest addiction to pornography can be overcome by taking practical steps to remove the temptation, by establishing an accountability structure, and by putting on the full armor of God (Ephesians 6:10–20). The covering described in Scripture as the full armor of God is an impenetrable barrier against which the fiery darts of the evil one are impotent. When we are clothed in the covering, we are invincible. When we are not, we are but pawns in the devil's malevolent schemes.

For further study, see Joe Dallas, "Darkening Our Minds: The Problem of Pornography among Christians," *Christian Research Journal* 27, 3 (2004): 12–21.

1 CORINTHIANS 10:13

"No temptation has seized you except what is common to man. And God is faithful; he will not let you be tempted beyond what you can bear. But when you are tempted, he will also provide a way out so that you can stand up under it."

DOES HOMOSEXUALITY DEMONSTRATE
THAT THE BIBLE IS
ANTIQUATED AND IRRELEVANT?

 popular sentiment today is that the Bible is increasingly irrelevant in a modern age of scientific enlightenment. Thus, when the Scripture's condemnation of homosexuality is referenced, it is not uncommon to see expressions of polite exasperation etched on the faces of the masses. After all, the Bible not only condemns homosexuality but also clearly teaches that Sabbath breakers must be put to death (Exodus 35:2).

First, it should be noted that while Sabbath-breaking had serious ramifications within ancient Israel, it is not a precedent for executing people today. Not only are we no longer under the civil and ceremonial laws of a Jewish theocratic form of government, but as the apostle Paul explains, the symbolism of the law has been fulfilled in Christ (Galatians 3:13–14). In his letter to the Colossian Christians, Paul underscores the Christian's freedom from adherence to Sabbath laws by pointing out that "these are a shadow of the things that were to come; the reality, however, is found in Christ" (Colossians 2:17). Thus, there is an obvious difference between enduring moral principles regarding homosexuality and temporary civil and ceremonial laws relegated to a particular historical context.

Furthermore, we would do well to recognize that the God of the Bible does not condemn homosexuality in an arbitrary and capricious fashion. Rather he carefully defines the borders of human sexuality so that our joy may be complete. It does not require an advanced degree in physiology to appreciate the fact that the human body is not designed for homosexual relationships. Spurious slogans and sound bites do not change the scientific reality that homosexual relationships are devastating not only from a psychological but also from a physiological perspective.

Finally, far from being irrelevant and antiquated, the Bible's warnings regarding homosexuality are eerily relevant and up to date. The book of Romans aptly describes both the perversion and the penalty: "Their women exchanged natural relations for unnatural ones. In the same way the men also abandoned natural relations with women and were inflamed with lust for one another. Men committed indecent acts with other men, and *received in themselves the due penalty for their perversion*" (1:26–27, emphasis added). It would be difficult to miss the relationship between Paul's words and the current health-care holocaust. More people already have died worldwide from AIDS than the United States of America has lost in all its wars combined. This is but the tip of an insidious iceberg. The homosexual lifestyle causes a host of complications including hemorrhoids, prostate damage, and infectious fissures. And even that merely scratches the surface. Nonviral infections transmitted through homosexual activity include gonorrhea, chlamydia, and syphilis. Viral infections involve condylomata, herpes, and hepatitis A and B.

While there are attendant moral and medical problems with sexual promiscuity in general, it would be homophobic in the extreme to obscure the scientific realities concerning homosexuality. It is a hate crime of unparalleled proportions to attempt to keep a whole segment of the population in the dark concerning such issues. Thus, far from demonstrating that the Bible is out of step with the times, its warnings regarding homosexuality demonstrate that it is as relevant today as it was in the beginning.

For further study, see Joe Dallas, *A Strong Delusion: Confronting the "Gay Christian" Movement* (Eugene, Ore.: Harvest House Publishers, 1996). See also Hank Hanegraaff, "President Bartlett's Fallacious Diatribe," available at www.equip.org.

ROMANS 1:26–27

"Even their women exchanged natural relations for unnatural ones. In the same way the men also abandoned natural relations with women and were inflamed with lust for one another. Men committed indecent acts with other men, and received in themselves the due penalty for their perversion."

SHOULD CHRISTIANS USE BIRTH CONTROL?

n light of recent advances in biotechnology
it is crucial to consider the issue of birth
control through the lens of a biblical
worldview.

First, while there is much debate among
Christians on the question of whether birth control
is appropriate in any form, there is no question that
birth control methods designed to destroy or prevent
the implantation of a fertilized egg (i.e., embryo)
should be avoided at all costs. From the moment of
conception, an embryo is a living, growing person
made in the image in God (Genesis 1:26–27; 9:6;
Exodus 20:13). Thus, the "abortion pill" (RU486)
must never be used! Similarly, the "morning after
pill" and oral contraceptives (i.e., the birth control
pill) must not be used because they are designed not
only to prevent fertilization but also to prevent
uterine implantation if fertilization should occur.

Furthermore, the necessary openness to children
that accompanies the sexual union serves to protect
against the abuse of sex for mere self–gratification.

When birth-control methods are employed out of a selfish unwillingness to have children, sex can quickly degenerate into nothing more than what Oxford's Oliver O'Donovan has aptly described as "a profound form of play."

Birth-control methods designed to destroy or prevent the implantation of a fertilized egg (i.e., embryo) should be avoided at all costs.

Finally, it is imperative that children be viewed as a blessing from above rather than a burden or blight. While birth control may be used for reasons of health or financial stewardship, birth control should never be employed out of purely selfish motives. If we consider a Cadillac more valuable than a child, our priorities are seriously skewed. Such an attitude toward the miracle of life and the blessings of parenthood pains our Father in heaven.

For further study, see Randy Alcorn, *Does the Birth Control Pill Cause Abortion?* 7th ed. (Gresham, Ore.: Eternal Perspective Ministries, 1997).

*"Then little children were brought to Jesus for him
to place his hands on them and pray for them.
But the disciples rebuked those who brought them.
Jesus said, 'Let the little children come to me,
and do not hinder them, for the kingdom
of heaven belongs to such as these.'"*

SHOULD CHRISTIANS USE
IN VITRO FERTILIZATION?

n vitro—literally "in glass"—fertilization
(IVF) is an increasingly popular form of
reproductive technology that should raise
significant moral concerns in the hearts and minds
of believers.

First, there are major moral concerns associated
with using biotechnology in place of the natural
means for procreation. The fertilization of an egg in
a glass dish can lead to viewing children as products
to be made (and disposed of) rather than gifts from
God. Indeed, IVF is already being used in the
production and genetic selection of "designer
babies." It is imperative that we guard against subtle
shifts in thinking that ultimately lead to the erosion
of our Christian worldview.

Furthermore, the introduction of third parties
through sperm or egg donation or through surrogate
motherhood is inconsistent with the biblical pattern
of continuity between procreation and parenthood
(Genesis 1:28; 2:24). Accordingly, if IVF is used at

all, the sperm and the egg must come from the husband and wife committed to raising the child. The potentially disastrous consequences of third–party involvement are clearly demonstrated in the lives of Abram, Sarai, and Hagar (Genesis 16).

Finally, because it is an established scientific fact that human life begins at conception (an embryo has a distinct human genetic code and exhibits metabolism, development, the ability to react to stimuli, and cell reproduction), discarding embryos or destroying them through experimentation is the moral equivalent of killing innocent human beings. Freezing embryos is likewise morally objectionable. Thus, if IVF is used, no more eggs should be fertilized than the couple is willing to give a reasonable chance at full–term life.

For further study, see Joni Eareckson Tada and Nigel M. de S. Cameron, *How to be a Christian in a Brave New World* (Grand Rapids: Zondervan, 2006).

PSALM 139:13–14

"For you created my inmost being; you knit me together in my mother's womb. I praise you because I am fearfully and wonderfully made; your works are wonderful, I know that full well."

WHAT IS ABORTION?

Those who continue to fight legislation restricting abortion are in reality *not* "pro-choice." Rather, they are singularly "pro-murder." While rhetoric has served to camouflage the carnage of abortion, it remains the *painful killing of an innocent human being.*

First, abortion is *painful* in that the methods employed to kill a preborn child involve burning, smothering, dismembering, and crushing. And such procedures are executed on live babies who have not been specifically anesthetized.

Furthermore, abortion involves *killing*. The zygote, which fulfills the criteria needed to establish the existence of biological life (metabolism, development, the ability to react to stimuli, and cell reproduction), is indeed terminated. In *Woman and the New Race*, Planned Parenthood founder Margaret Sanger tacitly acknowledged this point when she wrote: "The most merciful thing a large family can do for one of its infant members is to kill it."

Finally, abortion kills innocent *human beings*. The child who is terminated is the product of human parents and has a totally distinct human genetic code. Although the emerging embryo does not have a fully developed personality, it does have complete personhood from the moment of conception. Thus, far from deserving capital punishment, these innocent humans deserve care and protection.

Thankfully, in God's economy there is hope for those who have experienced the ravages of abortion. Not only can they receive God's forgiveness in the here and now, but they can yet look forward to the ecstasy of reuniting with their unborn loved ones in eternity.

ADAPTED FROM *The FACE*

For further study, see Francis J. Beckwith, *Politically Correct Death: Answering the Arguments for Abortion Rights*, (Grand Rapids: Baker Books, 1993).

PSALM 139:13–16

"For you created my inmost being; you knit me together in my mother's womb. I praise you because I am fearfully and wonderfully made; your works are wonderful, I know that full well. My frame was not hidden from you when I was made in the secret place. When I was woven together in the depths of the earth, your eyes saw my unformed body."

SHOULD ABORTION BE PERMITTED
IN THE CASE OF RAPE OR INCEST?

W hen the subject of abortion comes up, rape and incest are often used as an emotional appeal designed to deflect serious consideration of the pro–life position: "How can anyone deny a hurting woman safe medical care and freedom from the terror of rape or incest by forcing her to maintain a pregnancy resulting from the cruel and criminal invasion of her body?" The emotion of the argument often precludes serious examination of its merits.

First, it is important to note that the incidence of pregnancy as a result of rape is rare with studies estimating that approximately 1 percent to 4.7 percent of rapes result in pregancy. Thus lobbying for abortion on the basis of rape and incest is like lobbying for the removal of red lights because you might have to run one in order to rescue someone who is about to commit suicide. Even if we had legislation restricting abortion for all reasons other than rape or incest, we would save the vast majority of the 1.8 million preborn babies who die annually in the United States through abortion.

Furthermore, one does not obviate the real pain of rape or incest by compounding it with the murder of an innocent preborn child. Two wrongs do not make a right. The very thing that makes rape evil also makes abortion evil. In both cases, an innocent human being is brutally dehumanized.

The very thing that makes rape evil also makes abortion evil. In both cases, an innocent human being is brutally dehumanized.

Finally, the real question is whether abortion is the murder of an innocent human being. If so, abortion should be avoided at all costs. In an age of scientific enlightenment we now know that the embryo even at its earliest stages fulfills the criteria needed to establish the existence of biological life (including metabolism, development, the ability to react to stimuli, and cell reproduction); that a zygote is a living human being as demonstrated by its distinct genetic code; and that human personhood does not depend on size, location, or level of dependence.

Thus, abortion should be avoided even in cases of rape and incest.

For further study, see Hank Hanegraaff, "Annihilating Abortion Arguments," available through the Christian Research Institute (CRI) at www.equip.org.

PROVERBS 17:15

*"Acquitting the guilty and condemning the innocent—
the LORD detests them both."*

SHOULD CHRISTIANS SUPPORT A BAN ON EMBRYONIC STEM CELL RESEARCH?

n 2004 the cash–strapped state of California passed Proposition 71, allocating three billion dollars to finance the cloning of human embryos and their subsequent destruction through embryonic stem cell research. Support for this proposition was largely influenced by celebrities such as Brad Pitt, Nancy Reagan, and the late Christopher Reeve who reiterated the biotech industry's promises that embryonic stem cell research will lead to cures for debilitating diseases and spinal cord injuries. Other celebrities such as Mel Gibson and Joni Eareckson Tada, herself a paraplegic, rightly responded that all who are concerned for the sanctity of human life must support a complete ban on the use of this technology.

First, while an embryo does not have a fully developed personality, it does have full personhood from the moment of conception. You did not *come* from an adolescent; you once *were* an adolescent. Likewise, you did not *come* from an embryo; you once *were* an embryo. All human beings are created in the image of God and endowed with the right to life, regardless of size, location, or level of dependency. Make no mistake about it, extracting stem cells from an embryo kills the embryo.

Furthermore, while we should sympathize with those who suffer from debilitating diseases and injuries, cures and therapies must be sought within appropriate moral boundaries. Killing human embryos in the search for cures is tantamount to subjecting one class of people to harmful experimentation for the sake of another. To do so violates the biblical injunction against murdering humans made in the image of God (Genesis 1:26–27; 9:5–6), as well as the Nuremberg Code compiled by the tribunal responsible for judging the Nazis after World War II.

All who are concerned for the sanctity of human life must support a complete ban on the use of this technology.

Finally, in light of the promising results of adult stem cell research, state funding for the destruction of embryos is not only morally repugnant but fiscally irresponsible. Stem cells extracted from non–embryonic sources such as bone marrow, blood, brain cells, and baby teeth are similar to embryonic stem cells in their ability to grow into multiple types of tissues. While embryonic stem cells used in research have demonstrated a tendency to grow into tumors, adult stem cells have already shown success in human trials for treatment of multiple sclerosis, sickle cell anemia, stroke, Parkinson's disease, and more. The frightening conclusion is that the fervor over embryonic stem cell research is more a pretext for human cloning than a context for responsible medical progress.

For further study, see Charles W. Colson and Nigel M. de S. Cameron, *Human Dignity in the Biotech Century: A Christian Vision for Public Policy* (Downers Grove, Ill.: InterVarsity Press, 2004).

PROVERBS 24:11–12

*"Rescue those being led away to death;
hold back those staggering toward slaughter. If you say,
'But we knew nothing about this,' does not he
who weighs the heart perceive it? Does not he who
guards your life know it? Will he not repay each
person according to what he has done?"*

CAN HUMAN CLONING BE HARMONIZED
WITH A CHRISTIAN WORLDVIEW?

s has been well said, "The only thing necessary for evil to triumph is for good men to do nothing." The stark reality of this sentiment was borne out in 1973 when Christians quietly passed by a major battle in the war against abortion. Two and a half decades later, the far-reaching impact of that loss is being felt in a raging debate over human cloning. While Pandora's box is already open, Christians must do all that is permissible to prevent a human clone from emerging.

First, the issues concerning cloning and abortion are inextricably woven together. In other words, the prevailing logic that permits a woman to terminate the life of a child in the womb may well equally apply to cloning. For example, if defects were detected in developing clones, abortion might well be the solution of choice.

Furthermore, producing a human clone would of necessity require experimentation on hundreds if not thousands of live human embryos. Thus, the entire process would be the moral equivalent of human experiments carried out by Nazi scientists under Adolf Hitler.

Finally, it should be noted that cloning has serious implications regarding what constitutes a family. While children are the result of spousal reproduction, clones are essentially the result of scientific replication. Which raises the question: Who owns the clone? It is terrifying to think that the first human clone might well be owned and operated by the very scientists who conduct such ghastly experiments.

For further study, see Hank Hanegraaff, *The F.A.C.E. That Demonstrates the Farce of Evolution* (Nashville: Word Publishing, 1998), Appendix E "Human Cloning" and also Appendix D "Annihilating Abortion Arguments"; see also The Center for Bioethics and Human Dignity, 2065 Half Day Road, Bannockburn, IL 60015, www.cbhd.org.

JOB 33:4

"The Spirit of God has made me; the breath of the Almighty gives me life."

HOW SHOULD CHRISTIANS THINK
ABOUT GLOBAL WARMING?

lobal warming is hot … hot … hot! This morning I opened *USA Today* and encountered a full-page ad that begins as follows: *"Rising temperatures. Disastrous droughts. Melting glaciers and polar ice sheets. Polar bears headed to extinction. The climate crisis isn't on the way. It's here."* CNN founder Ted Turner is similarly pessimistic: *"We will be eight degrees hotter in 30 to 40 years and basically none of the crops will grow."* As a result, says Turner, *"most of the people will have died and the rest of us will be cannibals."* Former vice president Al Gore is equally emphatic. In his view, global warming is the single greatest threat facing our planet. Ellen Goodman of the *Boston Globe* puts global warming deniers on par with holocaust deniers. And prominent Baptist pastor Oliver "Buzz" Thomas has gone so far as to castigate spiritual leaders for failing to urge followers to have smaller families in light of this global catastrophe. Says Thomas, *"We must stop having so many children.*

Clergy should consider voicing the difficult truth that having more than two children during such a time is selfish. Dare we say sinful?" As Global Warming rhetoric continues to boil over, what is a Christian to do?

First, as Dr. Jay Richards, who holds a PhD in philosophy and theology, points out, we should learn to ask the right questions and to ask them in the right order. Our initial question should be: *Is global warming a reality?* The answer is a qualified, yes. If we appropriate accurate averages over a hundred and fifty years and carefully consider current satellite data, it appears likely that we are experiencing a slight warming trend. We must, however, exercise extreme caution in the extrapolation of trends. It is instructive to note that the first Earth Day (April 22, 1970) was observed amid the specter of a looming ice age. Indeed, four years later *Time* pontificated that the "tell-tale signs" of an ice age were evident "everywhere." The second question is this: *If the globe is warming, are humans a significant factor?* According to Dr. William M. Gray, a PhD in the geophysical sciences and a pioneer in the science of forecasting hurricanes, "The human impact on the atmosphere is simply too small to have a major effect on global temperatures." And Gray is not alone. A quick

Google search is sufficient to demonstrate that global warming is far from settled science. Third, we should ask: *Is global warming necessarily bad?* In response, Dr. Richards notes that a thousand years ago during a medieval warming period European agriculture experienced an increase in productivity. Moreover, more deaths result from cold winters than hot summers. While common sense might lead us to conclude that a warming trend is far less dangerous than a new ice age, reality is there hasn't been sufficient study to be sure. One thing is certain, however: sensationalism, sophistry, and sloppy journalism have done little to advance the ball. One need only think back a few years to Al Gore's dire warnings of global catastrophe as a result of the Millennium Bug. And Gore does not stand alone. Media, magazines, and ministers collectively rode the Millennium Bug hard. Indeed, when my primary research project—published as *The Millennium Bug Debugged*—revealed that Y2K would not even be a top-ten news story in the year 2000, I became the object of controversy and contempt. One well-known Christian broadcaster went as far as to suggest that I would have the blood of millions on my hands for causing complacency within the body of Christ. Truth is, the real danger is in the ready-fire-aim syndrome.

Furthermore, as Christians we should carefully consider the cost of having our eyes on the wrong ball. If we participate in promoting political policies involving trillions of dollars, there should be convincing evidence that global warming is, as Gore contends, the most pressing problem facing the planet. As Richards points out, the Kyoto Protocol (a legally binding agreement under which industrialized countries would reduce their collective emissions of greenhouse gases by 5.2% compared to 1990) would cost the global economy tens of trillions of dollars. By comparison, providing clean water for areas of the world that currently have contaminated water could be accomplished for around 200 billion. It is a genuine tragedy that while Christian leaders were hyping Y2K in America, millions of God's children were dying from malaria in Africa. And malaria is but one of the prevalent planetary problems. A whole range of issues from toxic waste to the war on terrorism could be addressed for a fraction of the cost. Point is: we dare not be wrong this time around!

Finally, what *is* incontrovertible is that Christians are called to be caretakers or stewards of God's creation. As such, not only are we called to carry out the Great Commission, but we are commissioned to carry out the cultural mandate. In the words of cultural apologist Nancy Pearcey, we are to "develop the social world: build families, churches, schools, cities, governments, laws" as well as "plant crops, build bridges, design computers, compose music." In other words, as crowning jewels of God's creation we are to care for the created order. The tragedy is that those who approach catastrophic human-induced global warming with a healthy dose of skepticism are routinely castigated as environmental enemies. Moral judgments are meted out with breathless abandon on everything from the size of one's family to the size of one's family car. The aforementioned Baptist preacher, Buzz Thomas, goes so far as to judge those who have more than two children as "selfish" and "sinful." In like fashion, leaders of the *Evangelical Environmental Network* have taken it upon themselves to posit that Jesus wouldn't drive an SUV. They seem blithely unaware that their idiosyncratic fundamentalism often flies in the face of the facts. As should be obvious, there are myriad factors to be considered with respect to family size. Whether one has two or twelve children is less important than whether those children grow up to be selfless producers as opposed to merely selfish consumers. Likewise, fuel savings do not necessarily dwarf such factors as family size or family safety. As Richards has well said, "Fuel economy doesn't trump the other factors, especially since some cars (such as hybrids) have better than average fuel economy, but require more energy both to construct and to recycle than do other, less fuel efficient cars. So an outside observer is in no position to make a moral judgment just by observing that you drive an SUV."

In an age in which Christians are all too often characterized as "poor, undereducated, and easily led," we should avoid lending credence to the stereotype. Instead we should commit ourselves to care for Christ's creation with tender hearts as well as with tenacious minds.

For further study, see the *Bible Answer Man* broadcast with guest Jay Richards, March 18 and 19, 2008, audio CDs; available through the Christian Research Institute at www.equip.org.

GENESIS 1:28

"God blessed them and said to them,
'Be fruitful and increase in number; fill the earth
and subdue it. Rule over the fish of the sea and
the birds of the air and over every living creature
that moves on the ground.'"

MONEY

What does the Bible teach about debt?

Not only has America become a debtor nation, but most Americans are drowning in debt. Our day–to–day dependence on debt begs the question: What does the Bible say about debt?

First, the Bible warns that "the borrower is servant to the lender" (Proverbs 22:7). As such, we are warned against the folly of being excessively indebted to those who may be unforgiving in their demands for repayment. We ought to take seriously the wisdom of the proverb "Do not be a man who strikes hands in pledge or puts up security for debts; if you lack the means to pay, your very bed will be snatched from under you" (Proverbs 22:26–27).

Furthermore, Scripture condemns the failure to repay our debts as wickedness. In the words of the psalmist, "the wicked borrow and do not repay, but the righteous give generously" (Psalm 37:21). Likewise, the apostle Paul urges believers to diligently repay their debts (Romans 13:8).

Finally, whether in the theocracy of ancient Israel or the democracy of modern America, God's people are called to be good stewards of the resources with which he has entrusted them. If we lend we should do so with kindness, and if we borrow we should do so with prudence.

God's people are called to be good stewards of the resources with which he has entrusted them.
If we lend we should do so with kindness, and if we borrow we should do so with prudence.

For further study, see Hank Hanegraaff, "Is the Tithe for Today?" *The Bible Answer Book Volume 1* (Nashville: J Countryman, 2004): 74–78.

ROMANS 13:8

"Let no debt remain outstanding, except the continuing debt to love one another, for he who loves his fellowman has fulfilled the law."

WHAT IS THE BIBLICAL VIEW OF WEALTH?

 am persuaded that the Bible teaches a form of Christian capitalism—in other words, responsibility associated with wealth. It does not promote the possession of money for the sake of money, but instead encourages us to use money for the sake of the kingdom. In short, a biblical view of wealth involves an eternal perspective.

First, it is crucial to realize that "the earth is the LORD's and everything in it, the world, and all who live in it" (Psalm 24:1). God is the Landlord; we are just tenants. We did not arrive with anything, and we will not take anything with us when we leave. Just remembering this fact of life will save us from a world of hurt.

Furthermore, poverty does not equal piety; nor do riches equal righteousness. God prospers some, and he puts others in more humble circumstances. If there were a one-to-one ratio between godliness and wealth, the godliest people in the world would be the wealthiest. A quick check of the Forbes 500 will quickly dash such an illusion.

Finally, it is important to view wealth with eternity in mind. In other words, lead your life here below as a responsible steward—whether you have a little or a lot—so that one day, at the judgment, God himself will richly reward you (Matthew 25:21). It is your bank statement in *heaven* that counts (Matthew 6:19–21); if you fix your hope on the one you have down here, you are bankrupt no matter how many digits you count next to your name.

ADAPTED FROM *Christianity in Crisis*

For further study, see John Piper, *Desiring God: Meditations of a Christian Hedonist* (Sisters, Ore.: Multnomah Publishers, 1986), chapter 7. Also see Hank Hanegraaff, *Christianity in Crisis* (Eugene, Ore.: Harvest House Publishers, 1993), Part 5.

MATTHEW 6:24

"No one can serve two masters.
Either he will hate the one and love the other,
or he will be devoted to the one and despise the other.
You cannot serve both God and Money."

IS THE TITHE FOR TODAY?

Of all the questions I am asked to answer, this is beyond a doubt the most difficult. Not only because the subject of tithing is hotly debated, but because I must confess that I personally have not always been faithful in giving a tenth or more to the work of the Lord. And I am not alone. Research demonstrates that not only do the vast majority of Christians not tithe regularly, but many give little or nothing at all. Thus, while addressing this question is incredibly convicting, it also is increasingly crucial.

First, as Randy Alcorn has well said, tithing may well be regarded as the training wheels of giving. As such, tithing is as important today as it has ever been. We all need to learn what it is to stride free and unfettered down the path of Christian stewardship. For in learning to give we also are learning to lean more heavily upon our heavenly Father and less heavily upon ourselves. Those who have traveled the Calvary road for any length of time surely can testify to the truth that God is ever faithful. Not only so, but as we weekly set aside our tithes and offerings we are reminded that all we are, or ever hope to be, is a gift from God.

Furthermore, as Moses communicated to the children of Israel, we tithe "so that [we] may learn to revere the Lord [our] God always" (Deuteronomy 14:23). As we all know, learning to reverence the name of God is a timeless principle—as crucial today as in the days of Moses. Long *before* Moses, the Bible records Jacob's promise to God: "Of all that you give me I will give you a tenth" (Genesis 28:22). Long *after* Moses, Jesus reaffirmed the practice of tithing (Matthew 23:23)—not for outward appearances but as an outward expression of an inward reality. Additionally, in the fourth century the great church father Jerome echoed the words of Malachi who intimated that failing to pay tithes and offerings was tantamount to "robbing" God—a prescription for financial ruin (Malachi 3:8).

Finally, it should be noted that tithing in the Old Testament not only prepared God's people to become hilarious givers but produced a temple of unparalleled splendor. The Israelites who pined for the pleasures and protection of pagan Egypt more than for the One who had miraculously parted the Red Sea had been transformed into joyful givers.

The Bible chronicles the prayer of David as he thanked God for the very privilege of being able to give to the work of the Lord: "But who am I, and who are my people, that we should be able to give as generously as this? Everything comes from you, and we have given you only what comes from your hand . . . and now I have seen with joy how willingly your people who are here have given to you" (1 Chronicles 29:14, 17).

What began as a spiritual discipline had evolved into sheer delight.

There is no telling what can be accomplished in our generation if we, too, may but catch the joy of contagious giving. Not only would we be empowered to spread the gospel around the globe, but we would be enabled to feed the hungry, clothe the naked, and care for the sick. Like our forefathers who founded great centers of Christian education, established countless hospitals, and funded myriad relief organizations, we might yet leave an indelible mark on our generation. For only when the training wheels of tithing come off will the world of free will giving become our playground.

For further study, see Randy Alcorn, *Money, Possessions and Eternity*, rev. ed. (Wheaton, Ill.: Tyndale House Publishers, 2003).

PROVERBS 3:9–10

*"Honor the LORD with your wealth, with the
firstfruits of all your crops;
then your barns will be filled to overflowing, and
your vats will brim over with new wine."*

My Budget

God's Money   100%

Tithing   10%

Taking care of the
family and neighbors
entrusted to me   70%
by God

Saving for times of need and
special opportunities   20%
to serve

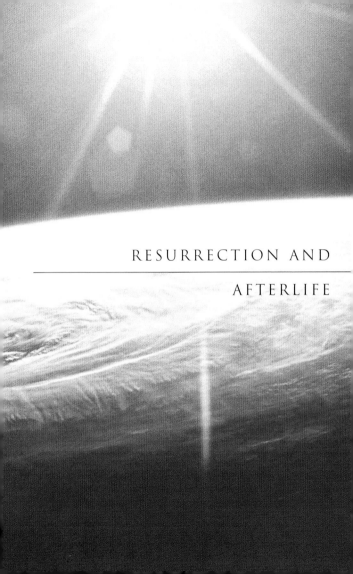

RESURRECTION AND

AFTERLIFE

– 1 4 8 –

WHEN DO WE RECEIVE
OUR RESURRECTED BODIES?

his is a question I encountered frequently after the death of my father. Family members and friends wanted to know whether my dad had become a disembodied soul or whether he received his resurrection body the moment he died.

First, Scripture clearly refers to the moment of death as disembodiment, not re–embodiment. In his second letter to the Corinthians, Paul makes it crystal clear that to be "at home with the Lord" is to be "away from the body" and to be "away from the body" is to be "at home with the Lord" (5:6, 8).

Furthermore, Scripture teaches that believers are not resurrected until the second coming of Christ. Paul explicitly says that when the Lord comes down from heaven, "the dead in Christ will rise first" (1 Thessalonians 4:16). Jesus himself taught that at his bodily return to earth "all who are in their graves will hear his voice and come out—those who have done good will rise to live, and those who have done

450   THE COMPLETE BIBLE ANSWER BOOK

evil will rise to be condemned" (John 5:28–29). If believers received their resurrected bodies at the moment of death, they obviously could not receive them at Christ's second coming.

Our resurrection body is not a second temporary body; rather it is our present body transformed.

Finally, our eternal bodies are numerically identical to the bodies we now possess. As Christ rose in the same physical body in which he died, so too we will be raised in the same physical body in which we die. In other words, our resurrection body is not a second temporary body; rather it is our present body transformed (1 Corinthians 15:42–43). While orthodoxy does not dictate that every cell of our present body will be restored in the resurrection, it does require continuity between the body that is and the body that will be.

One day, the very body of my father that I watched being lowered into the ground will rise from its grave. It was sown a perishable body, it will be raised imperishable; it was sown in dishonor, it will be raised in glory; it was sown in weakness, it will be raised in power; it was sown a natural body, it will be raised a spiritual body (1 Corinthians 15:42–44).

On that day, my dad's body will no longer be dominated by natural proclivities; instead he will have a supernatural, spiritual body dominated by the Holy Spirit and set free from slavery to sin.

For further study, see Hank Hanegraaff, *Resurrection* (Nashville: Word Publishing, 2000): 109–113.

1 CORINTHIANS 15:51–52

"Listen, I tell you a mystery: We will not all sleep,
but we will all be changed—in a flash,
in the twinkling of an eye, at the last trumpet.
For the trumpet will sound, the dead will be raised
imperishable, and we will be changed."

How old will we be in heaven?

Scripture does not specifically address the issue of apparent age; however it does provide glorious insights concerning the state of our resurrected bodies.

First, when God created Adam and Eve in Eden, he created them with apparent age and in the prime of life. Additionally, Jesus died and was resurrected at the prime of his physical development. Thus we are justified in believing that whether we die in infancy, in our prime, or in old age, we will be resurrected physically mature and perfect, as God originally intended.

Furthermore, our DNA is programmed in such a way that at a particular point we reach optimal development from a functional perspective. For the most part, it appears that we reach this stage somewhere in our twenties or thirties. Prior to this stage, the development of our bodies (anabolism) exceeds the devolution of our bodies (catabolism). From this point on, the rate of breakdown exceeds the rate of buildup, which eventually leads to physical death. All of this is to say that if the blueprint for our glorified bodies is in the DNA, then it would stand to reason that our bodies will be resurrected at the optimal stage of development determined by our DNA.

Finally, one thing can be stated with certainty—in heaven, there will be no deformities. The body, tarnished by humanity's fall into a life of constant sin terminated by death, will be utterly transformed. You will be the perfect you, and I will be the perfect me. Indeed, in heaven "there will be no more death or mourning or crying or pain, for the old order of things has passed away" (Revelation 21:4).

ADAPTED FROM *Resurrection*

For further study see, Peter J. Kreeft, *Everything You Ever Wanted to Know about Heaven, but Never Dreamed of Asking* (San Francisco: Ignatius Press, 1990).

ISAIAH 35:5–6

*"Then will the eyes of the blind be opened
and the ears of the deaf unstopped.
Then will the lame leap like a deer, and the
mute tongue shout for joy.
Water will gush forth in the wilderness
and streams in the desert."*

WILL THERE BE ANIMALS IN HEAVEN?

S cripture does not conclusively tell us whether our pets will make it to heaven. However, the Bible does provide us with some significant clues regarding whether or not animals will inhabit the new heaven and the new earth.

First, animals populated the garden of Eden. Thus, there is a precedent for believing that animals will populate Eden Restored as well. Animals are among God's most creative creations. Thus, it would seem incredible that he would banish such wonders in heaven.

Furthermore, while we cannot say for certain that the pets we enjoy today will be "resurrected" in eternity, I am not willing to preclude the possibility. Some of the keenest thinkers from C. S. Lewis to Peter Kreeft are not only convinced that animals in general but that pets in particular will be restored in the resurrection. If God resurrected our pets, it would be in total keeping with his overwhelming grace and goodness.

Finally, the Scriptures from first to last suggest that animals have souls. Both Moses in Genesis and John in Revelation communicate that the Creator endowed animals with souls. In the original languages of Genesis 1:20 and Revelation 8:9, *nephesh* and *psyche* respectively refer to the essence of life or soul. Not until Descartes and Hobbes and the Enlightenment did people think otherwise about animals. However, because the soul of an animal is qualitatively different from the soul of a human there is reasonable doubt that it can survive the death of its body. One thing is certain: Scripture provides us with sufficient precedence for believing that animals will inhabit the new heaven and new earth. In the words of Isaiah: "The wolf will live with the lamb, the leopard will lie down with the goat, the calf and the lion and the yearling together; and a little child will lead them" (Isaiah 11:6).

ADAPTED FROM *Resurrection*

For further study see, Hank Hanegraaff, *Resurrection* (Nashville: Word Publishing, 2000), chapter 13.

PSALM 145:13

"Your kingdom is an everlasting kingdom,
and your dominion endures through all generations.
The LORD is faithful to all his promises
and loving toward all he has made."

WILL THERE BE SEX IN HEAVEN?

What do you see in your mind's eye when the word "sex" is mentioned? An image of Madonna on MTV? A James Bond movie? *Cosmopolitan* magazine? Or does your mind immediately flash from sex to Scripture? Trust me, when it comes to sex, *Playboy* cannot hold a candle to Scripture. If you think that's an overstatement, just read a few pages of Solomon's Song of Songs. Tragically, what the Creator purposed to be pristine and pure, the creation has prostituted and perverted. But that is not where the story ends! God does not arbitrarily *remove* things—he *redeems* them. So will there be sex in the resurrection? Yes and no—it all depends on what you mean by sex.

First, by nature or essence we are sexual beings. Thus, sex is not just something you *do*. Sex is what you *are!* The foremost reason we can say with certainty that sex will exist in the resurrection is that sex is not merely a word that describes an erotic experience; it is what we are by essence—in the beginning God created us male and female (Genesis 1:27) and that is likely how it always will be.

Furthermore, we can safely surmise that there will be *sexuality* in heaven because heaven will personify enjoyment. Men and women will enjoy each another—not in a mere physical sense but in a metaphysical sense. This reality is virtually impossible for a crass materialist to grasp. The materialist views sexual pleasure as a function of fitting body parts together. Christians, however, see humanity as a psychosomatic unity of both body and soul. Thus, we are not solely sexual *somas* (bodies); we are sexual souls as well. In heaven, the pleasure that the male and female sex will experience in one another will be infinitely magnified, because in eternity our earthly conception of sex will have been eclipsed. In place of selfishness, we will take pleasure in selflessness.

Finally, we can safely assume that there will be sex in eternity because God created sex in Eden *before* humanity's fall into a life of constant sin terminated by death. Thus, in Eden restored we can rest assured that God will not *remove* our sexual nature; rather he will *redeem* it. In the new heaven and new earth, sex will no longer be for the purpose of procreation. Nor will it involve sexual intercourse—for "at the resurrection people will neither marry nor be given in marriage; they will be like the angels in heaven" (Matthew 22:30). In heaven we will experience a kind of spiritual intercourse that eludes our grasp on earth. In paradise, romance subverted will become romance sublime. It will be agape-driven rather than animal-driven. In Eden Restored our sexual bodies and sexual souls will fly full and free, unfettered by the stain of selfishness and sin.

Will there be sex in the resurrection? Again, yes and no. Yes, there will be *sexuality* in heaven in that *we* will be in heaven—and *we* by our very nature are sexual beings. And no, there is no warrant for believing there will be *sex* in heaven in terms of the physical act.

ADAPTED FROM *Resurrection*

For further study, see Hank Hanegraaff, *Resurrection* (Nashville: Word Publishing), Chapter 17. See also Peter J. Kreeft, *Everything You Ever Wanted to Know about Heaven, but Never Dreamed of Asking* (San Francisco: Ignatius Press, 1990).

GENESIS 1:27
"So God created man in his own image,
in the image of God he created him; male and
female he created them."

IF HEAVEN IS PERFECT,
WON'T IT BE PERFECTLY BORING?

n all-too-prevalent perception in Christianity and the culture is that heaven is going to be one big bore. That, however, is far from true. Rather, heaven will be a place of continuous learning, growth, and development. By nature, humans are finite, and that is how it always will be. While we will have an incredible capacity to learn, we will never come to the end of learning.

To begin with, we will never exhaust exploring our Creator. God by nature is infinite and we are limited. Thus, what we now merely apprehend about the Creator we will spend an eternity seeking to comprehend. Imagine finally beginning to get a handle on how God is one in nature and three in person. Imagine exploring the depths of God's love, wisdom, and holiness. Imagine forever growing in our capacities to fathom his immensity, immutability, and incomprehensibility. And to top it all off, the more we come to know him, the more there will be to know.

Furthermore, we will never come to the end of exploring fellow Christians. Our ability to appreciate one another will be enhanced exponentially. Imagine being able to love another human being without even a tinge of selfishness. Imagine appreciating, no, *reveling* in the exalted capacities and station that God bestows on another without so much as a modicum of jealousy.

Finally, we will never come to an end of exploring the Creator's creative handiwork. The universe literally will be our playground. Even if we were capable of exhausting the "new heaven and new earth" (Revelation 21:1), God could create brand-new vistas for us to explore.

Will heaven be perfect? Absolutely. Will it be boring? Absolutely not! We will learn without error—but make no mistake about it, *we will learn, we will grow, and we will develop*. Far from being dead and dull, heaven will be an exhilarating, exciting experience that will never come to an end.

ADAPTED FROM *Resurrection*

For further study, see Peter J. Kreeft, *Everything You Ever Wanted to Know about Heaven, but Never Dreamed of Asking* (San Francisco: Ignatius Press, 1990).

"You have made known to me the path of life;
you will fill me with joy in your presence,
with eternal pleasures at your right hand."

Degrees of reward in heaven are not often the subject of contemporary sermons. They were, however, a constant theme in the sermons of Christ. He explicitly points to *degrees* of reward that will be given for faithful service, self–sacrifice, and suffering. Indeed, the canon of Scripture is replete with references to rewards. While we are saved by God's grace through faith in Jesus Christ alone, what we do now counts for all eternity.

First, it is significant to note that in his most famous sermon, Christ repeatedly referred to rewards. In concluding the Beatitudes he said, "Blessed are you when people insult you, persecute you and falsely say all kinds of evil against you because of me. Rejoice and be glad, because great is your *reward* in heaven" (Matthew 5:11–12, emphasis added). Christ continued his message by warning the crowd that if they did their acts of righteousness to be seen by men, they would not receive a reward in heaven (Matthew 6:1–6, 16–18). Jesus Christ's message is crystal clear. Rather than fixate on earthly vanities, such as the admiration of men, we ought to focus on such eternal verities as the approval of the Master. He exhorted his followers to store up "treasures in heaven, where moth and rust do not destroy, and where thieves do not break in and steal" (Matthew 6:20).

The basis of our salvation is the finished work of Christ, but Christians can erect a building of rewards upon that foundation.

Moreover, Jesus made essentially the same point in his parables. In the parable of the talents (Matthew 25:14–30), Jesus tells the story of a man who entrusts his property to his servants before going on a long journey. Each servant received an amount commensurate with his abilities. To one he gave five talents, to another two talents, and to a third he gave one. The servant who received five talents doubled his money, as did the servant who had received two. The last servant, however, showed gross negligence and buried his master's money in the ground. When the master returned, he rewarded the faithful servants with the words, "Well done, good and faithful servant! You have been faithful with a few things; I will put you in charge of many things. Come and share your master's happiness!"

The unfaithful servant not only forfeited his reward but was thrown into outer darkness, "where there will be weeping and gnashing of teeth."

Furthermore, the canon of Scripture communicates degrees of reward in the resurrection. The basis of our salvation is the finished work of Christ, but Christians can erect a building of rewards upon that foundation. As Paul puts it, "no one can lay any foundation other than the one already laid, which is Jesus Christ. If any man builds on this foundation using gold, silver, costly stones, wood, hay or straw, his work will be shown for what it is, because the Day will bring it to light. It will be revealed with fire, and the fire will test the quality of each man's work. If what he has built survives, he will receive his reward. If it is burned up, he will suffer loss; he himself will be saved, but only as one escaping through the flames" (1 Corinthians 3:11–15).

Paul here illustrates the sober reality that some Christians will be resurrected with precious little to show for the time they spent on earth—they "will be saved, but only as one escaping through the flames." This conjures up images of people escaping burning buildings with little more than the charred clothes upon their backs. This will be the lot of even the most visible Christian leaders whose motives were selfish rather than selfless. Conversely, those who build selflessly upon the foundation of Christ using "gold, silver and costly stones" will receive enduring rewards. Indeed, a selfless Christian layman who labors in virtual obscurity will hear the words he has longed for throughout his life: "Well done, good and faithful servant! You have been faithful with a few things; I will put you in charge of many things. Come and share your master's happiness!" (Matthew 25:21). While deeds are our duty, not even the smallest act of kindness will go without its reward.

Some Christians will be resurrected with precious little to show for the time they spent on earth.

Finally, degrees of reward in eternity involve both enlarged responsibilities as well as enhanced spiritual capacities. An experience I had several years ago aptly underscores this biblical reality. I received an invitation to play Cypress Point, arguably the most spectacular golf course on planet Earth. While the invitation to play Cypress Point was free, I have seldom worked harder to prepare for anything in my life. For months I beat my body into submission. I lifted weights, worked on stretching exercises, and pounded thousands of golf balls, all the while dreaming of the day I would physically experience walking the fairways of Cypress Point. Without my strenuous preparation I would have still experienced the same cliff–side vistas and breathtaking views. I would still have been able to smell the fragrance of the Monterey Cypresses and feel the refreshing sting of the salt air upon my face. All the hard work, however, added immeasurably to the experience.

Degrees of reward in eternity involve both enlarged responsibilities as well as enhanced spiritual capacities.

That is how heaven will be. As a master musician can appreciate Mozart more than can an average music lover, so too my strenuous training allowed me to more fully appreciate the architectural nuances of Cypress Point. As phenomenal as Cypress Point is, it pales by comparison to what Paradise will be. I spent one day at a golf haven; I will spend an eternity in God's heaven. It stands to reason, therefore, that I would put a whole lot more effort into preparing for an eternity in heaven with God than I did for playing eighteen holes of golf. That is precisely the point Paul is driving at in one of his letters to the Corinthians. Pressing the analogy of athletics he writes, "Do you not know that in a race all the runners run, but only one gets the prize? Run in such a way as to get the prize. Everyone who competes in the games goes into strict training. They do it to get a crown that will not last; but we do it to get a crown that will last forever" (1 Corinthians 9:24–25). Thus, says Paul, "I do not run like a man running aimlessly; I do not fight like a man beating the air. No, I beat my body and make it my slave so that after I have preached to others, I myself will not be disqualified for the prize" (vv. 26–27).

For further study, see Hank Hanegraaff, *Resurrection* (Nashville: Word Publishing, 2000).

2 CORINTHIANS 5:10

"For we must all appear before the judgment seat
of Christ, that each one may receive what is
due him for the things done while in the body,
whether good or bad."

ARE THERE DEGREES
OF PUNISHMENT IN HELL?

O n the basis of the Bible we may safely conclude that not all existence in hell is equal.

First, the unified testimony of Scripture is that God is perfectly just and will reward and punish each person in accordance with what he or she has done (Psalm 62:12; Proverbs 24:12; Jeremiah 17:10; Ezekiel 18:20, 30; Romans 2:5–16; 1 Corinthians 3:8, 11–15; 2 Corinthians 5:10; Colossians 3:23–25; 1 Peter 1:17; Revelation 20:12).

Furthermore, the Bible is clear that with greater revelation and responsibility comes stricter judgment (cf. James 3:1). Jesus warned the Pharisees that they would "be punished most severely" for their willful hypocrisy (Luke 20:47). In denouncing the cities where most of his miracles had been performed, Jesus said, "Woe to you, Korazin! Woe to you, Bethsaida! If the miracles that were performed in you had been performed in Tyre and Sidon, they would have repented long ago in sackcloth and ashes" (Matthew 11:21). Thus, said Jesus, "It will be more bearable for

Tyre and Sidon on the day of judgment than for you" (v. 22). Moreover, Jesus used the metaphor of physical torture to warn his hearers that those who knowingly disobey will experience greater torment in hell than those who disobey in ignorance (Luke 12:47–48).

God is perfectly just and will reward and punish each person in accordance with what he or she has done.

Finally, the canon of Scripture ratifies the common-sense notion that not all sins are created equal (cf. John 19:11). To think a murderous thought is sin; to carry that thought to its logical conclusion is far graver sin. Every sin is an act of rebellion against a holy God, but some sins carry far more serious consequences than others and thus receive severer punishment in this life and the next. Indeed, according to Scripture the torment of Hitler's hell will greatly exceed that of the less wicked.

For further study, see Hank Hanegraaff, "Why should I believe in hell?" and "Is annihilationism biblical?" *The Bible Answer Book Volume 1* (Nashville: J Countryman, 2004): 211–218.

"And I saw the dead, great and small,
standing before the throne, and books were opened.
Another book was opened, which is the book
of life. The dead were judged according to
what they had done as recorded in the books."

Every sin is an act of rebellion against a holy God, but some
sins carry far more serious consequences than others
and thus receive severer punishment in this life and the next.

WHY SHOULD I BELIEVE IN HELL?

T he horrors of hell are such that they cause us to instinctively recoil in disbelief and doubt. Yet, there are compelling reasons that should cause us to erase such doubt from our minds.

First, Christ, the Creator of the cosmos, clearly communicated hell's irrevocable reality. He spent more time talking about hell than he did about heaven. In the Sermon on the Mount alone (Matthew 5–7), he explicitly warned his followers about the dangers of hell a half dozen or more times. In the Olivet Discourse (Matthew 24–25), Christ repeatedly warned his followers of the judgment that is to come. And, in his famous story of the Rich Man and Lazarus (Luke 16), Christ graphically portrayed the finality of eternal torment in hell.

Furthermore, the concept of choice demands that we believe in hell. Without hell, there is no choice. And without choice, heaven would not be heaven; heaven would be hell. The righteous would inherit a counterfeit heaven, and the unrighteous would be incarcerated in heaven against their wills, which would be a torture worse than hell. Imagine spending a lifetime voluntarily distanced from God only to find yourself involuntarily dragged into his loving presence for all eternity; the alternative to hell is worse than hell itself in that humans made in the image of God would be stripped of freedom and forced to worship God against their will.

Finally, common sense dictates that there must be a hell. Without hell, the wrongs of Hitler's Holocaust will never be righted. Justice would be impugned if, after slaughtering six million Jews, Hitler merely died in the arms of his mistress with no eternal consequences. The ancients knew better than to think such a thing. David knew that for a time it might seem as though the wicked prosper in spite of their deeds, but in the end justice will be served.

Common sense also dictates that without a hell there is no need for a Savior. Little needs to be said about the absurdity of suggesting that the Creator should suffer more than the cumulative sufferings of all of mankind, if there were no hell to save us from. Without hell, there is no need for salvation. Without salvation, there is no need for a sacrifice. And without sacrifice, there is no need for a Savior. As much as we may wish to think that all will be saved, common sense precludes the possibility.

Adapted from *Resurrection*

For further study, see Hank Hanegraaff, *Resurrection* (Nashville: Word Publishing, 2000), chapter seven.

DANIEL 12:2

"Multitudes who sleep in the dust of the earth will awake: some to everlasting life, others to shame and everlasting contempt."

IS ANNIHILATIONISM BIBLICAL?

J ust as universalism is the rage in liberal
Christianity, so too annihilation is
gaining momentum in conservative
Christian circles. The question of course is—
is annihilationism biblical?

First, common sense dictates that a God of
love and justice does not arbitrarily annihilate the
crowning jewels of his creation. Far from rubbing
us out, he graciously provides us the freedom to
choose between redemption and rebellion. It would
be a horrific evil to think that God would create
people with freedom of choice and then annihilate
them because of their choices.

Furthermore, common sense leads to the
conclusion that nonexistence is not better than
existence since nonexistence is nothing at all—as
Norman Geisler aptly puts it, "to affirm that nothing
can be better than something is a gigantic category
mistake." It also is crucial to recognize that not all
existence in hell is equal. We may safely conclude that

the torment of Hitler's hell will greatly exceed the torment experienced by a garden-variety pagan.

God is perfectly just, and each person who spurns his grace will suffer exactly what he deserves (Luke 12:47–48; Matthew 16:27; Colossians 3:25; Revelation 20:11–15; Proverbs 24:12).

Finally, humans are fashioned in the very image of God; therefore, to eliminate them would do violence to his nature. The alternative to annihilation is quarantine. And that is precisely what hell is.

ADAPTED FROM *Resurrection*

For further study, see Robert A. Peterson, *Hell on Trial: The Case for Eternal Punishment* (Phillipsburg, New Jersey: Presbyterian and Reformed Press, 1995).

REVELATION 14:9–11

*"If anyone worships the beast and his image and
receives his mark on the forehead or on the hand,
he, too, will drink of the wine of God's fury, which has
been poured full strength into the cup of his wrath.
He will be tormented with burning sulfur in the
presence of the holy angels and of the Lamb. And the
smoke of their torment rises for ever and ever.
There is no rest day or night for those who worship
the beast and his image, or for anyone
who receives the mark of his name."*

WHAT ABOUT PURGATORY?

Roman Catholicism teaches that believers incur debts that must inevitably be discharged in Purgatory "before the gates of heaven can be opened." While Purgatory is not equivalent to a second chance for unbelievers, it is nonetheless decidedly unbiblical.

First, the doctrine of Purgatory undermines the sufficiency of Christ's atonement on the cross. Scripture declares that Christ through "one sacrifice . . . has made perfect forever those who are being made holy" (Hebrews 10:14; see also Hebrews 1:3). Thus, we can rest assured that Christ received in his own body all the punishment we deserved, absolutely satisfying the justice of God on our behalf (Romans 3:25–26; 2 Corinthians 5:19, 21; 1 Peter 3:18; 1 John 2:2). When Jesus cried out from the cross, "It is finished!" (John 19:30) he was in effect saying, "The debt has been paid in full."

Furthermore, Roman Catholicism clearly undermines the seriousness of sin by forwarding the notion that there are venial sins that can be atoned for through temporal punishment in Purgatory. In reality, as the Bible makes clear, all our transgressions and iniquities are sins against a holy eternal God (Psalm 51:4). And as such, they rightly incur an eternal rather than a temporal debt (Ezekiel 18:4; Matthew 5–7; Romans 6:23; James 2:10).

Finally, while Purgatory was officially defined by the Council of Florence (1439) and officially defended by the Council of Trent in the late sixteenth century, nowhere is Purgatory officially depicted in the canon of Scripture. As *The New Catholic Encyclopedia* readily acknowledges, "the doctrine of Purgatory is not explicitly stated in the Bible." Thus, Catholicism is forced to appeal to the traditions of the fathers rather than the testimony of the Father—who through his Word has graciously provided salvation by grace alone, though faith alone, on account of Christ alone (Romans 4:2–8; 11:6; Ephesians 2:8–9).

For further study, see Norman L. Geisler and Ralph E. MacKenzie, *Roman Catholics and Evangelicals: Agreements and Differences* (Grand Rapids: Baker Books, 1995); James R. White, *The Roman Catholic Controversy* (Minneapolis: Bethany House, 1996), chapter 12.

Hebrews 10:14
"By one sacrifice he has made perfect forever those who are being made holy."

ESCHATOLOGY/REVELATION

DOES THE BIBLE MAKE A DISTINCTION
BETWEEN ISRAEL AND THE CHURCH?

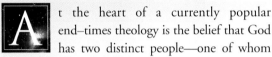

t the heart of a currently popular
end–times theology is the belief that God
has two distinct people—one of whom
must be raptured before God can continue his plan
with the other. Rather than teaching that God has
two categories of people, Scripture reveals only one
chosen people who form one covenant community,
beautifully symbolized by one cultivated olive tree.

First, far from communicating a distinction
between Israel and the church, the Scriptures from
beginning to end reveal that God has only ever had
one chosen people purchased "from every tribe and
tongue and language and nation" (Revelation 5:9).
As Paul explains, the "mystery is that through the
gospel the Gentiles are heirs together with Israel,
members together of *one* body, and sharers together
in the promise in Christ Jesus" (Ephesians 3:6,
emphasis added). Indeed, the precise terminology
used to describe the children of Israel in the Old
Testament is ascribed to the church in the New

Testament. Peter calls them "a chosen people, a royal priesthood, a holy nation, a people belonging to God" (1 Peter 2:9). Ultimately, they are the one chosen people of God not by virtue of their genealogical relationship to Abraham but by virtue of their genuine relationship to "the living Stone— rejected by men but chosen by God" (1 Peter 2:4).

Furthermore, just as the Old and New Testaments reveal only one chosen people, so too they reveal only *one covenant community*. While that one covenant community is physically rooted in the offspring of Abraham—whose number would be like that of "the stars" of heaven (Genesis 15:5) or "the dust of the earth" (Genesis 13:16)—it is spiritually grounded in one singular Seed. Paul makes this explicit in his letter to the Galatians: "The promises were spoken to Abraham and to his seed. The Scripture does not say 'and to seeds,' meaning many people, but 'and to your seed' meaning one person, who is Christ" (3:16, emphasis added). As Paul goes on to explain: "If you belong to Christ, then you are Abraham's seed, and heirs according to the promise" (v. 29). The faithful remnant of Old Testament Israel and New Testament Christianity are together the one genuine seed of Abraham and thus heirs according to the promise. This remnant is chosen not on the basis of religion or race but rather on the basis of relationship to the resurrected Redeemer.

"Not all who are descended from Israel are Israel.
Nor because they are his descendants are they all Abraham's
children. . . . In other words, it is not the natural children
who are God's children, but it is the children of
the promise who are regarded as Abraham's offspring."

Romans 9:6–8

Finally, the one chosen people, who form one covenant community, are beautifully symbolized in the book of Romans as *one cultivated olive tree* (Romans 11:11–24). The tree symbolizes Israel; its branches symbolize those who believe; and its root symbolizes Jesus—the root and the offspring of David (Revelation 22:16). Natural branches broken off represent Jews who reject Jesus. Wild branches grafted in represent Gentiles who receive Jesus. Thus says Paul, "Not all who are descended from Israel are Israel. Nor because they are his descendants are they all Abraham's children. . . . In other words, it is not the natural children who are God's children, but it is the children of the promise who are regarded as Abraham's offspring" (Romans 9:6–8).

Jesus is the one genuine seed of Abraham! And all clothed in Christ constitute *one* congruent chosen covenant community connected by the Cross.

Jesus is the one genuine seed of Abraham!
And all clothed in Christ constitute *one* congruent chosen covenant community connected by the Cross.

For further study, see Hank Hanegraaff, *The Apocalypse Code* (Nashville: Word Publishing, 2007).

GALATIANS 3:28–29

"There is neither Jew nor Greek, slave nor free, male nor female, for you are all one in Christ Jesus. If you belong to Christ, then you are Abraham's seed, and heirs according to the promise."

IS "COMING ON CLOUDS" A REFERENCE TO CHRIST'S SECOND COMING?

any modern skeptics, following scholars such as Bertrand Russell and Albert Schweitzer, have believed Jesus to be a false prophet because he predicted his "coming on clouds" within the lifetime of his disciples. Did Jesus have the Second Coming in mind or does "coming on clouds" have a different meaning?

First, when Jesus told Caiaphas and the court that condemned him to death that he was the Son of Man who would come *on the clouds of heaven* he was not speaking of his second coming but of the coming judgment of Jerusalem (Matthew 26:63–64). As Caiaphas and the court well knew, clouds were a common Old Testament symbol pointing to God as the sovereign judge of the nations. In the words of Isaiah, "See, the Lord rides on a swift *cloud* and is *coming* to Egypt. The idols of Egypt tremble before him, and the hearts of the Egyptians melt within them" (Isaiah 19:1, emphasis added). Like the Old Testament prophets, Jesus employs the symbolism of clouds to warn his hearers that as judgment fell on Egypt, so would judgment soon befall Jerusalem.

Furthermore, the "coming on clouds" judgment metaphor was clearly intended for Caiaphas and the first–century crowd who condemned Christ to death. In the words of our Lord, "I say to all of *you*: In the future *you* will *see* the Son of Man sitting at the right hand of the Mighty One and coming on the clouds of heaven" (Matthew 26:64, emphasis added). The generation that crucified Christ would *see* the day that he was exalted and enthroned at "the right hand of the Mighty One."

Finally, Jesus' "coming on clouds" to judge Jerusalem in the first century points forward to the end of time when he will appear again "to judge the living and the dead" (2 Timothy 4:1; cf. 1 Peter 4:5). Indeed, as Jesus promised, a day is coming when "all who are in their graves will hear his voice and come out—those who have done good will rise to live, and those who have done evil will rise to be condemned" (John 5:28–29). Or as the writer of Hebrews put it, "he will appear a second time, not to bear sin, but to bring salvation to those who are waiting for him" (9:28).

For further study, see Hank Hanegraaff, *The Apocalypse Code* (Nashville: W Publishing Group, 2007).

"Look, he is coming with the clouds and every eye
will see him, even those who pierced him;
and all the peoples of the earth will mourn because
of him. So shall it be! Amen."

WHICH GENERATION IS "THIS GENERATION"?

⟆

I n the Olivet Discourse, Jesus said, "I tell you the truth, this generation will certainly not pass away until all these things have happened" (Matthew 24:34). Which generation did Jesus have in mind?

First, when Jesus says, "this generation," *this* means *this*. *This* does not mean *that*. The phrase "this generation" appears multiple times in the Gospels and *always* refers to Jesus' contemporaries. Allow me to state the obvious. Our Lord was not grammatically challenged in the least. Had he wanted to draw the attention of his disciples to a generation nineteen hundred years hence, he would not have confused them with the adjective *this*.

Furthermore, the suggestion that *generation* means *race* is equally gratuitous. Indeed, rendering generation "race" would make the time parameter in Jesus' prophecy virtually meaningless. Common sense alone dictates that in answering his disciples' question, "When will these things happen?" (v. 3) Jesus does not respond by saying, "I tell you the truth, this *race of people* will certainly not pass away until all these things have happened."

Finally, grammatical gyrations, such as rendering *this* "that" and *generation* "race," are ultimately unnecessary. All the things Jesus prophesied came to pass just as he said they would—not the least of which was his "coming on clouds."

For further study, see Hank Hanegraaff, *The Apocalypse Code* (Nashville: W Publishing Group, 2007); see also "Is 'coming on clouds' a reference to Christ's second coming?" p. 484.

MATTHEW 12:41–42

"The men of Nineveh will stand up at the judgment with this generation and condemn it; for they repented at the preaching of Jonah, and now one greater than Jonah is here. The Queen of the South will rise at the judgment with this generation and condemn it; for she came from the ends of the earth to listen to Solomon's wisdom, and now one greater than Solomon is here."

WHO ARE THE 144,000 OF REVELATION?

Jehovah's Witnesses believe there is a "little flock" of 144,000 (Revelation 7:4) who get to go to heaven and a "great crowd" (Revelation 7:9) of others who are relegated to earth. What does Revelation really reveal?

First, the 144,000 and the great multitude are not two different peoples but two different ways of describing the same purified bride. As Richard Bauckham explains, literarily, the 144,000 and the great multitude are comparable to the Lion and the Lamb. Just as John is *told* about a Lion and turns to *see* a Lamb (Revelation 5:5–6), so he is *told* about the 144,000 and turns to *see* a great multitude (Revelation 7). Thus, the 144,000 is to the great multitude what the Lion is to the Lamb, namely, the same entity seen from two different vantage points. From one vantage point the purified bride is numbered; from another, she is innumerable—a great multitude that no one can count.

Furthermore, to suggest that the 12,000 from each of the twelve tribes means exactly 12,000—not

11,999 or 12,001—must surely stretch the credulity of even the most literalistic Jehovah's Witness beyond the breaking point. To begin with, ten of the twelve tribes lost their national identity almost three thousand years ago in the Assyrian exile. The other two, Judah and Benjamin, were largely decimated two thousand years ago by Roman hordes. Moreover, the pattern of Scripture is to refer to the community of faith, whether Jew or Gentile, with Jewish designations. New Jerusalem itself is figuratively built on the foundation of the twelve apostles and is entered through twelve gates inscribed with the names of the twelve tribes of Israel. Not only so, but its walls are twelve times twelve or 144 cubits thick (Revelation 21:12–17). As such, it is far more likely that 144,000 is a number that represents the 12 apostles of the Lamb multiplied by the 12 tribes of Israel, times 1,000. The figurative use of the number 12 and its multiples is well established in biblical history. For example, the tree of life in Paradise restored is said to bear twelve crops of fruit, yielding its fruit every month (Revelation 22:2), and the great Presbytery in heaven is surrounded by twenty–four elders (Revelation 4:4; 5:8; 11:16; 19:4). Likewise, the figurative use of the whole number 1,000 is common in Old Testament usage. God increased the number of the Israelites 1,000 times (Deuteronomy 1:11); God keeps his covenant to 1,000 generations (Deuteronomy 7:9); God owns the cattle on 1,000 hills (Psalm 50:10); the least of Zion will become 1,000 and the smallest a mighty nation (Isaiah 60:22); better is a day in God's courts than 1,000 elsewhere (Psalm 84:10); God shows love to 1,000 generations (Exodus 20:6); "Even if a thousand shekels were weighed out into my hands, I would not lift my hand against the king's son" (2 Samuel 18:12). A thousand more examples (figuratively speaking) could easily be added to the list.

The 144,000 represent true Israel as it was intended to be— in perfect symmetry and providentially sealed.

Finally, the 144,000 represent true Israel as it was intended to be—in perfect symmetry and providentially sealed. Who can help but think back to Ezekiel's epic depiction of a man clothed in linen etching a mark on the foreheads of those who grieved and lamented over all the detestable things done in Jerusalem prior to its destruction by the Babylonians six centuries before Christ (Ezekiel 9:4)? Or fail to realize that those who were marked were the earnest of the 144,000 sealed prior to Jerusalem's destruction in AD 70? She is the purified bride from every nation, tribe, people, and language that will step over Jordan into the New Jerusalem prepared for her from the very foundations of the world. Indeed, the 144,000 is the limitless great multitude of all whose names are written in the Book of Life and who will inhabit the courts of God for all eternity.

For further study, see Hank Hanegraaff, *The Apocalypse Code* (Nashville: W Publishing, 2007).

REVELATION 7:14

"These are they who have come out of the great tribulation; they have washed their robes and made them white in the blood of the Lamb."

WHO ARE THE TWO WITNESSES
OF REVELATION?

evelation is an apocalypse. Not just in the sense of recording an unveiling but also in terms of its composition in what might best be described as a language system or matrix deeply embedded in the Old Testament. As such, to rightly identify the two witnesses of Revelation 11, it is crucial to have the background music of the Old Testament coursing through our minds. We must neither attempt to draw exact parallels between the apocalyptic imagery and their Old Testament referents nor attempt to press the language system of Revelation into a literalistic labyrinth such that the two witnesses literally turn their mouths into blowtorches.

First, the two witnesses are a metaphorical reference to Moses and Elijah. Old Testament jurisprudence mandated at least two witnesses to convict of a crime (Deuteronomy 19:15), and in this case the two witnesses accuse Israel of apostasy. The imagery also harkens back to a familiar Old Testament passage in which Zechariah sees two olive trees on the right and the left of a lampstand which symbolize "the two who are anointed to serve the Lord of all the earth" (Zechariah 4:14). The two witnesses in Zechariah were identified as Zerubbabel, the governor of Judah who returned to Jerusalem to lay the foundation of a second temple, and Joshua, the high priest commissioned to preside over its altar. In Revelation this imagery is invested in two witnesses who preside over the judgment and destruction of Jerusalem and the second temple. Like Moses the witnesses have power to turn water into blood. And like Elijah they have power to call down fire from heaven to consume their enemies and to shut up the sky so that it will not rain for three and a half years (1 Kings 17; Luke 4:25).

We must neither attempt to draw exact parallels between the apocalyptic imagery and their Old Testament referents nor attempt to press the language system of Revelation into a literalistic labyrinth such that the two witnesses literally turn their mouths into blowtorches.

Furthermore, the mission of the two witnesses can rightly be identified with the person and work of Jesus Christ. Like Jesus they are sacrificial lambs.

Indeed, their corpses unceremoniously litter the streets of Jerusalem—the very city in which their Lord was crucified. The city is figuratively called Sodom in that it epitomizes human wickedness and heavenly wrath, and Egypt in that it is emblematic of the slavery from which only Jesus Christ can emancipate. Their resurrection after three and a half days parallels the resurrection of Christ in much the same way that their three–and–a–half–year ministry mirrors that of Messiah.

Finally, the description of these witnesses as "clothed in sackcloth" (Revelation 11:3) identifies them with the tradition of Hebrew prophets from Elijah to John the Baptist who wore sackcloth in mourning over Israel's apostasy (e.g., 2 Kings 1:8; Isaiah 20:2; Matthew 3:4). As such, the two witnesses form a composite image of the Law and the Prophets culminating in the life, death, resurrection, and ascension of a Prophet and Priest who is the earnest of all who are his witnesses and who will reign with him in a New Jerusalem wherein dwells righteousness.

In light of biblical imagery, the two witnesses are revealed not as two literal people, such as a future reincarnation of Moses and Elijah, but rather as literary characters in John's apocalyptic narrative representing the entire line of Hebrew prophets in testifying against Israel and warning of soon-coming judgment of God on Jerusalem.

For further study, see Hank Hanegraaff, *The Apocalypse Code* (Nashville: W Publishing Group, 2007); see also David Chilton, *The Days of Vengeance: An Exposition of the Book of Revelation* (Ft. Worth, Tex.: Dominion Press, 1987): 276-8.

REVELATION 11:3–5

"And I will give power to my two witnesses, and they will prophesy for 1,260 days, clothed in sackcloth. These are the two olive trees and the two lampstands that stand before the Lord of the earth. If anyone tries to harm them, fire comes from their mouths and devours their enemies."

– 1 6 3 –

WHO IS THE ANTICHRIST?

For centuries Christians have speculated about the identity of Antichrist. Likely candidates have included princes and popes of the past as well as potentates and presidents in the present. Rather than joining the sensationalistic game of pin–the–tail–on–the–Antichrist, Christians need only go to Scripture to find the answer.

First, the apostle John exposed the identity of Antichrist when he wrote, "Who is the liar? It is the man who denies that Jesus is the Christ. Such a man is the antichrist—he denies the Father and the Son. No one who denies the Son has the Father; whoever acknowledges the Son has the Father also" (1 John 2:22). In his second epistle, John gives a similar warning: "Many deceivers, who do not acknowledge Jesus Christ as coming in the flesh, have gone out into the world. Any such person is the deceiver and the antichrist" (v. 7).

Furthermore, John taught that all who deny the incarnation, messianic role, and deity of Jesus are instances of antichrist. As such the term "antichrist" refers not only to the apostasy of individuals but to the apostasy of institutions and ideologies as well. In this sense, institutions such as modern–day cults and world religions as well as ideologies such as evolutionism and communism can rightly be considered antichrist.

All who deny the incarnation, messianic role, and deity of Jesus are instances of antichrist.

Finally, in the book of Revelation, John identifies both an individual and an institution that represent the ultimate personification of evil—the archetypal antichrist. He refers to this archetypal antichrist as "a beast who deceived the inhabitants of the earth" (Revelation 13:14). Drawing on Daniel's apocalyptic depiction of evil world powers (Revelation 13; cf. Daniel 7–8), John describes an emperor in his own epoch of time who arrogantly sets himself and his empire against God (13:5–6), violently persecuting the saints (13:7), and grossly violating the commandments through a long litany of disgusting demonstrations of depravity, not the least of which was his demand to be worshiped as Lord and God (13:8, 15).

For further study, see Hank Hanegraaff, *The Apocalypse Code* (Nashville: W Publishing Group, 2007).

"Dear children, this is the last hour; and as you have heard that the antichrist is coming, even now many antichrists have come. This is how we know it is the last hour. They went out from us, but they did not really belong to us. For if they had belonged to us, they would have remained with us; but their going showed that none of them belonged to us."

WHAT IS THE MEANING OF 666?

ultitudes today assume that 666 is a number representing a modern-day beast about to be revealed. Placing the beast in the twenty-first century, however, may well pose insurmountable difficulties.

First, John, the author of Revelation, told a first-century audience that with "wisdom" and "insight" they would be able to "calculate the number of the beast, for it is man's number. His number is 666" (Revelation 13:18). Obviously no amount of wisdom and insight would have enabled a first-century audience to calculate the number of a twenty-first-century beast. It would have been cruel and dangerously misleading for John to suggest to first-century Christians that they could identify the beast if, in fact, the beast was a twenty-first-century individual or institution.

Furthermore, unlike today, transforming names into numbers (*gematria*) was common in antiquity. For example, in the *Lives of the Twelve Caesars* Roman historian Suetonius identifies Nero by a numerical designation equal to a nefarious deed. This numerical equality (*isopsephism*) is encapsulated in the phrase: "Count the numerical values of the letters in Nero's name, and in 'murdered his own mother' and you will find their sum is the same." In Greek the numerical value of the letters in Nero's name (Greek: Νέρων, English transliteration: Neron) totaled 1,005, as did the numbers in the phrase *murdered his own mother*. This ancient numerical cryptogram reflected the widespread knowledge that Nero had killed his own mother.

Finally, while "Nero" in Greek totaled 1,005, the reader of John's letter familiar with the Hebrew language could recognize that the Greek spelling of "Nero Caesar" (Greek: Νέρων Καῖσαρ, English transliteration: Neron Kaisaros) transliterated into Hebrew (ברון קסד) equals 666. Moreover, the presence in some ancient manuscripts of a variation in which 666 is rendered 616 lends further credence to Nero as the intended referent. The Hebrew transliteration of the Latin spelling of "Nero Caesar" totals 616, just as the Hebrew transliteration of the Greek, which includes an additional letter (Greek: "ν"=50, English transliteration: "n"=50), renders 666. Thus, two seemingly unrelated numbers lead you to the same doorstep—that of a beast named Nero Caesar.

Twenty-first-century believers, like their first-century counterparts, can be absolutely certain that *666* is the number of Nero's name and that Nero is the beast who ravaged the bride of Christ in a historical milieu that included three and a half years of persecution. In the end, Peter and Paul themselves were persecuted and put to death at the hands of this Beast. Indeed this was the only epoch in human history in which the Beast could directly assail the foundation of the Christian Church of which Christ himself was the cornerstone.

For further study, see Hank Hanegraaff, *The Apocalypse Code* (Nashville, W Publishing Group, 2007); see also, "Who is the Antichrist?" p. 497 and "Is the mark of the Beast a microchip?" p. 504.

REVELATION 13:8

"This calls for wisdom. If anyone has insight, let him calculate the number of the beast, for it is man's number. His number is 666."

Nero Caesar in Greek (Νέρων Καῖσαρ) transliterated into Hebrew (קסד ברון) adds up to 666 = (נ = 50) + (ר = 200) + (ו = 6) + (ן = 50) + (ק = 100) + (ס = 60) + (ר = 200)

Nero Caesar in Latin (Nero Caesar) transliterated into Hebrew (קסר ברו) adds up to 616 = (נ = 50) + (ר = 200) + (ו = 6) + (ק =100) + (ס =60) + (ר = 200)

Nero in Greek (Νέρων) adds up to 1,005 = (N=50) + (έ=5) + (ρ=100) + (ω=800) + (ν=50)

murdered his own mother in Greek (ἰδίαν μητέρα ἀπέκτεινε) adds up to 1,005

α	=	1	=	א	ν	=	50	= נ or ן
β	=	2	=	ב	ξ	=	60	= ס
γ	=	3	=	ג	ο	=	70	= ע
δ	=	4	=	ד	π	=	80	= פ
ε	=	5	=	ה	ϙ	=	90	= צ
ς	=	6	=	ו	ρ	= 100		= ק
ζ	=	7	=	ז	σ	= 200		= ר
η	=	8	=	ח	τ	= 300		= ש
θ	=	9	=	ט	υ	= 400		= ת
ι	=	10	=	י	φ	= 500		= חק
κ	=	20	=	כ	χ	= 600		
λ	=	30	=	ל	ψ	= 700		
μ	=	40	=	מ	ω	= 800		

Is the mark of the Beast a microchip?

In October 2004 the Food and Drug Administration approved the marketing of a microchip implantable under the skin of humans for medical identification. Paranoid prophecy pundits immediately began touting Verichip technology as the mark of the Beast spoken of in Revelation 13. Contrary to such newspaper eschatology, there is no biblical basis for believing that the mark of the Beast is a silicon microchip.

First, biblically, the mark of the Beast is a parody of the mark of the Lamb. Just as the mark on the foreheads of the 144,000 in Revelation 14 symbolizes identity with the Lamb, so the mark in Revelation 13 symbolizes identity with the Beast. Likewise, when Jesus says that on him who overcomes he will *write* "the name of my God, and the name of the city of my God . . . I will also write on him my new name" (Revelation 3:12), we intuitively realize he does not have a magic marker in mind.

Furthermore, the forehead and the hands are Old Testament symbols of a person's beliefs and behavior (cf. Exodus 13:9; Deuteronomy 6:8; 11:18; Ezekiel 9). In other words, what you believe and how you behave mark you as either belonging to God or belonging to Satan. As such, John's reference to the mark of the Beast in Revelation is securely tethered to Scripture. Conversely, the notion that the mark of the Beast is Sunday worship, a social security card number, or a silicon microchip has no biblical basis whatsoever.

The mark of the Beast is not something that can be taken inadvertently. It is the intentional denial in thought, word, and deed of the lordship of Jesus Christ.

Finally, the mark of the Beast is not something that can be taken inadvertently. It is the intentional denial in thought, word, and deed of the lordship of Jesus Christ. Thus, rather than fearfully avoiding microchip technology, we should with fear and trembling resist the temptation to be conformed to the evil systems of this world. Instead, we must boldly accept the mark of the Lamb by offering our bodies as living sacrifices and by being transformed by the renewing of our minds (Romans 12).

For further study, see Hank Hanegraaff, *The Apocalypse Code* (Nashville: W Publishing Group, 2007).

There is no biblical basis for believing

that the mark of the Beast is a silicon microchip.

– 1 6 6 –

WHO OR WHAT IS THE GREAT PROSTITUTE
OF REVELATION 17?

What has puzzled me over the years is not the identity of "the great prostitute," but how so many could mistake her historical identity. On the one hand, hundreds of prophecy experts misidentify the great prostitute as the contemporary Roman Catholic Church. On the other, hundreds of commentators identify the great harlot as ancient (or revived) imperial Rome. The application of the historical principle of biblical interpretation, however, demonstrates that, either way, this is a clear case of mistaken identity.

First, in biblical history only one nation is inextricably linked to the moniker "harlot." *And that nation is Israel!* Anyone who has read the Bible even once has flashbacks to the graphic images of apostate Israel when they first encounter the great prostitute of Revelation. From the Pentateuch to the Prophets, the image is repeated endlessly. Verse by verse, the painful picture of a people who prostitute themselves with pagan deities emerges (see, e.g., Jeremiah 2:20–24;

3:2–3; Ezekiel 23:9–20). The prostituted bride had little interest in seeking intimacy with God in his temple. Instead, she craved intimacy with foreign gods on the threshing floors of perverse temples (Hosea 9:1).

Furthermore, the fact that Revelation is a virtual recapitulation of Ezekiel adds credibility to the notion that apostate Israel is the great prostitute depicted in Revelation 17. Nowhere are the parallels more poignant than in Ezekiel 16 and Revelation 17—sequentially linked and memorable. In both Ezekiel and Revelation, the prostitute commits adultery with the kings of the earth; is dressed in splendor; glitters with gold and precious jewels; and is intoxicated with the blood of the righteous. And that is but a glimpse of her unveiling. In Ezekiel, the prostitution of Jerusalem made that of her sisters—Samaria and Sodom—look insignificant by comparison. And in Revelation she is in bed with imperial Rome. In the end, the great prostitute aligns herself with Caesar in piercing Christ and persecuting Christians. The golden cup in her hand is filled with "the blood of prophets and of the saints and of all who have been killed on the earth" (Revelation 18:24). Shrouded in mystery, she was glorious—like "the most beautiful of jewels" (Ezekiel 16:7). Unveiled as apostate Israel, she is grotesque.

Finally, when we consider the fact that the essence of Revelation involves a contrast between the purified bride and a prostituted bride, the identity of apostate Israel as the great prostitute becomes unmistakable. While the prostituted bride bears the mark, "Mystery, Babylon the great, the mother of prostitutes, and of the abominations of the earth" (17:5), the purified bride bears the moniker of the Lord and the Lamb on her forehead. Unlike "the synagogue of Satan" (2:9)—those who claim to be Jews though they are not—she need not fear the judgment about to befall Jerusalem, for she has been sealed by "the Lamb that was slain from the creation of the world" (13:8). In fact, before apostate Israel is judged, true Israel must be sealed. Says John: "[An angel] called out with a loud voice . . . : 'Do not harm the land or the sea or the trees until we put a seal on the forehead of the servants of our God.' Then I heard the number of those who were sealed: 144,000 from all the tribes of Israel" (Revelation 7:3–4).

For further study, see "Who are the 144,000 of Revelation?" p. 489; and Hank Hanegraaff, *The Apocalypse Code: Find Out What the Bible Really Says about the End Times...and Why It Matters Today* (Nashville: Thomas Nelson, 2007).

"I saw a woman sitting on a scarlet beast
that was covered
with blasphemous names and had seven heads and
ten horns. The woman was dressed in purple and scarlet,
and was glittering with gold, precious stones and
pearls. She held a golden cup in her hand, filled with
abominable things and the filth of her adulteries.
This title was written on her forehead:
MYSTERY
BABYLON THE GREAT
THE MOTHER OF PROSTITUTES
AND OF THE ABOMINATIONS
OF THE EARTH."

WHO WROTE REVELATION?

In the same way that buildings contain clues that unveil the identity of their architects, so too books contain clues that unveil the identity of their authors. In the case of Revelation, three possibilities have been put forward, but only one fits the design.

First is a notion that can be dismissed rather rapidly, namely, the idea that Revelation was written pseudonymously. Pseudonymity (writing under a false name) was largely practiced by writers who lack authority. Thus, they borrow the names of authentic eyewitnesses to the life and times of Christ to create an air of credibility. In sharp contrast, the book of Revelation provides ample internal evidence that it was written by a Jew intimately acquainted with the historical events and locations he wrote about. Only a handful of extremists today even countenance the possibility that Revelation could have been written pseudonymously.

Furthermore, it is commonly argued that Revelation was written by a shadowy figure named

John the Elder. Like pseudonymity, this contention has its feet firmly planted in mid-air. It would be better grounded if there were even a shred of historical certainty that John the Elder existed in the first place. (According to eminent New Testament scholar R. C. H. Lenski, the reason the "Elder theory" caught on in the first place is not historical evidence but distaste for chiliasm—i.e., millenarianism.) It is far more likely that John the Elder is just another way of referring to John the apostle. Indeed, John describes himself as "the Elder," not to distinguish himself from "the apostle," but to emphasize his authority and seniority. In short, there is scant evidence that a distinct John the Elder even existed and there is sufficient evidence that John the Elder and John the apostle are one and the same.

Finally, while there is little to commend the notion that a shadowy figure named John the Elder wrote the book of Revelation, there is ample evidence that it was written by John the apostle. The very fact that the author of the apocalypse simply calls himself *John* is a dead giveaway that he was well known throughout the churches in Asia Minor. Additionally, the fingerprints of John the apostle are all over the apocalypse! One need only open their eyes and ears to apprehend the clues. For example,

John, and John alone, identifies Jesus as the Word, or Logos (John 1:1, 14; Revelation 19:13). Likewise, John alone identifies Jesus as the true witness (John 5:31–47; 8:14–18; Revelation 2:13; 3:14), and it is John who most exploits the Mosaic requirement of two witnesses (John 8:12–30; Revelation 11:1–12). Added to this, there is undeniable commonality in the symbolic use of the number seven that transcends its literal meaning. It is also noteworthy that like the gospel of John, Revelation is a literary masterpiece.

Identifying John as the author of the apocalypse goes a long way toward shutting the door to speculations that Revelation was a late first-century—or even a second- or third-century pseudepigraphal gospel like the Gospel of Judas. Moreover, the later the date the less the likelihood that Revelation was written by an apostle or an associate of an apostle as posited by the early Christian church. The conclusion of the matter is this: there is no evidence that Revelation was written pseudonymously or by an imaginary *John the Elder*. The evidence convincingly points instead to John the apostle as the author of the apocalypse. Just as the architects' fingerprints are all over our residence, so the apostle's fingerprints are all over Revelation.

For further study, see Hank Hanegraaff, *The Apocalypse Code: Find Out What the Bible Really Says about the End Times…and Why It Matters Today* (Nashville: Thomas Nelson, 2007).

REVELATION 1:9–11

"I, John, your brother and companion in the suffering
and kingdom and patient endurance that are ours
in Jesus, was on the island of Patmos because
of the word of God and the testimony of Jesus. On the
Lord's Day I was in the Spirit, and I heard behind
me a loud voice like a trumpet, which said:
'Write on a scroll what you see and send it to the seven
churches: to Ephesus, Smyrna, Pergamum, Thyatira,
Sardis, Philadelphia and Laodicea.'"

— 168 —

WAS REVELATION WRITTEN BEFORE
OR AFTER THE DESTRUCTION OF
THE TEMPLE IN AD 70?

ust as it is common to describe Patmos as a barren Alcatraz, misidentify the great prostitute as the Roman Catholic Church, or identify the 144,000 as exclusively Jewish male virgins, so too it is common to contend that Revelation was written long after the destruction of the temple in AD 70. Thus, according to modern-day prophecy pundits, Revelation describes events that will likely take place in the twenty-first century rather than the first century.

First, if the apostle John were indeed writing in AD 95—long after the destruction of the temple—it seems incredible that he would make no mention whatsoever of the most apocalyptic event in Jewish history—the demolition of Jerusalem and the destruction of the temple at the hands of Titus. Imagine writing a history of New York today and making no mention of the destruction of the twin towers of the World Trade Center at the hands of terrorists on September 11, 2001. Or, more directly, imagine writing a thesis on the future of terrorism in America and failing to mention the Manhattan Massacre. Consider another parallel. Imagine that you are reading a history concerning Jewish struggles in Nazi Germany and find no mention whatsoever of the Holocaust. Would it not be reasonable to suppose that this history was written prior to the outbreak of World War II? The answer is self-evident. Just as it stretches credulity to suggest that a history of the Jews in Germany would be written in the aftermath of World War II and yet make no mention of the Holocaust, so too it is unreasonable to think that Revelation was written twenty-five years after the destruction of Jerusalem and yet makes no mention of the most apocalyptic event in Jewish history.

Furthermore, those who hold that the book of Revelation was written long after the destruction of the temple in AD 70 face an even more formidable obstacle! Consider one of the most amazing prophecies in all of Scripture. Jesus is leaving the temple when his disciples call his attention to its buildings. As they gaze upon its massive stones and magnificent buildings, Jesus utters the unthinkable:

"I tell you the truth, not one stone here will be left on another; every one will be thrown down" (Matthew 24:2; Mark 13:2; Luke 21:6). One generation later this prophecy, no doubt still emblazoned on the tablet of their consciousness, became a vivid and horrifying reality. As noted by Josephus, the temple was doomed August 30, AD 70, "the very day on which the former temple had been destroyed by the king of Babylon." As incredible as Christ's prophecy and its fulfillment one generation later are, it is equally incredible to suppose that the apostle John would make no mention of it. As the student of Scripture well knows, New Testament writers were quick to highlight fulfilled prophecy. The phrase "This was to fulfill what was spoken of by the prophet" permeates the pages of Scripture. Thus, it is inconceivable that Jesus would make an apocalyptic prophecy concerning the destruction of Jerusalem and the Jewish temple and that John would fail to mention that the prophecy was fulfilled one generation later just as Jesus had predicted it.

Finally, let me highlight an additional piece of internal evidence that should give pause to those who are overly dogmatic about the late-dating of Revelation. In Revelation 11 John says, "I was given a reed like a measuring rod and was told, 'Go and measure the temple of God and the altar, and count the worshipers there. But exclude the outer court; do not measure it, because it has been given to the Gentiles. They will trample on the holy city for 42 months'" (vv. 1–2). In context, Jesus has sent his angel "to show his servants what must soon take place." Thus, the prophecy concerns a future event, not one that took place twenty-five years earlier.

In summary, among the reasons we can be certain that the book of Revelation was not written twenty-five years after the destruction of Jerusalem, three tower above the rest. First, just as it is unreasonable to suppose that someone writing a history of the World Trade Center in the aftermath of September 11, 2001, would fail to mention the destruction of the twin towers, so too it stretches credulity to suggest that Revelation was written in the aftermath of the devastation of Jerusalem and the Jewish temple and yet makes no mention of this apocalypse. Additionally, if John is writing in AD 95, it is incredible to suppose he would not mention the fulfillment of Christ's most improbable and apocalyptic vision. Finally, New Testament documents—including the book of Revelation— speak of Jerusalem and the Jewish temple intact at the time they were written. If Revelation was written *before* AD 70, it is reasonable to assume that the vision given to John was meant to reveal the apocalyptic events surrounding the destruction of Jerusalem—events that were still in John's future but are in our past. This, of course, does not presuppose that *all* the prophecies in Revelation have already been fulfilled. Just as thoughtful Christians should distance themselves from the fully futurist fallacy, they should disavow a predominantly preterist (i.e., past) perspective.

For further study, see Hank Hanegraaff, *The Apocalypse Code: Find Out What the Bible Really Says about the End Times and Why It Matters Today* (Nashville: Thomas Nelson, 2007).

REVELATION 1:1–3

"The revelation of Jesus Christ, which God gave him
to show his servants what must soon take place.
He made it known by sending his angel to his servant
John, who testifies to everything he saw—that is,
the word of God and the testimony of Jesus Christ.
Blessed is the one who reads the words of this prophecy,
and blessed are those who hear it and take to heart
what is written in it, because the time is near."

BIBLICAL INTERPRETATION

WHAT DOES IT MEAN TO INTERPRET THE BIBLE LITERALLY?

or more than a decade popular TV personality Bill Maher has made a cottage industry out of ridiculing Christianity. Maher has gone so far as to dogmatically pontificate that the Bible was "written in parables. It's the idiots today who take it literally." Even a cursory reading reveals that Scripture is a treasury replete with a wide variety of literary styles ranging from poetry, proverbs, and psalms to historical narratives, didactic epistles, and apocalyptic revelations. To dogmatically assert that the Bible was written in parables and that those who read it *literally* must be "idiots" is at best an idiosyncratic form of fundamentalism and at worst a serious misunderstanding of the literal principle of biblical interpretation. In order to read the Bible for all its worth, it is crucial that we interpret it just as we would other forms of communication—in its most obvious and natural sense. As such, we must read it as literature, paying close attention to *form, figurative language*, and *fantasy imagery*.

First, in order to interpret the Bible literally we must pay special attention to what is known as form or genre. In other words, to interpret the Bible as literature, it is crucial to consider the kind of literature we are interpreting. Just as a legal brief differs in form from a prophetic oracle, so too there is a difference in genre between Leviticus and Revelation. This is particularly important when considering writings that are difficult to categorize, such as Genesis, which is largely a historical narrative interlaced with symbolism and repetitive poetic structure.

If Genesis were reduced to an allegory conveying merely abstract ideas about temptation, sin, and redemption devoid of any correlation with actual events in history, the very foundation of Christianity would be destroyed. If the historical Adam and Eve did not eat the forbidden fruit and descend into a life of habitual sin resulting in death, there is no need for redemption. On the other hand, if we consider Satan to be a slithering snake, we would not only misunderstand the nature of fallen angels but we might also suppose that Jesus triumphed over the work of the devil by stepping on the head of a serpent (Genesis 3:15) rather than through his passion on the cross (Colossians 2:15).

> To read the Bible for all its worth, it is crucial that we interpret it just as we would other forms of communication—in its most obvious and natural sense. As such, we must read it as literature, paying close attention to *form, figurative language,* and *fantasy imagery.*

A literalistic method of interpretation often does as much violence to the text as does a spiritualized interpretation that empties the text of objective meaning. A "literal–at–all–costs" method of interpretation is particularly troublesome when it comes to books of the Bible in which visionary imagery is the governing genre. For example, in Revelation the apostle John sees an apocalyptic vision in which an angel swinging a sharp sickle gathers grapes into "the great winepress of the wrath of God." The blood flowing out of the winepress rises as high as "the horse bridles, by the space of a thousand and six hundred furlongs" (Revelation 14:19–20). Interpreting apocalyptic imagery in a woodenly literal sense inevitably leads to absurdity.

Furthermore, it is crucial to recognize that Scripture—particularly apocalyptic portions of Scripture—is replete with figurative language. Such language differs from literal language, in which words mean exactly what they say. Figurative language requires readers to use their imagination in order to comprehend what the author is driving at. Such imaginative leaps are the rule rather than the exception in that virtually every genre of literature contains metaphorical language. In point of fact, we might well say that figurative language is the principal means by which God communicates spiritual realities to his children. In other words, God communicates spiritual realities through means of earthly, empirically perceptible events, persons, or objects—what might best be described as living metaphors.

A metaphor is an implied comparison that identifies a word or phrase with something that it does not literally represent. Far from minimizing biblical truth, metaphors serve as magnifying glasses that identify truth we might otherwise miss. This identification creates a meaning that lies beyond a woodenly literal interpretation and thus requires an imaginative leap in order to grasp what is meant. For example, when Jesus said, "I am the bread of life" (John 6:48), he obviously was not saying that he was literally the "staff of life" (i.e., physical bread). Rather he was metaphorically communicating that he is the "stuff of life" (i.e., the essence of true life). Biblical metaphors are never to be regarded as vacuous occasions for subjective flights of fantasy. On the contrary, biblical metaphors are always objectively meaningful, authoritative, and true.

Hyperbole is another figure of speech particularly prevalent in prophetic passages. In essence hyperbole employs exaggeration for effect or emphasis. If you step onto a scale and exclaim, "O my goodness, I weigh a ton" you are obviously not intending to say that you literally weigh two thousand pounds. Similarly, when an NBA commentator looks up at the clock, sees a minute left and says, "There's a world of time left in this game" he is using hyperbole to communicate that in the NBA a lot can happen in sixty seconds.

While hyperbole is commonly used in our culture, it is ubiquitous in the Bible. This is particularly true of prophetic passages. The prophet Isaiah used hyperbolic language when he predicted judgment on Babylon: "See, the day of the Lord is coming—a cruel day, with wrath and fierce anger—to make the land desolate and destroy the sinners within it. *The stars of heaven and their constellations will not show their light. The rising sun will be darkened and the moon will not give its light*" (Isaiah 13:9–10, emphasis added). To those unfamiliar with biblical language these words may well be taken to mean that the end of the world was at hand. In reality, Isaiah was prophesying that the Medes were about to put an end to the glories of the Babylonian empire.

Biblical metaphors are always objectively meaningful, authoritative, and true.

In evidence one need only read the preceding verses which are packed with prophetic hyperbole: "Wail for the day of the Lord is near; it will come like destruction from the Almighty. Because of this, *all hands will go limp, every man's heart will melt*. Terror will seize them, pain and anguish will grip them; they will writhe like a woman in labor. They will look aghast at each other, *their faces aflame*" (vv. 6–8, emphasis added). Even the most pedantic literalist intuitively recognizes that Isaiah is not literally intending to infer that all hands will literally go limp and that every heart will literally melt. Nor is he literalistically predicting that every Babylonian face will be on fire any more than John is using wooden literalism to prophesy that the two witnesses in Revelation will literally emit flames of fire from their mouths (Revelation 11:5).

Finally, it is crucial to correctly interpret fantasy imagery in apocalyptic passages—such as an enormous red dragon with seven heads and ten horns (Revelation 12:3); locusts with human faces, women's hair, and lions' teeth (9:7); and a beast that resembled a leopard, but with feet like a bear and a mouth like a lion (13:2). What is distinct about such fantasy images is that they do not correspond to anything in the real world. But while fantasy images are unreal, they provide a realistic means by which to ponder reality.

Fantasy imagery, of course, is fraught with danger. That danger, however, lies not in its use but in its abuse. In Revelation 12 the apostle John describes "an enormous red dragon with seven heads and ten horns and seven crowns on his heads. His tail swept a third of the stars out of the sky and flung them to the earth" (vv. 3–4). Many Christians abuse such imagery by interpreting it in a woodenly literalistic fashion, thus missing the point of the passage. Not only would a single star—let alone a third of the stars—obliterate earth, but dragons are the stuff of mythology not theology. Thus, the danger does not lie in the use of fantasy imagery but in uncritically impregnating these images with unbiblical notions.

> The Scriptures are uniquely inspired by the Spirit. . . .
> We must therefore fervently pray that the Spirit, who inspired
> the Scriptures, illumines our minds to what is *in* the text.

While the Scriptures must indeed be read as literature, you and I must ever be mindful that the Bible is also far more than literature. Instead, the Scriptures are uniquely inspired by the Spirit. As Peter put it, "no prophecy of Scripture came about by the prophet's own interpretation. For prophecy never had its origin in the will of man, but men spoke from God as they were carried along by the Spirit" (2 Peter 1:20–21). We must therefore fervently pray that the Spirit, who inspired the Scriptures, illumines our minds to what is *in* the text.

For further study, see Hank Hanegraaff, *The Apocalypse Code* (Nashville: W Publishing Group, 2007).

2 TIMOTHY 2:15
"Do your best to present yourself to God as one approved, a workman who does not need to be ashamed and who correctly handles the word of truth."

170

WHAT IS THE SIGNIFICANCE OF BIBLICAL TYPOLOGY?

 type (from the Greek word *typos*) is a person, event, or institution in the redemptive history of the Old Testament that prefigures a corresponding but greater reality in the New Testament. A type is thus a copy, a pattern, or a model that signifies an even greater reality. The greater reality to which a type points and in which it finds its fulfillment is referred to as an *antitype*. The writer of Hebrews specifically employs the word *antitype* to refer to the greatness of the heavenly sanctuary of which the Holy Land, the Holy City, and the holy temple are merely types or shadows (Hebrews 9:23–24).

First, in Hebrews, as in the rest of the New Testament, the Old Testament history of Israel is interpreted as a succession of types that find ultimate fulfillment in the life, death, and resurrection of our Lord. As such, far from being peripheral, typology is central to a proper interpretation of the infallible Word of God. Indeed, throughout the New

Testament Jesus is revealed as the antitype of the Hebrew prophets through his preaching of repentance, his ministry of healing, his concern for the poor and the social outcasts, and his death near Jerusalem (Luke 13:33). This, of course, is not to confuse the biblical principle of typology with an allegorical method of biblical interpretation that ignores or rejects the historical nature of the Old Testament narratives. On the contrary, typology is firmly rooted in historical fact and always involves historical correspondence.

Furthermore, biblical typology, as evidenced in the writings of the New Testament, always involves a heightening of the type in the antitype. It is not simply that Jesus replaces the temple as a new but otherwise equal substitute. No, Jesus is far greater than the temple! It is not as though Jesus is simply another in the line of prophets with Moses, Elijah, Isaiah, and Jeremiah. No, Jesus is much greater than the prophets! The new covenant is not a mere "plan B" that God instituted as a parenthesis between two phases of his redemptive work with Israel. The new covenant is far greater than the old covenant—"a better covenant" (Hebrews 7:22)—rendering the old "obsolete" (Hebrews 8:13)! Just as Joshua is a type of Jesus who leads the true children of Israel into the eternal land of promise, so King David is a type of the "King of kings and Lord of lords" who forever rules and reigns from the New Jerusalem in faithfulness and in truth (Revelation 19:16). In each case, the lesser is fulfilled and rendered obsolete by the greater.

Finally, it is important to point out that antitypes themselves may also function as types of future realities. Communion, for example, is the antitype of the Passover meal. Each year the Jews celebrated Passover in remembrance of God's sparing the firstborn sons in the homes of the Israelite families that were marked by the blood of the Passover lamb (see Luke 22; cf. Exodus 11–12). Jesus' celebration of the Passover meal with his disciples on the night of his arrest symbolically points to the fact that he is the ultimate Passover Lamb "who takes away the sin of the world" (John 1:29). Though the Last Supper and the corresponding sacrament of communion serve as the antitype of the Passover meal, they also point forward to their ultimate fulfillment in "the wedding supper of the Lamb" (Revelation 19:9; cf. Luke 22:15–18). On that glorious day the purified bride—true Israel—will be united with her Bridegroom in the new heaven and the new earth (Revelation 21:1–2). Thus the fulfillment of the promise is itself a guarantee of the final consummation of the kingdom of God.

In sum, as eschatology is the thread that weaves the tapestry of Scripture into a glorious mosaic; typology is the material out of which that thread is spun.

For further study, see Hank Hanegraaff, *The Apocalypse Code: Find Out What the Bible Really Says about the End Times…and Why It Matters Today* (Nashville: Thomas Nelson, 2007).

HEBREWS 10:1–2

"The law is only a shadow of the good things that are coming—not the realities themselves. For this reason it can never, by the same sacrifices repeated endlessly year after year, make perfect those who draw near to worship. If it could, would they not have stopped being offered?"

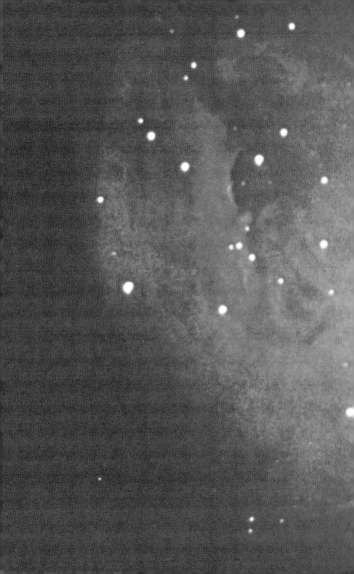

FINAL THOUGHTS

171

How can I develop
an eternal perspective?

f we are looking for the personification of an eternal perspective, we need look no further than our Lord and Savior Jesus Christ. He immersed himself in Scripture, sacrificed himself for the needs of others, and treasured fellowship with his heavenly Father. Like the Master, we are called to elevate our gaze from earthly vanities to eternal verities.

First, we develop an eternal perspective by saturating ourselves with Scripture. Jesus modeled daily devotion to the Word of God. In the ultimate spiritual battle, Jesus took up the sword of the Spirit, which is the Word of God. He had mined, memorized, and meditated on Scripture. Thus, when the slanderer sought to tempt the Savior to turn stones into bread, Jesus was prepared. "It is written," he said, "'man does not live on bread alone, but on every word that comes from the mouth of God'" (Matthew 4:4).

Furthermore, we begin to view this world with an eye toward eternity by focusing on the needs of others. As our Master sacrificed himself for the sins of the world, we must learn to live selflessly rather than selfishly. At the Judgment those who fed the hungry, gave drink to the thirsty, clothed the naked, cared for the sick, and visited those in prison will be rewarded as if they had done these things for the Lord himself (Matthew 25:31–40).

We develop an eternal perspective by saturating ourselves with Scripture, by focusing on the needs of others, and by withdrawing from the invasive sounds of this world so that we can hear the sounds of another place and another voice.

Finally, we develop an eternal perspective by withdrawing from the invasive sounds of this world so that we can hear the sounds of another place and another voice. Dr. Luke tells us that "Jesus often withdrew to lonely places and prayed" (Luke 5:16). Unlike the religious leaders of his day he did not pray to be seen by men. He prayed because he treasured fellowship with his Father. If you too wish to develop the kind of perspective that leads to abundant living both now and for all eternity, "go into your room, close the door and pray to your Father, who is unseen. Then your Father, who sees what is done in secret, will reward you" (Matthew 6:6).

For further study see, Dallas Willard, *The Divine Conspiracy* (San Francisco: Harper San Francisco, 1998); see also Hank Hanegraaff, *The Prayer of Jesus* (Nashville: Word Publishing, 2001) and *Resurrection* (Nashville: Word Publishing, 2000).

MATTHEW 6:19–21

"Do not store up for yourselves treasures on earth, where moth and rust destroy, and where thieves break in and steal. But store up for yourselves treasures in heaven, where moth and rust do not destroy, and where thieves do not break in and steal. For where your treasure is, there your heart will be also."

HOW CAN A PERSON
FIND MORE BIBLE ANSWERS?

he *Complete Bible Answer Book Collector's Edition* addresses some of the most significant questions I've been asked during nearly twenty years of hosting the *Bible Answer Man* radio broadcast. In well over three thousand live broadcasts I've answered thousands more. I invite you to ask me *your* questions live on the *Bible Answer Man* broadcast by dialing toll-free 1.888.ASK.HANK, Monday through Friday, 5:50 to 7:00 PM, Eastern Time. You can find a listing of radio stations carrying the program at www.equip.org.

Furthermore, the Christian Research Institute exists to provide carefully researched biblical answers to questions concerning Christianity and the culture as well as the kingdom of the cults and the world of the occult. As such, you can find answers to your questions in our award-winning magazine, *Christian Research Journal*, or online at www.equip.org.

Finally, it is crucial that you get into the Word of God and get the Word of God into you. If you fail to eat well-balanced meals on a regular basis, you eventually will suffer the physical consequences. Likewise, if you do not regularly feed on the Word of God, you will suffer spiritual consequences. Jesus said, "Man does not live on bread alone, but on every word that comes from the mouth of God" (Matthew 4:4). Great physical meals are one thing; great spiritual M-E-A-L-S are quite another:

Memorize: As a result of teaching memory seminars for over twenty years I am convinced that anyone, regardless of age or acumen, can memorize Scripture. God has called you to write his Word on the tablet of your heart (Proverbs 7:1–3; Deuteronomy 6:6), and with the call he has provided the ability. Your mind is like a muscle. If you exercise it, you will increase its capacity to remember and recall information. If you do not, like a muscle, it will atrophy. A good place to start memorizing is Joshua 1:8: "Do not let this Book of the Law depart from your mouth; meditate on it day and night, so that you may be careful to do everything written in it. Then you will be prosperous and successful."

Examine: As mentioned above, the Berean believers daily examined the Scriptures to see if what Paul taught was true. For that they were commended as being noble in character. Ultimate authority was not placed in the revelation of men but in the revelation of God. The apostle Paul urged Christians to test all things (1 Thessalonians 5:21) and to be transformed by the renewing of their minds in order to discern the will of God (Romans 12:2). Examining the Scriptures requires discipline, but the dividends are dramatic.

Apply: As wonderful and worthwhile as it is to memorize and examine Scripture, it is not enough! You must take the knowledge you have gleaned from the Word of God and *apply* it in your daily life—*wisdom is the application of knowledge.* As the Master put it: "Everyone who hears these words of mine and puts them into practice is like a wise man who built his house on the rock. The rain came down, the streams rose, and the winds blew and beat against that house; yet it did not fall, because it had its foundation on the rock. But everyone who hears these words of mine and does not put them into practice is like a foolish man who built his house on sand. The rain came down, the streams rose, and the winds blew and beat against that house, and it fell with a great crash" (Matthew 7:24–27). James the brother of Jesus used irony to drive home the same point. In essence, he said that anyone who hears the Word and does not apply it is like a man who looks in a mirror and sees that his face is dirty, but doesn't wash it (James 1:23–24).

Listen: In order to apply God's directions to life experiences, you must first *listen* carefully as God speaks to you through the mystery of his Word. Like Samuel, you should say, "Speak, [Lord,] for your servant is *listening*" (1 Samuel 3:10, emphasis added). One of the most amazing aspects of Scripture is that it is alive and active, not dead and dull. Indeed, God still speaks today through the mystery of his Word. The Holy Spirit illumines our minds so that we may understand what he has freely given us (1 Corinthians 2:12). As Jesus so beautifully put it, "My sheep *listen* to my voice; I know them, and they follow me" (John 10:27, emphasis added).

Study: In *examining* Scripture, it is typically best to stick with one good Bible translation. This not only provides consistency but facilitates the process of Scripture memorization. In *studying*, however, it is helpful to use a number of good translations. To further your study of Scripture, it is necessary to have access to study tools. The toolbox of serious Scripture students should include a concordance, a commentary, and a Bible dictionary. You also might consider obtaining some of the resources suggested in *The Bible Answer Book*.

Jesus said, "I am the bread of life. He who comes to me will never go hungry, and he who believes in me will never be thirsty" (John 6:35). May the acronym M-E-A-L-S daily remind you to nourish yourself by partaking of the Bread of life.

ADAPTED FROM *Christianity in Crisis*

PHILIPPIANS 4:8–9

"Finally, brothers, whatever is true, whatever is noble, whatever is right, whatever is pure, whatever is lovely, whatever is admirable—if anything is excellent or praiseworthy—think about such things."

Memorize

Examine

Apply

Listen

Study

ADDITIONAL RESOURCES

Richard Abanes, *One Nation Under Gods* (New York: Four Walls Eight Windows, 2003).

Randy Alcorn, *Does the Birth Control Pill Cause Abortion?* 7th ed. (Gresham, Ore.: Eternal Perspective Ministries, 1997).

Randy Alcorn, *Money, Possessions and Eternity*, rev. ed. (Wheaton, Ill.: Tyndale House Publishers, 2003).

Gleason L. Archer, *New International Encyclopedia of Bible Difficulties* (Grand Rapids: Zondervan, 1982), 79–80.

Gleason Archer, *Encyclopedia of Bible Difficulties* (Grand Rapids: Zondervan, 1982).

Francis J. Beckwith, "Baha'i–Christian Dialogue: Some Key Issues Considered," *Christian Research Journal* 11, 3 (1989), available through the Christian Research Institute (CRI) at www.equip.org.

Francis J. Beckwith, "Intelligent Design in the Schools: Is it Constitutional?" *Christian Research Journal* 25, 4 (2003), available through the Christian Research Institute (CRI) at www.equip.org.

Francis J. Beckwith, *Politically Correct Death: Answering the Arguments for Abortion Rights*, (Grand Rapids: Baker Books, 1993).

Craig L. Blomberg, *Jesus and the Gospels* (Nashville: Broadman and Holman Publishers, 1997).

Gregory A. Boyd, *Oneness, Pentecostals, and the Trinity* (Grand Rapids: Baker Books, 1992).

Gary M. Burge, *Whose Land? Whose Promise?* (Cleveland, OH: The Pilgrim Press, 2003).

D. A. Carson, ed., *From Sabbath to Lord's Day: A Biblical, Historical, and Theological Investigation* (Eugene, Oregon: Wipf and Stock Publishers, 1999, originally published by Zondervan, 1982)

The Center for Bioethics and Human Dignity —www.cbhd.org—2065 Half Day Road, Bannockburn, IL 60015 USA, Voice: 847.317.8180.

J. Daryl Charles, "Sentiments as Social Justice: The Ethics of Capital Punishment," *Christian Research Journal*, Spring/Summer 1994.

David Chilton, *The Days of Vengeance: An Exposition of the Book of Revelation* (Ft. Worth, Tex.: Dominion Press, 1987).

Charles W. Colson and Nigel M. de S. Cameron, *Human Dignity in the Biotech Century: A Christian Vision for Public Policy* (Downers Grove, Ill.: InterVarsity Press, 2004).

Paul Copan and William Lane Craig, *Creation out of Nothing: A Biblical, Philosophical, and Scientific Exploration* (Grand Rapids: Baker Academic, 2004).

Paul Copan, *That's Just Your Interpretation: Responding to Skeptics Who Challenge Your Faith* (Grand Rapids: Baker Books, 2001), 171–178.

Paul Copan, *"True for You, But not for Me": Deflating the Slogans that Leave Christians Speechless* (Minneapolis: Bethany House Publishers, 1998).

William Lane Craig, *Reasonable Faith* (Crossway Books, 1994).

Joe Dallas, "Darkening Our Minds: The Problem of Pornography among Christians," *Christian Research Journal* 27, 3 (2004), available through the Christian Research Institute (CRI) at www.equip.org.

Joe Dallas, *Desires in Conflict*, updated edition (Eugene, Ore.: Harvest House Publishers, 2003).

Joe Dallas, *A Strong Delusion: Confronting the "Gay Christian" Movement* (Eugene, Ore.: Harvest House Publishers, 1996).

William Dembski, *The Design Revolution* (Grand Rapids: IVP, 2004).

Millard J. Erickson, *What Does God Know and When Does He Know It?* (Grand Rapids: Zondervan, 2003).

Millard J. Erickson, *The Word Became Flesh: A Contemporary Incarnational Christology* (Grand Rapids: Baker Book House, 1996).

Gordon Fee and Douglas Stewart, *How to Read the Bible for All Its Worth*, 3rd ed. (Grand Rapids: Zondervan, 2003).

R. Douglas Geivett and Gary R. Habermas, eds., *In Defense of Miracles: A Comprehensive Case for God's Action in History* (Downers Grove, Ill.: InterVarsity Press, 1997).

Timothy George, *Is the Father of Jesus the God of Muhammad?* (Grand Rapids: Zondervan, 2002).

Norman L. Geisler & Abdul Saleeb, *Answering Islam* (Grand Rapids: Baker Books, 2002).

Norman L. Geisler, *Baker Encyclopedia of Christian Apologetics* (Grand Rapids: Baker Books, 1999), 553–554; see also 283–288.

Norman L. Geisler, *Christian Ethics: Options and Issues* (Grand Rapids: Baker Book House, 1989), chapter 7.

Norman L. Geisler and Douglas E. Potter, "From Ashes to Ashes: Is Burial the Only Christian Option?" *Christian Research Journal*, summer 1998, available at www.equip.org/free/dc765.htm.

Norman L. Geisler and Ralph E. MacKenzie, *Roman Catholics and Evangelicals: Agreements and Differences* (Grand Rapids: Baker Books, 1995).

Duane T. Gish, *Evolution: The Fossils Still Say No!* (El Cajon, Calif.: Institute for Creation Research, 1995).

Douglas R. Groothuis, *Unmasking the New Age* (Downers Grove, Ill.: InterVarsity Press, 1986).

Os Guinness, *Time for Truth* (Grand Rapids: Baker Books, 2000).

Os Guinness, *Unspeakable: Facing up to Evil in an Age of Genocide and Terror* (San Francisco: Harper San Francisco, 2005).

Gary R. Habermas and J. P. Moreland, *Beyond Death: Exploring the Evidence for Immortality* (Wheaton, Ill.: Crossway Books, 1998).

Gary R. Habermas and Michael R. Licona, *The Case for the Resurrection of Jesus* (Grand Rapids: Kregel, 2004).

Dean Halverson, *The Illustrated Guide to World Religions* (Minneapolis: Bethany House Publishers, 2003).

Hank Hanegraaff and Tom Fortson, *7 Questions of a Promise Keeper* (Nashville: J. Countryman, 2006).

Hank Hanegraaff, "Annihilating Abortion Arguments," available through the Christian Research Institute (CRI) at www.equip.org.

Hank Hanegraaff, *The Apocalypse Code* (Nashville: W Publishing Group, 2007).

Hank Hanegraaff, *The Bible Answer Book Volume 1* (Nashville: J. Countryman, 2004).

Hank Hanegraaff, "Bringing Baptism into Biblical Balance," *Christian Research Journal*, 19, 1 (1996) available through the Christian Research Institute at www.equip.org.

Hank Hanegraaff, *Christianity in Crisis* (Eugene, Ore.: Harvest House Publishers, 1993), Part 2.

Hank Hanegraaff, *Counterfeit Revival: Looking for God in All the Wrong Places*, rev. ed. (Nashville: Word Publishing, 2001).

Hank Hanegraaff, *The Covering: God's Plan to Protect You from Evil* (Nashville: W Publishing Group, 2002).

Hank Hanegraaff and Paul L. Maier, *The Da Vinci Code: Fact or Fiction?* (Wheaton, IL: Tyndale House, 2004).

Hank Hanegraaff, "Does your relationship with God make you sure you will go to heaven when you die?" pamphlet, available through Christian Research Institute, P.O. Box 7000, Rancho Santa Margarita, California 92688; 1–888–7000–CRI; www.equip.org.

Hank Hanegraaff, *The F.A.C.E. That Demonstrates the Farce of Evolution* (Nashville: Word Publishing, 1998).

Hank Hanegraaff, *Fatal Flaws: What Evolutionists Don't Want You To Know* (Nashville: W Publishing, 2003).

Hank Hanegraaff, "How to Find a Healthy Church" (Rancho Santa Margarita, Calif.: Christian Research Institute, 2003), pamphlet.

Hank Hanegraaff, "The Indwelling of the Holy Spirit," *Christian Research Journal*, Spring 1997, available at www.equip.org/free/DS575.pdf.

Hank Hanegraaff, "Karla Faye Tucker and Capital Punishment," *CRI Perspective* CP1304, Christian Research Institute, P O Box 7000, Rancho Santa Margarita, Calif., 92688; 1–888–7000–CRI.

Hank Hanegraaff, "Magic Apologetics," *Christian Research Journal* 20, 1 (1997) available through the Christian Research Institute (CRI) at www.equip.org.

Hank Hanegraaff, *The Prayer of Jesus: Secrets to Real Intimacy with God* (Nashville: W Publishing Group, 2001).

Hank Hanegraaff, *Resurrection* (Nashville: Word Publishing, 2000).

Hank Hanegraaff, "Safe and Secure" (Rancho Santa Margarita, Calif.: Christian Research Institute, 1996).

Hank Hanegraaff, "The Search for Jesus Hoax," *Christian Research Journal* 23, 2 (2000), available through the Christian Research Institute (CRI) at www.equip.org.

Hank Hanegraaff, *The Third Day* (Nashville: W Publishing Group, 2003).

Hank Hanegraaff, "The Unforgivable Sin," available from Christian Research Institute at www.equip.org/free/DU250.htm.

Hank Hanegraaff, "The Untouchables: Are 'God's Anointed' Beyond Criticism?" available through the Christian Research Institute (CRI) at www.equip.org.

Hank Hanegraaff, "What about Halloween?" (Rancho Santa Margarita, Calif.: Christian Research Institute, 2001), pamphlet.

Carl F. H. Henry, *Basic Christian Doctrines*, (Grand Rapids: Baker Book House, 1962).

Richard G. Howe, "Modern Witchcraft: It may not be what you think," *Christian Research Journal* 28, 1 (2005) available through the Christian Research Institute (CRI) at www.equip.org.

Phillip E. Johnson, *Darwin on Trial*, second edition (Downers Grove, Ill.: InterVarsity Press, 1993).

Walter C. Kaiser, Jr., Peter H. Davids, F.F. Bruce, and Manfred T. Brauch, (eds.), *Hard Sayings of the Bible* (Downers Grove, Ill.: InterVarsity Press, 1996).

Peter J. Kreeft, *Everything You Ever Wanted to Know About Heaven, but Never Dreamed of Asking* (San Francisco: Ignatius Press, 1990).

Robert Letham, *The Holy Trinity: In Scripture, History, Theology, and Worship* (Phillipsburg, New Jersey: P&R Publishing, 2004).

C. S. Lewis, *Mere Christianity* (New York: Macmillan, 1952).

C. S. Lewis, *The Screwtape Letters* (New York: Macmillan, 1982).

Gordon R. Lewis, "Attributes of God," in Walter A. Elwell, ed., *Evangelical Dictionary of Theology*, 2nd edition (Grand Rapids: Baker Academic, 2001), 492–499.

John MacArthur, *Hard to Believe: The High Cost and Infinite Value of Following Jesus* (Nashville: Thomas Nelson Publishers, 2003).

John MacArthur, *Why One Way? Defending an Exclusive Claim in an Inclusive World* (Nashville: W Publishing Group, 2002).

Paul Maier, *The First Christmas* (Grand Rapids: Kregel Publications, 2001).

Paul Marston and Roger Forster, *God's Strategy in Human History*, 2nd ed. (Wipf and Stock Publishers, 2000).

Josh McDowell and Bob Hostetler, *The New Tolerance* (Wheaton, IL: Tyndale House Publishers, 1998).

Elliot Miller, *A Crash Course on The New Age Movement* (Grand Rapids: Baker Book House, 1989).

Bruce Milne, *Know the Truth: A Handbook of Christian Belief* (Downers Grove, Ill.: InterVarsity Press, 1999).

Marcia Montenegro, "Kabbalah: Getting Back to the Garden," *Christian Research Journal* 28, 2 (2005) available through the Christian Research Institute (CRI) at www.equip.org.

James Moore, *The Darwin Legend* (Grand Rapids: Baker Books, 1994).

J. P. Moreland's two-part Christian Research Journal series on "The Euthanasia Debate" available through the Christian Research Institute (CRI) at www.equip.org.

J. P. Moreland, *Love Your God with All Your Mind: The Role of Reason in the Life of the Soul* (Colorado Springs: NavPress, 2007).

J. P. Moreland and William Lane Craig, *Philosophical Foundations for a Christian Worldview* (Downers Grove, Ill: InterVarsity Press, 2003).

J. P. Moreland, *Scaling the Secular City: A Defense of Christianity* (Grand Rapids: Baker Book House, 1987).

J. P. Moreland and John Mark Reynolds, eds., *Three Views on Creation and Evolution* (Grand Rapids: ZondervanPublishingHouse, 1999).

Thomas V. Morris, *The Logic of God Incarnate* (Ithaca, NY: Cornell University Press, 1986).

Ronald H. Nash, *The Gospel and the Greeks* (Richardson, Texas: Probe Books, 1992).

Ronald Nash, *Is Jesus the Only Savior?* (Grand Rapids: Zondervan, 1994).

J. I. Packer, *Knowing God* (Downers Grove, Ill.: InterVarsity Press, 1993).

Bob and Gretchen Passantino, "Christians Criticizing Christians: Can it be Biblical?" available through the Christian Research Institute (CRI) at www.equip.org.

Adam Pelser, "Genuine Temptation and the Character of Christ" available through the Christian Research Institute (CRI) at www.equip.org.

Robert A. Peterson, *Hell on Trial: The Case for Eternal Punishment* (Phillipsburg, New Jersey: Presbyterian and Reformed Press, 1995).

John Piper, *Desiring God: Meditations of a Christian Hedonist* (Sisters, Ore.: Multnomah Publishers, 1986), chapter 7.

"Questions and Answers: Genesis 6:4," available from Christian Research Institute, P O Box 7000, Rancho Santa Margarita, Calif. 92688, or call 1–888–7000–CRI.

Scott B. Rae, *Moral Choices*, 2nd ed. (Grand Rapids: Zondervan, 2000).

David A. Reed, *Answering Jehovah's Witnesses: Subject by Subject* (Grand Rapids: Baker Book House, 1996).

Robert L. Reymond, *Jesus, Divine Messiah* (Tain, Ross–shire, Scotland: Christian Focus Publications, 2003).

Ron Rhodes, *The Challenge of the Cults and New Religions* (Grand Rapids: Zondervan, 2001).

Ron Rhodes, *Reasoning from the Scriptures with the Jehovah's Witnesses* (Eugene, Ore.: Harvest House Publishers, 1993).

Richard Robinson, "Understanding Judaism: How to Share the Gospel with Your Jewish Friends," *Christian Research Journal* 19, 4 (1997) available through the Christian Research Institute (CRI) at www.equip.org.

James W. Sire, *The Universe Next Door: A Basic Worldview Catalog*, third ed. (Downers Grove, Ill.: InterVarsity Press, 1997).

R. C. Sproul, *Justified by Faith Alone* (Wheaton, IL: Crossway Books, 1999).

R. C. Sproul, *Not A Chance: The Myth of Chance in Modern Science and Cosmology* (Grand Rapids: Baker Book House, 1994).

R. C. Sproul, *Reason to Believe* (Grand Rapids: Zondervan, 1982).

Lee Strobel, *The Case for a Creator* (Grand Rapids: Zondervan, 2004).

Lee Strobel, *The Case for Christ* (Grand Rapids: Zondervan, 1998).

Lee Strobel, *The Case for Faith* (Grand Rapids: Zondervan, 2000).

Charles R. Strohmer, *America's Fascination with Astrology: Is it Healthy?* (Greenville, South Carolina: Emerald House, 1998).

Charles Strohmer, *The Gospel and the New Spirituality* (Nashville: Thomas Nelson, 1996).

Charles Strohmer, "Is there a Christian Zodiac, a Gospel in the Stars?" *Christian Research Journal* 22, 4 (2000) available through the Christian Research Institute (CRI) at www.equip.org.

Eric D. Svendsen, *Who Is My Mother?* (Amityville, NY: Calvary Press, 2001).

Joni Eareckson Tada and Nigel M. de S. Cameron, *How to be a Christian in a Brave New World* (Grand Rapids: Zondervan, 2006).

Joni Eareckson Tada and Steven Estes, *When God Weeps* (Grand Rapids: Zondervan, 1997).

Jerald and Sandra Tanner, *The Changing World of Mormonism* (Chicago: Moody, 1980).

Peter Toon, *The Ascension of our Lord* (Nashville: Thomas Nelson, 1984).

John Weldon, "Scientology: From Science Fiction to Space–Age Religion," *Christian Research Journal* 16, 1 (1993) available through the Christian Research Institute (CRI) at www.equip.org.

Jonathan Wells, *Icons of Evolution: Science or Myth?* (Washington D.C.: Regnery, 2000).

James R. White, *The Forgotten Trinity* (Minneapolis: Bethany House, 2001).

Dallas Willard, *The Divine Conspiracy* (San Francisco: Harper San Francisco, 1998).

N. T. Wright, "Women's Service in the Church: The Biblical Basis," available at www.ntwrightpage.com.

J. Isamu Yamamoto's four–part *Christian Research Journal* series on Buddhism in North America available through the Christian Research Institute (CRI) at www.equip.org.

J. Isamu Yamamoto, "Zest for Zen: North Americans Embrace a Contemplative School of Buddhism" *Christian Research Journal* 17, 3 (1995) available through the Christian Research Institute (CRI) at www.equip.org.

CONTACT CHRISTIAN RESEARCH INSTITUTE:

By Mail:
CRI United States
P.O. Box 8500, Charlotte, NC 28271-8500

In Canada:
CRI Canada
56051 Airways P.O., Calgary, Alberta T2E 8K5

By Phone:
U.S. 24–hour Toll–Free Credit Card Line 1 (888) 7000–CRI
U.S. Customer Service (704) 887-8200
Fax (704) 887-8299

Canada Toll-Free Credit Card Line 1 (800) 665–5851
Canada Customer Service (403) 571–6363

On the Internet: www.equip.org

On the Broadcast:
To contact the *Bible Answer Man* broadcast with your
questions, call toll free in the U.S. and Canada,
1 (888) ASK HANK (275– 4265), Monday-Friday, 5:50
P.M. to 7:00 P.M. Eastern Time.

For a list of stations airing the *Bible Answer Man* or to listen
to the broadcast via the internet, log on to our Web site at
www.equip.org.

Hank Hanegraaff serves as president and chairman of the board of the North Carolina-based Christian Research Institute International. He is also host of the *Bible Answer Man* radio program, which is broadcast daily across the United States and Canada—as well as around the world through the Internet at www.equip.org.

Widely considered to be one of the world's leading Christian apologists, Hanegraaff is deeply committed to equipping Christians to be so familiar with truth that when counterfeits loom on the horizon they recognize them instantaneously. Through his live call-in radio broadcast, Hanegraaff equips Christians to read the Bible for all it's worth; answers questions on the basis of careful research and sound reasoning; and interviews today's most significant leaders, apologists, and thinkers.

Hanegraaff is the author of award-winning bestsellers, including *The Prayer of Jesus, Christianity in Crisis,* and *Resurrection*, the latter providing a stirring and persuasive defense of the central event in Christianity. *Resurrection* and *Christianity in Crisis* both won the Gold Medallion for excellence in Christian Literature awarded by the Evangelical Christian Publisher's Association. Two other books by Hanegraaff, *Counterfeit Revival* and *The FACE that Demonstrates the Farce of Evolution,* each won the Silver Medallion.

The Prayer of Jesus was honored as a top 10 best-selling nonfiction book in both 2001 and 2002 by the Christian Bookseller's Association, while the small group video presentation *The Prayer of Jesus EZ Lesson Plan* taught by Hanegraaff won a Telly Award in 2003.

Recent releases include *The Apocalypse Code: Find Out What the Bible REALLY Says about the End Times…And Why It Matters Today* and *The Legacy Study Bible.* He is also co-author of The Last Disciple fiction trilogy; *Fuse of Armageddon, The Da Vinci Code: Fact or Fiction?* and *Seven Questions of a Promise Keeper.* Other books include, *The Covering: God's Plan to Protect You from Evil, The Third Day,* and *Fatal Flaws: What Evolutionists Don't Want You to Know.*

Hanegraaff is a regular contributor to *Christian Research Journal* and *The Plain Truth* magazine. A popular conference speaker, he addresses churches, schools, and businesses worldwide and appears on national media broadcasts to discuss a wide range of issues.

Hanegraaff and his wife, Kathy, live in North Carolina and have nine children—Michelle, Katie, David, John Mark, Hank Jr., Christina, Paul, Faith, and baby Grace—as well as five grandchildren.